Designing Case

Research Methods Series

General Editors: **Bernhard Kittel**, Professor and Head of Department, Department of Economic Sociology, University of Vienna, Carl von Ossietzky Universität Oldenburg, Germany and **Benoît Rihoux**, Professor of Political Science, Université catholique de Louvain (UCL), Belgium

In association with the European Consortium for Political Research (ECPR), Palgrave Macmillan is delighted to announce the launch of a new book series dedicated to producing cutting-edge titles in Research Methods. While political science currently tends to import methods developed in neighbouring disciplines, the series contributes to developing a methodological apparatus focusing on those methods which are appropriate in dealing with the specific research problems of the discipline.

The series provides students and scholars with state-of-the-art scholarship on methodology, methods and techniques. It comprises innovative and intellectually rigorous monographs and edited collections which bridge schools of thought and cross the boundaries of conventional approaches. The series covers both empirical-analytical and interpretive approaches, micro and macro studies, and quantitative and qualitative methods.

Titles include:

Joachim Blatter and Markus Haverland
DESIGNING CASE STUDIES
Explanatory Approaches in Small-N Research

Alexander Bogner, Beate Littig and Wolfgang Menz (*editors*)
INTERVIEWING EXPERTS

Michael Bruter and Martin Lodge (*editors*)
POLITICAL SCIENCE RESEARCH METHODS IN ACTION

Isabelle Engeli and Christine Rothmayr Allison
COMPARATIVE POLICY STUDIES
Conceptual and Methodological Challenges

Bernhard Kittel, Wolfgang J. Luhan and Rebecca B. Morton (*editors*)
EXPERIMENTAL POLITICAL SCIENCE
Principles and Practices

Audie Klotz and Deepa Prakash (*editors*)
QUALITATIVE METHODS IN INTERNATIONAL RELATIONS
A Pluralist Guide

Lane Kenworthy and Alexander Hicks (*editors*)
METHOD AND SUBSTANCE IN MACROCOMPARATIVE ANALYSIS

Ingo Rohlfing
CASE STUDIES AND CAUSAL INFERENCE
An Integrative Framework

Research Methods Series
Series Standing Order ISBN 978–0–230–20679–3 hardcover
Series Standing Order ISBN 978–0–230–20680–9 paperback
(*outside North America only*)

You can receive future titles in this series as they are published by placing a standing order. Please contact your bookseller or, in case of difficulty, write to us at the address below with your name and address, the title of the series and one of the ISBNs quoted above.

Customer Services Department, Macmillan Distribution Ltd, Houndmills, Basingstoke, Hampshire RG21 6XS, England

Designing Case Studies

Explanatory Approaches in Small-N Research

Joachim Blatter

Professor of Political Science, Department of Humanities and Social Sciences, University of Lucerne, Switzerland

and

Markus Haverland

Professor of Political Science, Department of Public Administration, Erasumus University Rotterdam, The Netherlands

First published 2012
Published in paperback 2014 by
PALGRAVE MACMILLAN

Palgrave Macmillan in the UK is an imprint of Macmillan Publishers Limited, registered in England, company number 785998, of Houndmills, Basingstoke, Hampshire RG21 6XS.

Palgrave Macmillan in the US is a division of St Martin's Press LLC, 175 Fifth Avenue, New York, NY 10010.

Palgrave Macmillan is the global academic imprint of the above companies and has companies and representatives throughout the world.

Palgrave® and Macmillan® are registered trademarks in the United States, the United Kingdom, Europe and other countries.

ISBN 978–0–230–24969–1 hardback
ISBN 978–1–137–47257–1 paperback

This book is printed on paper suitable for recycling and made from fully managed and sustained forest sources. Logging, pulping and manufacturing processes are expected to conform to the environmental regulations of the country of origin.

A catalogue record for this book is available from the British Library.

A catalog record for this book is available from the Library of Congress.

Transferred to Digital Printing in 2014

We dedicate this book to
Lisa
as well as to
Judith, Anou, and Maud

Contents

Figures and Tables

Figures

Tables

Abbreviations

ACF	Advocacy Coalition Framework
CC	Core concepts
CC	Contextual conditions
CEEC	Central and Eastern European Countries
CON	Congruence analysis
COV	Co-variational analysis
CPT	Causal-process tracing
csQCA	Crisp Set Qualitative Comparative Analysis
EC	European Community
EOI	Export-oriented industrialization
EU	European Union
fsQCA	fuzzy set Qualitative Comparative Analysis
GATT	General Agreement on Tariffs and Trade
IBK	Internationale Bodenseekonferenz
IR	International relations
ISI	Import-substitution industrialization
N	Number of cases
NATO	North Atlantic Treaty Organization
PC	Peripheral concepts
QCA	Qualitative Comparative Analysis
RT	Regime Theory
SC	Sufficient condition
UK	United Kingdom
US	United States
W	Causal Configuration
WTO	World Trade Organization
X	Independent variable
Y	Dependent variable
β	Regression coefficient

Preface to the Paperback Edition

We are very glad that Palgrave has made it possible to present our book on how to design case studies in a paperback edition. This makes it even more likely that it will be used by students. The setup of the book is especially suited as a textbook for teaching and learning case studies and uses extensively existing case studies which might serve as role models.

Our book has been the first of the latest wave of books devoted to qualitative methods, case studies and (causal-)process tracing (for an overview see Vol. 11, No. 1 of the Newsletter of the American Political Science Association Organized Section for Qualitative and Multi-Method Research, Spring 2013). We are now faced with different accounts on how to conduct case studies. Students and practitioners are especially confronted with quite distinct understandings of "causal mechanism" and "(causal-) process tracing." We are convinced that our three-fold approach, which includes a co-variational approach that accounts for the difference that a causal factor makes, an outcome-centred causal-process tracing approach, and a paradigmatic theory-centred congruence analysis approach, is one of the most helpful ways to guide case study researchers.

We cannot provide a full-fledged methodological discussion at this place, but want to briefly highlight what we see as unique advantages of our book:

- With our three approaches, we provide the broadest account to case studies. All other books are narrower and have clear affinities to a single ontological and epistemological stance. Furthermore, we believe that it makes no sense to put all alternatives to the classic co-variational or comparative approach to case studies in one box, but rather to delineate two distinct approaches to within-case analysis. This reveals not only more alternative techniques for making or testing causal claims, but it embeds these techniques into coherent research approaches.
- Taking terminology seriously, we follow George and Bennett (2005) in putting timing or temporality at the heart of the endeavour when we talk about tracing "processes". In addition, we deliberatively exchanged the term "process tracing" – which has already become

a very fuzzy catch-all phrase – for the more specific and therefore precise notion of "causal-process tracing."

The paperback edition contains only a few changes in comparison to the hard back edition of 2012. Primarily, we tried to improve some of the tables, which serve as crucially important guiding posts for the user of the book.

We changed only one significant aspect/term. We do not talk anymore of "most-likely cases" and "least-likely cases" when we specify the meaning of "crucial cases" within the congruence analysis approach (p. 176–178). Instead, we use the terms "very likely cases" and "very unlikely cases". The terms "most-likely cases" and "least-likely cases" suggest that case selection of the case study takes place on the basis of an ex-ante analysis of an existing population of cases, as it is often advised in the context of "multi-method research". They furthermore suggest that based on such a large-N study, cases with extreme values on dependent and/or independent variables are selected for more detailed within-case analysis. These reasons for case selection make sense when the techniques of process tracing are used for testing the internal validity of a specific hypothesis which has already gained leverage by a correlational analysis or for developing a modified hypothesis by selecting a deviant case (see chapter 5.4). Nevertheless, the reflection on the likeliness of a specific case to be explained by a specific theory within a congruence analysis does follow a different rational and there is no need to know the location of a case in a population of similar cases. What is necessary is a reflection – based on the antecedent or context conditions of specific cases – whether the case is very likely or very unlikely to be explained by a specific theory (and ideally, this should be done for all theories). This means, we do not know – or more precisely: we do not have to know – whether the case is "the" most-likely case or whether it is "just" a very likely case. In consequence, we exchange the term "most-likely case" with "very likely case" and the term "least-likely case" with "very unlikely case" when we describe how to select "crucial cases" and how to draw "theoretical generalizations."

We would like to thank Andrew Baird for helping us to come up with this paperback edition and hope that it serves what it is meant to do: to provide guidance for conducting good case study research.

Joachim Blatter and Markus Haverland

Preface and Acknowledgements

We conducted projects involving extensive case study research before we began teaching case study methods and reflecting more intensively on the methodology of small-N research. These experiences made clear the challenges scholars face when studying cases 'in-depth' and led to the development of a certain sense of pragmatism. We both found that the methodological advice on case study research that was available in the mid-1990s, when we conducted the research for our PhD theses, was scant and often not very helpful, but we have been impressed by the tremendous progress that has been made since then. Methodological reflections on 'qualitative inquiry' and 'case studies' have grown substantially in number, and these reflections make it possible to escape the narrow confines of methodological advice that implicitly or explicitly understand case studies or small-N studies (we use both expressions synonymously) as the 'smaller brothers' of large-N statistical studies – an understanding that implies inferiority.

As a result, we are now faced with a different situation: the methodological debate on case studies has become so broad that it is difficult for students and more experienced scholars alike to avoid confusion regarding these methods. We believe that the main challenge today lies in streamlining the diversity of advice found in the methodological literature into coherent approaches to case study research.

The core message of this book is that it makes sense to distinguish three approaches to case study research (Blatter and Blume 2008). All approaches strive for explanation, but they vary in their research goals and questions, the corresponding criteria for proper case selection, techniques of drawing causal inferences, possible directions of generalization, and the best format for presenting results. Distinguishing between these approaches allows for stronger internal coherence in case studies. It also allows for more explicit and reflective combinations of the elements of various case study approaches.

The core of this book consists of three chapters that develop each of the three approaches, which we name by coining the terms 'co-variational analysis' (COV), 'causal-process tracing' (CPT), and 'congruence analysis' (CON). The final chapter shows how to combine different case study approaches and how to connect case studies with large-N studies (applying statistics as a technique of data analysis) and medium-N studies (applying Qualitative Comparative Analysis as a technique of data analysis) to strengthen the internal and external validity of explanations.

With our book, we seek to help students as well as beginning and advanced scholars to design and execute compelling case studies in political science, public administration, international relations, European studies, urban studies, organizational studies, and related branches of the social sciences. We draw on methodological debates and provide examples of the best practices from these disciplines and fields of study.

We try to strike a balance between a hands-on approach that contains useful advice for designing and conducting case studies and the need to locate our approaches in the lively and sometimes confusing methodological debate on case study research, and to substantiate our choices. Those who read this book with largely pragmatic intentions may want to skip the next parts of this introduction and turn immediately to the overview of the approaches in Section 1.7 to determine which approach fits their research goals best. They may also find the second section of each of the three main chapters unnecessary because it is here that the epistemological foundations of our three case study approaches are discussed. Although it is certainly enlightening to dig deeper into the epistemological foundations of the case study approach that one applies, we have organized the book in such a way that it is possible to learn how to design and execute convincing case studies without focusing too much on the philosophy behind the approaches. The core chapters of the book are structured in a way that is similar to the sequence of the research process, starting with the research question and ending with suggestions on how to present findings. The book contains many examples of case studies that we perceive as models for the various approaches, and we present some of these examples comprehensively. We believe that good case study research demands both knowledge of abstract methodological concepts and familiarity with concrete 'showcases' that provide a practical orientation on how to conduct good case study research.

We strongly believe that case study research gains substantially from applying the rigor of formal logic. The use of formal logic for data analysis within the co-variational approach has been paramount in making this approach the dominant one since the 1970s – at least within the methodological literature. In this book we invest heavily in order to also bring the rigor of formal logics to the newer approaches.

Nevertheless, we also strongly believe that social science benefits from a sensitivity to language and terminology. We take major terms such as 'observation', 'causal-process tracing', or 'smoking guns' very seriously. In consequence, we invest heavily in defining these terms in a way that makes sense for case study research and in recognizing the connotations of these terms in colloquial language. Finally, we hope that the readers share our conviction that the alternation of 'she' and 'he' in the text is a solution that represents sensitivity to gender and to language.

Several draft chapters of the book have been tested in the classroom. We thank the participants of the following courses for acting as our guinea pigs and for helpful feedback: General Methodology at the Netherlands Institute of Government (NIG), which is the Dutch national graduate school for public administration and political science; Case Study Designs at the University of Freiburg (i.Brsg.), Germany; Research Methods in Political Science at the University of Lucerne, Switzerland; and Research Design of the Master's in International Public Management and Policy at the Erasmus University Rotterdam, The Netherlands.

Several scholars have also shared their precious time to read one or more of our draft chapters. We thank Patrick Emmenegger, Gary Goertz, Dirk Leuffen, Hidde Koornstra, Deborah Rice, Frank Schimmelfennig, Matthias Stepan, Maarten Vink, and Claudius Wagemann for their insightful and constructive comments. Andrea Blättler and Samuel Schmid have done a great job in formatting and streamlining the book and the list of references. A grant given by the NIG for language editing of the book manuscript is also gratefully acknowledged.

Moreover, we wish to thank the following for permission to reproduce copyright material:

Elsevier Science Inc., for table 1, from Elizabeth J. Wilson and Arch G. Woodside, 'Degrees-of-Freedom Analysis of Case Data in Business Marketing Research' in *Industrial Marketing Management* (1999), 28(3), 215–29.

The University of Chicago Press, for figure 1, from James Mahoney, 'Nominal, Ordinal, and Narrative Appraisal in Macrocausal Analysis' in *The American Journal of Sociology* (1999), 104(4), 1154–96.

Finally, we wish to thank the editors of the series, the reviewers, and Liz Holwell at Palgrave Macmillan for their interest in our book as well as for their patience and support.

1
Relevance and Refinements of Case Studies

Case studies are an interesting phenomenon in the social sciences. On the one hand, they have played a pivotal role in theory development and are still popular in almost all fields of the social sciences, with the notable exception of economics. On the other hand, they have been treated by most methodologists with skepticism and disdain. Many classic works in the social sciences illustrate the relevance – even prevalence – of case study research for most of the twentieth century. Developments in ontological reasoning, theory building, and epistemology, together with the sophistication of statistical techniques, seemed to reduce the appeal of the case study approach in the last decades of the twentieth century and led to the rise of large-N studies. Nevertheless, in recent years, we have witnessed a resurgent interest in case study research, accompanied by intensive methodological reflection.

In this first chapter, we begin by illustrating the theoretical relevance of case studies to the scientific discourse in many fields of research with some illustrative examples (Section 1.1). Second, we point to recent changes in social reality and in the social sciences that have revived interest in case studies (Section 1.2). Third, we clarify our epistemological stance as anti-fundamentalist and differentiated. All three case study approaches that we present are located in the 'epistemological middle-ground', but they have distinct affinities with the main epistemological/methodological camps that currently populate the literature on the philosophy of science (Section 1.3). Before we define our own understanding of case studies (Section 1.5), we briefly address some major contributions to case study methodology (Section 1.4) and explain where we agree with and build on these contributions and where we diverge. In addition, we clarify what we mean when we talk about 'observations' (Section 1.6). We close our introduction with an overview of the main features of our three approaches to case study research (Section 1.7).

1.1   Case studies as cornerstones for theories and research programs

In many disciplines and fields in the social sciences, we can point to case studies that have attained the status of classics, because they have strongly influenced the scientific discourse and triggered broad-based research programs. In political science, for instance, Robert E. Goodin and Hans-Dieter Klingemann (1996) identify as classics Robert A. Dahl's *Who Governs?* (1967 [1961]), Graham T. Allison's *Essence of Decision* (1971), and Theda Skocpol's *States and Social Revolutions* (1979), among other works. In what follows, we discuss the core contributions and impact of these three studies and of Arend Lijpharts' *The Politics of Accommodation* (1975 [1968]), an influential work in comparative politics.

Robert A. Dahl's case study *Who Governs?* focuses on power, a core concept in political science. His intensive investigation of the formal and informal power structures in the city of New Haven was a landmark work. He showed that governance is not characterized by a single power structure or one single power elite, as was previously commonly believed, but is rather characterized by pluralism. He found that, in the three areas he studied, urban renewal, public education, and primary elections, different actors hold power. This pluralist vision of power in democracies has strongly influenced empirical work in public policy making, urban politics, and interest group research. It has also provided a foundation for further theoretical work by Theodor Lowi, Mancur Olson, and others. That work has culminated in what is now known as 'neopluralism' in interest group research and related areas of studies (see McFarland 2007). Bibliometric data have provided empirical evidence of the enormous academic reach of Dahl's case study of a single American city. Dahl's book has been cited in more than 1,600 academic journal articles covered by the *Web of Science* and in more than 4,000 studies covered by *Google Scholar*. In methodological terms, Dahl's approach to the study of power favors the intensive analysis of policy processes in specific policy areas. To reveal the exercise of power, actors' preferences and behaviors need to be identified, and there must be an emphasis on the temporal dimension of politics or on the time and timing of political action. This emphasis resonates well with one of the approaches we present in this book: causal-process tracing.

Allison's *Essence of Decision* is an intensive case study of a short, although very important, episode in the history of the Cold War: the Cuban Missile Crisis. Allison studies three decisions that determined the course of the Cuban Missile Crisis: the Soviet Union's decision to place offensive missiles in Cuba, the decision by the United States (US) to respond with a blockade, and the Soviet Union's withdrawal of the missiles. Yet, far from being an idiosyncratic treatment of 13 days in history, it is a study that is heavily informed by theories of decision-making and provides general lessons that reach far beyond this particular event. The study has informed research in public administration, public policy, foreign policy analysis, and international relations (IR), among other disciplines. With regard to its impact on teaching, it not only provided the intellectual foundation for the Harvard School of Government – one of the world's most important public policy schools and the school at which Allison became Dean soon after he published the book (see Marks 2000) – but also, in fact, became standard teaching material on government decision-making in many classrooms in the US, Europe, and beyond. The book has been cited in more than 700 academic journal articles covered by the *Web of Science* and in more than 6,500 studies covered by *Google Scholar*. The second edition (co-authored with Zelikow) alone has been cited in more than 4,000 documents since its publication in 1999. According to Allison's website, the book has sold more than 400,000 copies (Allison 2011). This indicates that the book's ideas have traveled well beyond the academic community. With its systematic elaboration of ex-ante formulated propositions, the book represents an important example for our congruence approach, which we present and discuss in Chapter 4.

Skocpol's *State and Social Revolutions* has been a milestone in comparative sociology. In her study, she seeks to identify the conditions which lead to social revolutions. She compares the Chinese, French, and Russian revolutions with various cases in which revolutionary overhauls of a political system were possible but did not occur. One of Skocpol's key contributions was her emphasis on the independent role of rulers and their (lack of) resources in explaining revolutions. This study has thus been a major impetus for 'bringing the state back in' when engaging in political analysis (Evans, Rueschemeyer, and Skocpol 1985) or more generally for the neo-institutional turn in political science and related disciplines (for example, Mahoney and Rueschemeyer 2003). Again, the academic reach of this work is extensive, with 1,400 references in the *Web of Science* and approximately 4,000 hits in *Google Scholar*. Skocpol's book influenced theoretical discourse due to her emphasis on the state and her development and empirical testing of a theoretical approach that was previously marginalized. In addition, her study has been widely discussed in methodological debates because she used a broad set of techniques to draw causal inferences. We will discuss her approach mainly as a best practice for the causal-process tracing approach, because she draws effectively on causal conjunctures and causal chains in her explanation of the Chinese, French, and Russian revolutions (Mahoney 1999). We will also return to her work in our discussion of combinations of approaches, because she nests causal-process tracing in a comparative design that is related to our co-variational approach.

A seminal study in comparative politics is Lijphart's *The Politics of Accommodation* – a single case study of political culture in the Netherlands (1975 [1968]). Lijphart took issue with the argument from 'pluralist theory' that culturally heterogeneous societies can only be stable democracies if the cleavages in the country (language, religion) are cross-cutting. This means that a society that is culturally heterogeneous and has no cross-cutting cleavages cannot become a stable democracy. Lijphart's study showed, however, that the Netherlands was culturally heterogeneous and segmented into different cultural pillars in the period 1920–70, but was extremely politically stable at the same time. Lijphart explained that cooperation among political elites was an example of a 'politics of accommodation' that is constituted by particular rules of the game. Consociationalism was the key concept in this study. Consociationalism and its related concepts, 'consensus democracy' and 'power sharing democracy', became major analytical instruments for the description and comparison of democratic political systems and their institutions, and for gauging their effects in terms of democratic quality and policy outcomes (see Lijphart 2008). Various editions of *Politics of Accommodation* have been cited in approximately 700 academic journal articles covered by the *Web of Science* and in more than 1,800 studies covered by *Google Scholar*.

What is striking when we look at these influential case studies is the fact that they investigate only a single case or, more precisely – as Dahl and Allison have differentiated their cases internally into multiple cases – that cross-case comparison is not the main technique for drawing causal inferences. Interestingly, when these influential case studies emerged, the methodological discourse had begun to emphasize the need for cross-case comparison, and Lijphart himself contributed tremendously to this trend with two influential articles advocating large-N approaches (Lijphart 1971, 1975; see Section 1.4). Based on insights from his study on the Netherlands, Lijphart initiated a research program that took him from comparative case studies toward large-N studies (Lijphart 1999, 2008). Nevertheless, in methodological discourse, it is Lijphart's original study of a single case that received the most attention. Gary King, Robert O. Keohane, and Sidney Verba state that Lijphart's work on the Netherlands is 'the case study that broke the pluralist camel's back' (2004: 186). This statement can be interpreted as an assumption on the part of the authors that the previously dominant 'pluralist theory' had been 'falsified' by a case study, an assumption that would be in accordance with their positivist or critical rationalist stance with respect to epistemology. Others would argue that Lijphart had 'only' shown that there is another possible path to stable democracy. Overall, our discussion of important case studies indicates that we must delve deeper into the theoretical, epistemological, and methodological foundations of case study research to understand why these studies have become cornerstones of theory building.

1.2 The case for case study research

In this section, we make a plea for case study research built on various theoretical and organizational developments in the social sciences. We observe that in important fields of the social sciences recent theoretical developments highlight ontological assumptions that are best addressed using case study research. Furthermore, we argue that recent perforations of the boundaries between social science disciplines and sub-disciplines have led to a situation in which scholars now have a broader set of theoretical approaches available when studying a specific theme. Case studies are uniquely predisposed to taking into account a broad and diverse set of explanatory factors.

1.2.1 The growing relevance of timing, cognition, and interdependence

Peter Hall (2003) has argued that recent theoretical approaches are built implicitly or explicitly on ontological assumptions that make it reasonable to turn to case study research. Hall emphasizes the fundamental theoretical relevance of 'timing', 'interaction effects', and 'contexts' (2003: 384–5) in recent theoretical explanations and in varying analytical approaches such as Game Theory and Historical Institutionalism. The logical methodological conclusion from these theoretical developments is that a turn toward '*systematic process analysis*' in small-N research designs is warranted (2003: 391–5). A further theoretical trend is the increasing relevance of cognitive factors like norms, ideas, and discourses as cornerstones of analytic frameworks – for example, the *Advocacy Coalition Framework* (Sabatier and Jenkins-Smith 1993) in policy studies or the role of 'epistemic communities' in international Regime Theory (Haas 1992). Although the latter trend has served primarily to stimulate the growth of various forms of content, discourse, and frame analysis, it also serves as a justification for turning to case studies for those who are interested in explaining the specific processes and results of political decision-making. Case studies are superior to large-N studies in helping the researcher to understand the perceptions and motivations of important actors and to trace the processes by which these cognitive factors form and change.

Another line of argumentation points to developments in the social world that produce problems for established forms of large-N research. The processes of globalization and transnationalization lead to diffusion effects between nation states. This in turn undermines one of the core assumptions in correlation-based comparative analysis – that the cases are fully independent. Although there are means to account for this phenomenon (often called 'Galton's problem') in correlation-based analysis, case study designs are better predisposed to take into account both 'internal' and 'external' explanatory factors (Hall 2003: 382; Patzelt 2005: 47).

1.2.2 Perforated boundaries in social reality and the social sciences

Another change that has taken place in the last 20 years as a result of globalization and transnationalization processes is the perforation of boundaries between scientific (sub-)disciplines. Typical (sub-)disciplines in the social sciences are products of the twentieth century, when the modern social sciences emerged as intellectual and institutionalized entities. For example, in political science, four major sub-disciplines have been established: (1) political theory/philosophy; (2) a sub-discipline that concentrates on domestic politics, for example, American politics; (3) comparative politics; and (4) international relations. Although there have always been more or less established fields of study that transcended the boundaries of disciplines (such as public administration, urban studies, European studies, or policy analysis), an unprecedented blurring of boundaries between the main sub-disciplines has taken place in the last 20 years as a result of transnationalization and globalization. Scholars in the fields of political theory, domestic politics, and comparative politics have begun to take into account the transnational and supra-national dimensions of their fields of inquiry. IR scholars, in turn, have begun to take into account a broader set of actors in 'international politics', for example, sub-national governments. Furthermore, the research agenda of IR has been broadened substantially and in such a way that IR scholars have to rely more and more on concepts from other sub-disciplines, for example, from political philosophy, when dealing with issues like cosmopolitan governance or the (alleged) democratic deficit of the European Union (EU) and other international institutions. As a result, scholars have a larger set of concepts, theories, and analytical frameworks that they can apply when studying phenomena in a transnationalizing world. Case studies are especially well suited for taking into account a broader range of theories, because the diverse set of information necessary to test complex theories can very often be collected only for one case or a few cases.

1.2.3 Building bridges between paradigmatic camps

Our major ontological argument for advocating case study research is that case studies are not only able to take more theoretical frameworks into account but can also take very diverse theoretical frameworks into account. Therefore, they are able to build bridges across the cleavages that have emerged between different paradigmatic camps within the social sciences.

The basic pair of ontological questions in the social sciences reads as follows:

– What are the basic entities of the social world?
– How are they related?

Major disputes have focused primarily on the first question: the controversy between Materialism and Idealism and the so-called agency-structure problem (often equated with the micro–macro problem). Materialist accounts assume that factors independent of the human mind matter in social reality, whereas idealists assume that reality consists of representations that are created in the human mind and that social reality is made up of shared interpretations. The agency-structure problem refers to the question of whether the building of social science theory should start with the behavior of individual agents or with the constituting and regulating functions of social structures. In each discourse, some scholars argue for the primacy of one dimension and for the 'reduction' of the other dimension in building causal explanations. Others claim that a thorough understanding and explanation of the social world cannot be based on such a reductionist conceptualization and that theoretical approaches that take full account of multiple dimensions are required (Wight 2006). Case studies are uniquely disposed to fulfill the latter demand.

Very often, the introduction of explanatory frameworks that take a broad spectrum of causal factors into account goes hand in hand with the use of case studies in their empirical application. We believe that there is a logical connection. Namely, given that all empirical research is restricted by limited resources, concentrating one's empirical investigation on one or a few cases allows for two things:

– taking a broader set of theoretical approaches into account and
– collecting more finely grained empirical evidence (in comparison to large-N studies).

Furthermore, tracking empirical developments over time and in a detailed manner makes it possible to explore two kinds of processes in the same study: the (re-)constitution of agents (their interests, identities, and institutional features) through social structures and the (re-)constitution of social structures through the cognitive processes and social interactions of the agents. By taking into account structure and agency as well as material factors (for example, economic interests, resource-based power relations) and ideas (for example, normative and causal beliefs and hegemonic discourses and frames), case study researchers can overcome the supposedly incommensurable differences between 'constitutive' and 'causal' approaches in explaining social realities (for a similar line of argumentation, see, for example, Vennesson 2008: 232). Two case studies that we extensively present in Chapter 4 (Tannenwald 1999, 2007) and Chapter 5 (Blatter 2009) provide proof for this claim.

Some of the above-mentioned developments on the theoretical and ontological level can be used to promote case study research in general, for example, the growing relevance of cognitive and communicative factors. Other developments, by contrast, point to the growing relevance of specific case study approaches. The increasing recognition that time and timing play an important role in explaining social events and the corresponding theoretical reflections bolster the widespread conviction that causal-process tracing is a crucial technique for drawing causal inferences. The observation that boundaries between (sub-)disciplines and cleavages between paradigmatic camps are eroding makes congruence analysis an especially promising approach.

1.3 The case for a non-fundamentalist and pluralist epistemology

As we show in the following section, case study methodology has been dominated since the 1970s by methodological advice that is rooted in the same epistemology that underlies large-N studies, which draw causal inferences with the help of statistics. Actual case study research never fully complied with the corresponding advice, but only in recent years have alternative epistemological foundations for drawing causal inference in case studies been clearly explicated. Developments in case study methodology, which we outline in the next section, are embedded in broader epistemological developments. To provide a clearer understanding of various ways of generating explanatory knowledge, we briefly delve into a discussion of the philosophy of science. We distinguish three major 'camps' with respect to ways of understanding knowledge creation in the social sciences. Our own epistemological stance is located in the 'middle ground' between these camps and rejects all radical epistemological positions. Furthermore, it is differentiated and pluralistic. Each of the three distinct case study approaches that we lay out in the major chapters of this book has an affinity to a specific epistemological camp. Such a pragmatic and pluralist stance has two major advantages. First, it allows for the formulation of internally consistent methodological approaches, and second, it makes it possible to combine and connect the approaches.

1.3.1 Empiricism/Positivism and Critical Rationalism

The first epistemological camp can be called Empiricism/Positivism and Critical Rationalism. Positivism has its origins in the writings of Auguste Comte in the nineteenth century and in the logical positivism of the Vienna Circle in the 1920s. It draws heavily on the empirical tradition of David Hume and combines it with the rationality of formal logics/mathematics. This position is epistemologically foundationalist; it assumes not only that an 'objective' reality outside the subjective minds of the researchers exists but also that sense impressions or observations provide us with information that corresponds with this external reality. Therefore, the external social reality influences the process of scientific knowledge generation at least as much as the internal mental maps of the researchers and the interpretative frameworks within the scientific community. As a result, it is possible to reach a better correspondence between scientific knowledge and objective reality by putting our theoretical propositions to an empirical test.

Positivists do not claim that we can observe all aspects of the social world nor that we need to. But, they presume that it is possible to observe human behavior and that formal logic helps us to draw descriptive and causal conclusions from these empirical observations.

Whereas positivists strive for the verification of theoretical claims through empirical observations and inductive reasoning, critical rationalists turn to deductive reasoning and to the falsification of deductively developed hypotheses as major goals of social science. Crucially important is the belief that theoretical (descriptive and causal) statements can be falsified or – to put it the other way round – that theoretical statements have to be formulated in such a way that they can be falsified. Scientific progress is seen primarily to lie in the reduction of unwarranted beliefs. Critical rationalists have a critical stance toward existing belief systems such as established theories in the social sciences. They believe that empirical observations can be used to test theoretical propositions, although they do not strive for 'proof' but for mere 'tentative refutation'.

1.3.2 Constructivism/Conventionalism and Critical Theory

The most direct alternative camp can be labeled 'Constructivism/Conventionalism and Critical Theory'. The proponents of this camp assume that interpretation and communication are at the core of knowledge generation in the social sciences and that interpretation is primarily influenced by pre-existing cognitive frames in the mind of the researcher and by dominant theoretical frameworks in the scientific community; sensory impressions from the external world are only a secondary influence. In other words, this position takes an anti-foundationalist epistemological stance, often combined with an emancipatory attitude.

The epistemology of this camp has its origins in hermeneutics and phenomenology, but adherents of post-Marxist critical theorists from Jürgen Habermas to Michel Foucault share its basic assumptions. Proponents of hermeneutics assume that knowledge about the social world depends on an understanding of the meanings that people attach to social behavior. Social science knowledge is nothing more than an interpretation of the interpretations of social actors. Processes of double hermeneutics and the fusion of horizons between the researcher and social actors lead to a joint understanding of the social world – a shared convention that is renewed and reconstructed primarily by taking into account new concepts and frameworks but also by empirical evidence that provides justifications for specific concepts and frameworks.

Empirical evidence consists not so much of observations as of the communicative explications of social actors. Empirical evidence is not used to verify or falsify theoretical propositions but provides arguments in the ongoing discussion about the most important theoretical framework for understanding and creating social reality. As with Empiricism/ Positivism and Critical Rationalism, we can detect turns from induction to deduction and toward less ambitious goals in the more recent philosophies of this camp.

Post-structural and post-modern philosophies of science also stress the importance of language, communication, and interpretation in knowledge generation. In contrast to adherents of hermeneutics and to modern critical theorists such as Habermas, post-structuralists and post-modernists do not believe that it is possible to produce commonly shared understandings of the social world. Instead, divergent theoretical frameworks lead to highly different interpretations of the same empirical observations, and knowledge generation in the social world is conceived as a discursive struggle for hegemony between competing theoretical (ideological and ontological) frames. For post-modern critical theorists such as Michel Foucault, this leads to a radical epistemological anti-foundationalist stance and the abandonment of any search for 'truth' in the social sciences. Furthermore, most critical theorists hold the conviction that theoretical discourses in the social sciences are strongly connected to ideological discourses in the social world. As a result, for them, the question 'which interpretation is true or convincing?' must be replaced with the question 'which interpretations are possible and who profits from each interpretation?' Nevertheless, not all those who see interpretation at the core of social science take such a relativist epistemological stance; some defend the (relative) autonomy of social science knowledge generation. For example, Mark Bevir and Rod A. W. Rhodes state:

> Although we do not have access to pure facts that we can use to declare particular interpretations and narratives to be true or false, we can still hang on to the idea of objectivity.... We judge one narrative better than another because it best meets such criteria as: accuracy, comprehensiveness, consistency, and opening new avenues of inquiry. Objectivity arises from criticizing and comparing rival webs of interpretation about agreed facts.
>
> (Bevir and Rhodes 2002 [1995]: 141–2)

For us, Critical Theory, understood as an epistemological stance, is an approach that is critical with respect to the dominant theories in a field

of research, and compares the relative merits of established or even hegemonic theories with other theories by using these theories as competing
interpretative frameworks for making sense out of a broad and diverse
cluster of empirical information about social processes and outcomes.

1.3.3   Pragmatism/Naturalism and Critical Realism

A third epistemological camp can be called Pragmatism/Naturalism and
Critical Realism. This position is foundationalist in its epistemological
stance, which means that its adherents assume that there is an 'objective' social reality beyond the minds of the researchers that plays a
central role in the process of scientific knowledge generation. Whereas
Roy Bhaskar, as the major representative of this philosophical position,
has sometimes called his approach 'naturalism' (Bhaskar 1979), it is usually referred to as Critical Realism (see, for example, Joseph and Wight
2010, or Cruickshank 2003 and other books in the series *Routledge Studies on Critical Realism*). In contrast to positivists, critical realists do not
rely only on sense impressions and on the observation of behavior as
major forms of empirical evidence. Furthermore, they do not rely on formal logic and on the search for invariant regularities among variables as
core tools for inferring causality. Instead, they believe it is necessary to
dig deeper into the social world by having a closer look at the processes,
temporal sequences, underlying mechanisms, and conditionalizing contexts that constitute social entities and that have causal effects in the
social world. Like the hermeneuticists, critical realists try to understand
the perceptions and intentions of social actors and the cultural and
communicative contexts of social interaction, but there is less emphasis on linguistic analysis, and critical realists also have different primary
research goals.

   Following pragmatic predecessors such as William James and John
Dewey, proponents of this position aim at generating useful, practical knowledge for social actors. They are doubtful of the value of
law-like patterns of co-variation among variables that positivists strive
for in making predictions. Instead, there is a strong affinity with
'configurational thinking', which leads to less ambitious goals with
respect to generalization across populations. Critical realists strive for
explaining specific cases or for contingent generalizations instead of
universal laws. Furthermore, because critical realists start from the ontological assumption that social reality consists of very different kinds
of entities on various levels and that these entities are linked in very
different ways, they accept a much broader array of methods to draw

descriptive and causal inferences than positivists. For example, Bhaskar proposes that there are two distinct levels of reality beyond the level of the 'empirical', or experiences based on sensual impressions. First, there is the level of the 'actual', consisting of events and the actual state of affairs, and second, there is the level of the 'real', consisting of unobservable real structures and mechanisms that, in interactions with other real structures and mechanisms, bring about outcomes and make empirical observations possible (Bhaskar 1989: 16; Kurki 2008: 163–4). Critical realists propose not only a 'deep' but also a 'broad' conception of causation, including both agency-centered and structural accounts and both idealist and materialist explanations (Kurki 2008: 218–30). This approach leads to a holistic position on epistemology and methodology. Causal inference depends equally on observations, logical conclusions, and interpretations. Critical realists argue for the integration of the supposedly incommensurate approaches of *erklären* ('explaining') versus *verstehen* ('understanding') in social research (Kurki 2008). They embrace Jon Elster's dictum: 'In my view, to interpret is to explain' (Elster 2007: 52). Nevertheless, Critical Realism is not just a plea for overcoming the fundamental divide between positivist and constructivist ontologies and epistemologies. It has its own distinct epistemological stance based on the assumption that 'causation is a relation in nature, not in logic' (Wendt 1999: 81), which leads to different ways of drawing causal inferences. The natural aspects of temporality and spatial contiguity in particular play an important role in explanatory approaches based on a critical realist epistemology. As a result, this epistemological stance has a strong affinity with the methodology on which the discipline of history is based (for example, George and Bennett 2005).

1.3.4   The epistemological 'middle ground': Anti-fundamentalist and pluralistic

The epistemological 'middle ground' can be best defined as a rejection of all fundamentalist (not to be confounded with foundationalist) epistemological positions. First, descriptive and causal inferences should not be drawn using empirical observation and formal logic alone (as radical positivists assume); instead, theory-led interpretation, understood as intensive reflection on the relationship between empirical evidence and abstract concepts, is a core element of all social science research, and case studies are especially well suited for this task. Second, there exists no incommensurable gap between theoretical frameworks or between abstract concepts and empirical observations that can render any search for a 'better' theory meaningless (as radical constructivists believe). Therefore, empirical evidence can be used to judge the adequacy of concepts and theories and their relative merits in providing adequate understandings and stimulating meanings of the social world. Finally, it is not only impossible but also useless to strive for a full-fledged representation of social reality. Instead, social scientists can reduce the complexity of social reality by focusing on events, structures, actions, and mechanisms that are relevant for social practices. Furthermore, temporality and proximity provide some 'natural' hints for explaining social processes and outcomes, but we have to be aware that even these aspects of social reality are to a large part influenced by our conceptual understanding of time and proximity.

Although we think that all empirical case study research should be grounded in the ideals of an anti-fundamentalist epistemological middle ground, it makes sense to differentiate the various approaches to case study design according to their affinity with the three epistemological camps. There are three major arguments for this stance.

– Firstly, there exists a clear affinity between specific research goals on one hand and specific epistemological stances and corresponding ways of drawing causal inferences on the other hand. The pro-typical question 'does the factor X make a difference?' implies a very different research approach than do the pro-typical questions 'what makes the outcome Y possible?' and 'which explanatory approach provides more/new insights?' For the first question, we propose using the co-variational analysis approach, which has strong affinities with Critical Rationalism; for the second question, the causal-process tracing approach, which has strong affinities with Critical Realism, is most appropriate; and for the last question, the congruence analysis approach is ideal because it embraces a specific understanding of Critical Theory as a critical stance toward hegemonic approaches in scientific discourses.
– Secondly, only by differentiating among the various approaches to case study research can we provide consistent advice for conducting case study research. The various approaches are based on different understandings of how causal inferences can be drawn. This fact leads to sometimes differing advice with regard to case selection, data collection, and data analysis, as well as to different understandings of generalization.
– Thirdly, we believe that differentiation and plurality are necessary to make progress in case study methodology. Major contributions and

existing textbooks on case study methodology are either exclusively based on one epistemological stance or blur and confuse the different epistemological foundations, leading to inconsistent advice for conducting case study research. We will return to this point in the following sections.

1.4 Case study methodology: A brief history and recent contributions

Having discussed basic epistemological positions in the literature and clarified our own position, we proceed with a short overview of the history of case study methodology, with an emphasis on the most recent contributions and their epistemological orientations. This overview provides another rationale for distinguishing among the three approaches to case study research.

Four volumes on *Case Study Research* edited by Matthew David (2006) illustrate nicely that since the introduction of case study research, led by the Chicago School of Sociology at the beginning of the twentieth century, there has been a lively debate on the nature and the (dis-) advantages of case studies. As a first trend, we can identify a change from seeing case studies as the study of a single case with an emphasis on its embeddedness within a specific (local or national) context to the use of case studies in comparative analysis based on abstract theoretical concepts and typologies that stresses the configurative nature of cases (Hall 2003: 378). The beginning of the 1970s brought another turn in case study research toward the variable-centered logic of causal analysis that characterizes the statistical techniques used in large-N studies. A textbook by Adam Przeworski and Henry Teune (1970) and the articles of Arend Lijphart (1971, 1975) drew on John Stuart Mill's (1875) methods of agreement and difference and established an understanding of case studies that is based on cross-case comparisons and the search for constant conjunction among variables. Such an understanding of case studies led to the conclusion that 'because the comparative method must be considered the weaker method, it is usually advisable to shift to the statistical method if sufficient cases are available for investigation' (Lijphart 1975: 165). Lijphart and most methodologists followed this advice, but case studies and small-N research survived in most social science disciplines, although very often without sufficient methodological reflection. Nevertheless, the situation changed again in the 1990s when Gary King, Robert O. Keohane, and Sidney Verba (1994) tried to reemphasize that small-N research should apply the same logic of descriptive and causal inference as large-N research. Their book, entitled *Designing Social Inquiry: Scientific Inference in Qualitative Research*, triggered a strong reaction by many scholars who sought to defend the distinctive logic of case-based research. The book *Rethinking Social Enquiry: Diverse Tools, Shared Standards*, edited by Henry E. Brady and David Collier (2004), contains a broad spectrum of arguments in favor of distinct tools for drawing causal inference in small-N studies. Additionally, Charles Ragin has summed up his own set alternative to the correlational/co-variational template proposed by King, Keohane, and Verba in his book *Redesigning Social Inquiry: Fuzzy Sets and Beyond* (2008).

At the same time, two book-length treatments of case study research that carry the promise of being comprehensive and internally consistent guides to case study research emerged: John Gerring's *Case Study Research: Principles and Practices* (2007a) and Alexander L. George and Andrew Bennett's *Case Studies and Theory Development in the Social Sciences* (2005). What strikes us most about these books in the context of our endeavor is that, although they both use the words 'case study' in their titles, they approach case study research very differently. They are based on different epistemological foundations, define case studies in different ways, advocate different techniques of causal inference, and have different visions concerning generalization. Both treatments have been very helpful in advancing case study methodology, but both represent specific and therefore limited approaches to case study research.

John Gerring's *Case Study Research: Principles and Practice* (2007a) essentially follows King, Keohane, and Verba's statistical template in presenting guidelines for research design, although Gerring differs in that he emphasizes the intrinsic value of case studies. Epistemologically, the book is grounded in positivist thought, with some emphasis on Critical Rationalism as advanced by Popper. A clear reference to large-N research is implied by a number of traits of the book. First, in defining case studies, Gerring emphasizes that the goal of case studies is at least in part to say something about a large class or population of cases (2007a: 20). Second, the virtues and vices of case studies are elaborated by contrasting case studies with large-N research (called cross-case research by Gerring). Third, he enumerates and discusses a variety of case selection criteria that are all related to their location in a population. The location in the population is ideally already determined by a large N-study. These features make the book particularly useful for those who are conducting large-N statistical research and want to complement this work with case study research.

George and Bennett's *Case Study and Theory Development in the Social Sciences* (2005) represents a contrasting view on case studies. While Gerring is largely in line with King, Keohane, and Verba, George and Bennett are critical of this approach. Their book is grounded in a critical realist epistemology, to which they devote a whole chapter (Chapter 3). Accordingly, they emphasize causal mechanisms and assume that these mechanisms exist in the real world and that researchers should seek to find traces of the workings of these mechanisms. At the core of their book is the advancement of two techniques for drawing causal inference: causal-process tracing, for which the authors are widely known, and the congruence method. Although George and Bennett's book has enabled case study research to escape the narrow confines of co-variational thinking and although it provides plenty of helpful examples, it has its own limits. Its structure makes it ill-suited for use as a textbook on case study research. Its conceptual richness is a strength but also a weakness because it allows practitioners of case study research to pick specific statements without taking into account the premises and further consequences. George and Bennett's treatment of causal-process tracing is extremely brief and provides little help for students who actually want to conduct a causal-process tracing study. There is a real danger that a fuzzy understanding of causal-process tracing can provide an 'escape/excuse clause' for those who conduct case studies without engaging in methodological reflection. Furthermore, the authors' stance against strongly theory-driven research leads to a limited understanding of the benefits of a methodological approach that draws causal inferences on the basis of a systematic analysis of the congruence between theoretical expectations and empirical observations. One of the main messages of our book is that causal-process tracing is not the only alternative to the co-variational template!

Our textbook straddles the methodological cleavage that has emerged in the current debate on case studies, not by proposing an encompassing approach to case study research, but by laying out three distinct approaches to case study research.[1] This allows us to present three internally consistent approaches with respect to major research goals, underlying epistemological assumptions and corresponding methodological concepts, selection of cases (and theories), the logic of causal inference, the direction of generalization, and ways of presenting research results. Our first approach follows the co-variational template that also underlies Gerring's book. Our second approach, causal-process tracing, builds on George and Bennett's book but is more specific in respect to basic terms such as 'process' and 'mechanism'. Our third approach, which we call congruence analysis, also shares some features with the approach presented by George and Bennett. However, we believe congruence analysis has unique epistemological presuppositions, research goals, and directions of generalization; in other words, congruence analysis represents a distinct approach to case study research.

1.5   Case studies: Towards a generic and multidimensional definition

There is little general consensus on what case studies are. After scrutinizing various and often contradictory ways of describing case studies, we provide a generic definition that highlights the differences between large-N studies and small-N studies and at the same time reveals distinct dimensions that allow for different approaches to case study research.

In the literature, we find a broad spectrum of definitions and descriptions of case studies (Blatter, Janning, and Wagemann 2007: 123–4; see Gerring 2007a: 17, 2008 for slightly different overviews):

- case studies are empirical studies focusing on a single phenomenon or outcome (for example, Stake 1995; Muno 2003: 21);
- case studies are studies that are primarily interested in the causes of effects and less in the effects of causes (for example, Goertz 2003a: 55); they are centered on the dependent variable (Y) in contrast to other research designs that focus on the independent variable (X) (for example, Ganghof 2005, who advocates a change in small-N research toward more X-centered designs);
- case studies are small-N studies conducted with the aim of generalizing across a population of similar cases (for example, King, Keohane, and Verba 1994: 51–3);
- case studies comprise a few, 'comparable' cases (for example, Lijphart 1971, 1975);
- case studies are 'case-centered', whereas large-N studies are 'variable-centered'. Case-centered research is based on configurational thinking; in contrast to variable-centered approaches, it starts with the assumption that there are strong interaction effects between individual causal factors and between specific factors and contexts (for example, Ragin 2000: 39, 2008: 109–23; Patzelt 2005: 21–4);
- case studies are studies in which no clear-cut boundary between the phenomenon of interest and its context exist (Yin 2009: 18); in contrast to large-N studies that take established socio-political entities such as nations or nation states as cases, case study researchers

are 'casing' (Ragin 1992: 218): they are defining the object and the boundaries of the object through their research project (Vennesson 2008: 230);
- case studies are characterized by the technique of 'process tracing' (George and Bennett 2005); their primary goal is to uncover 'causal mechanisms' rather than 'causal effects' (Brady and Collier 2004: 277).

Although all of these definitions are appropriate for some types of case study research, they are too specific to serve as a generic definition, and they do not capture one of the most important features of case study research (our fourth aspect in the following list). For us, case study research is defined as a non-experimental research approach that differs from large-N studies in the following four characteristics:

1. a small number of cases;
2. a large number of empirical observations per case;
3. a huge diversity of empirical observations for each case; and
4. an intensive reflection on the relationship between concrete empirical observations and abstract theoretical concepts.

The first element of our definition represents a categorical decision; we do not make a fundamental distinction between the study of a single case and the study of a few cases, because the core characteristics are the same for all small-N studies. The small number of cases makes it easier for researchers to select cases that have no clear-cut boundaries, but have to be delineated and specified on the basis of abstract theoretical concepts (for example, policy reforms or international regimes). Therefore, case studies are ideal for investigating new, complex, or abstract phenomena.

In each of the three approaches to case study research that we advance in this book, one of the other three elements of our definition is predominant. The co-variational approach in case study research approximates in many ways statistical analysis, but there exists one major difference between the comparative method in small-N studies and correlation analysis in large-N studies: the number of observations that researchers take into account to arrive at the score for each variable and each case is much higher in case study research (and the reflection on the correct measurement is much more intensive). For the second approach, causal-process tracing, a large number of observations per case is also a key feature, but the variety of diverse observations is even more important here. In this approach, the observations need not be aggregated into standardized scores, because causal inference is not based on cross-case comparison. Instead, a large set of diverse observations is necessary to produce 'comprehensive storylines', 'smoking guns', and 'confessions', which form the empirical basis for drawing causal inferences.

Probably the most important feature of case studies is the fact that limiting the research to one or a few cases allows the researcher to invest time and intellectual energy in reflecting on the relationship between empirical observations and the abstract concepts that form the core elements of hypotheses, theories, and mechanism-based explanations. Many strengths and advantages of case study research result from this fact. For example, theories in which difficult-to-observe cognitive aspects of individual actors (for example, their problem perception) play a central role can be included in case studies with much higher levels of validity in comparison to large-N studies. Furthermore, internal validity is enhanced because case study researchers can more easily employ context-specific indicators for theoretical concepts. Finally, case study researchers can take into account a broader set of theories and more abstract theories when analyzing and interpreting cases. In our third and last approach to case study research, congruence analysis, these features take center stage and lead to a specific research design.

Although it makes sense to distinguish the three different approaches in order to provide internally consistent ideal-types, it is important to realize that all approaches share the characteristics of the generic definition – albeit with a different emphasis.

1.6   Observations: Towards an adequate understanding for case studies

'Observation' is another important term for which the existing literature fails to provide a definition that is adequate for a pluralistic understanding of case study research. To highlight the unique use of empirical information as a basis for drawing causal inferences in qualitative research in contrast to quantitative research, David Collier, Henry E. Brady, and Jason Seawright introduce the term 'causal-process observation' and contrast it with the term 'data-set observation'. In the glossary of the book, Jason Seawright and David Collier define these terms as follows:

> Data-set observation: All the scores in a given row, in the framework of a rectangular data set. It is thus the collection of scores

for a given case on the dependent variable and all the independent variables. This includes intervening and antecedent variables. Put another way, it is 'all the numbers for one case'. A data point in a two- or multidimensional scatterplot is a data-set observation.

(Seawright and Collier 2004: 283)

Causal-process observation: An insight or piece of data that provides information about context, process, or mechanism, and that contributes distinctive leverage in causal inference. A causal-process observation sometimes resembles a 'smoking gun' that confirms a causal inference in qualitative research, and is frequently viewed as an indispensable supplement to correlation-based inference in quantitative research as well.

(Seawright and Collier 2004: 277/278)

These definitions are not satisfying for case study researchers, mainly because they have been developed with the goal of distinguishing case study research in general from statistical analysis, and the terminology has been explicitly chosen with an eye to quantitatively oriented scholars (Collier, Brady, and Seawright 2004: 253). As a result, they are not suitable for a more nuanced understanding of different case study approaches.

The first problem with these definitions arises from the fact that the two definitions apply the same term – observation – on two different levels of abstraction. In line with statistical methodology, a 'data set observation' refers to the scores that we assign to a case for the variables of interest. Variables are usually abstract concepts (for example, democracy) that cannot be directly observed but have to be operationalized through the specification of indicators on a lower level of abstraction. The indicators are usually on the same level of abstraction as the concrete pieces of information that the researcher finds 'out there' (for example, regular elections). As a result, a 'data-set observation' is not really an observation but the result of a data generation process in which empirical information has been transformed into a score for a variable, and all of these scores can be represented as a single 'data point' on a scatter plot. In contrast, the definition of causal-process observation seems to indicate that these kinds of observations are located on the lower level of abstraction. In the context of qualitative or case study research, it is wise to use the term 'observation' more literally and restrict its meaning to those pieces of information that are located on the lowest level of abstraction. In other words, an 'observation' is information that we find 'out there', and we need a further step to connect these kinds of information to the more abstract concepts that form the core elements of our hypotheses, mechanism-based explanations, and theories.

A second problem with the above definitions is that a 'data-set observation' is in fact a set of individual data (the set of the scores for a case for all variables), whereas a causal-process observation seems to be a single piece of information. First, using the same term in these two ways is inconsistent; it makes sense only if we want to highlight the fact that a data point is a configuration of variable scores, which is not generally the case in case study research. Second, both definitions are of limited value for the fine-grained understanding of case study research that is the focus of this book. For the co-variational (COV) case study approach, each individual score of a case on the independent and dependent variables is of crucial importance, as the conclusions that we can draw from case study research depend much more on the correct scoring of each variable than is the case within large-N studies. As a result, case study researchers invest heavily in making sure that each score is valid and tend to employ a large number of empirical observations for this task (see Section 2.6). As a result, the crucial step in this research approach is the process of transforming the information that we find 'out there' in the social world into scores for individual variables and not so much the following step of data analysis. Thus, we should call the empirical information that we use for generating a score for individual variables 'variable-scoring observations'. Note that we deliberately use the plural in 'variable-scoring observations', because the scoring of a variable in the COV approach is usually based on a plurality of observations. Nevertheless, these observations are not yet integrated into a data set. Such integration takes place within a co-variational case study approach as well, and it is a necessary step for drawing causal inferences (see Section 2.5), but this data analysis step does not take as central a place as it does in large-N studies.

For delineating a specific and helpful causal-process tracing (CPT) approach, the definition of causal-process observations must be more clearly specified. Such a specification should highlight the fact that these observations have to contribute to determining the temporal sequence of a social process. In other words, we should take the term 'process' seriously. Furthermore, we find the equalization of 'causal mechanisms' with 'intervening variables' in the same volume (Seawright and Collier 2004: 277) confusing. As we will argue in Chapter 3, it seems wise to use a distinct terminology for the CPT approach in contrast to the variable-centered terminology of the COV approach. Finally, Jason Seawright and David Collier's definition does not take into account the fact that, in CPT, we always need a plurality of empirical information/concrete observations to determine the status of a causal condition as necessary or sufficient. For example, the observation of a smoking gun is only a strong piece of evidence if it is complemented by further observations that document the consequences of the shooting on the basis of temporal and spatial contiguity (see Section 3.5.2).

As a result of these reflections, we propose to use the following terminology:

Variable-scoring observations: A cluster of empirical information that is used to determine the score or value of a case for a specified and operationalized variable. Usually, the search for these kinds of empirical information is guided by indicators and measurement scales for the variables that are determined ex-ante – although in case study research, the actual research process is much more iterative than in large-N studies with respect to specifying indicators and measurement scales, and collecting empirical information.

Process-tracing observations: A cluster of empirical information that is used (a) to determine the temporal order in which causal factors work together to produce the outcome of interest, (b) to determine the status of these causal factors as individually necessary and jointly sufficient for the outcomes in the cases under investigation, and/or (c) to identify and to specify the social mechanisms that form the basis for mechanism-based explanations.

1.7 Three approaches to case study research: An overview

In this section, we provide a short comparative overview of our three explanatory approaches to small-N research. This overview reveals how the three approaches differ in terms of their main research goals, their focus, the selection of cases (and theories), data generation and data analysis, and the understanding and direction of generalization. In the following chapters of this book, we present each approach separately to display the internal consistency of each approach; each aspect is delineated in great detail and illustrated with examples. These chapters also contain extensive explanations and definitions of the terminology that we have introduced only briefly in this overview.

1.7.1 Research goals and questions

Each empirical research project, whether or not it follows a case study approach, starts with a research question that needs to be answered to achieve the goal of the research project. The co-variational approach (COV) to case study research typically aims to investigate whether a specific factor makes a difference. For example: Does government reorganization reduce public spending? Are humanitarian interventions successful? As this kind of research is interested in the effect of a specific causal factor, or independent variable, this research can be labeled X-centered research. But the focus on 'independent variables' has a further, deeper meaning, because the COV approach assumes that the causal factors function independently of each other; this approach is based on the ontological assumption of autonomous causal factors.

Contrast this with research projects that start with an interest in a specific (kind of) outcome. They ask what factors lead to a concrete outcome or what makes a specific kind of outcome possible. For example: What factors led to World War I? Which conditions lead to social revolution? Because the researcher is interested in a relatively complete explanation of an outcome or a full-fledged understanding of a social process rather than the effect of a specific variable, this approach can be called Y-centered research. Nevertheless, with respect to causal analysis, the main difference between the causal-process tracing approach (CPT) and the COV approach is that, within CPT, the researcher starts with the assumption that a plurality of factors work together to produce the outcome of interest. Such a holistic ontological starting point leads to the search for configurations of causal conditions or social mechanisms.

Other case studies are conducted with the aim of contributing to the theoretical debate in a discipline or field of research. Typical research questions read as follows: Which theory of organizational decision-making is most consistent with the real decision-making processes in business organizations? Is Liberal Intergovernmentalism the best explanation for European Integration? Such research questions recognize that paradigms and theories have an important function in the process of knowledge generation because they provide the anchor points for research programs and structure the scientific discourse. In the congruence analysis approach (CON), theories are not reduced to single independent variables (as in the COV approach) but are treated as comprehensive worldviews that are specified through a set of constitutive and causal propositions. Case studies are used to elucidate and to compare the explanatory merits of competing or complementary theories.

1.7.2   Case and theory selection

For the COV approach, case selection is crucial to demonstrate that it was indeed variation in X and not another factor that caused the effect (variation in Y). In other words, case selection is crucial to making valid causal inferences. A plurality of cases is selected according to the experimental template. This means that the cases must express strong differences with respect to the main independent variable of interest, and they must be as similar as possible with regard to variables associated with other potential explanations. This design is described using the term 'most similar system design' (Przeworski and Teune 1970) or, alternatively, a term that emphasizes the underlying logic, the 'method of difference' (Mill 1875); this design also corresponds to the 'comparable cases' approach of Lijphart (1975).

Because causal-process tracing depends on gaining a comprehensive overview over the temporal unfolding of the causal-process, the ability to provide a dense description of critical moments, and the possibility of gaining deep insights into the perceptions and motivations of important actors, the accessibility of a case is the primary precondition for investigation. Causal-process tracing is a within-case analytical technique; therefore, we need not select more than one case, although we do have the option to do so. In the ideal-typical form of the CPT approach, those cases that show a strong positive result with respect to the outcome of interest are selected. In a second step, further 'possible' cases can be selected to test the relevance of specific factors that have been identified as necessary for the outcome in the first study.

Within the CON approach, the selection of theories has to be done more explicitly than in the other approaches. Ideally, this step precedes the selection of cases. We advocate selecting more than one theory and avoiding the ex-ante integration of those theories in a synthetic explanatory approach. The researcher should consider a plurality of theories and should reflect on the status of these theories in the scientific discourse. This allows for selecting a 'crucial case' – whereby the 'crucialness' of the case depends on the 'likeliness' that it is congruent with the expectations that we can deduce from the selected theories. This ex-ante likeliness, in turn, depends on some prior knowledge of the cases.

When we apply the above guidelines for case selection, it becomes obvious that for the COV and the CON approaches significant prior knowledge about the cases is necessary if we want to select optimal cases. Nevertheless, this knowledge is often not available ex-ante or it turns out to be superficial when we learn more about the cases. For the CON approach, selecting a non-crucial case only undermines the impact of the study on the theoretical discourse, but for the COV approach, the selection of non-similar cases can be devastating because it undermines the possibility of drawing valid causal inferences. This is one major

Table 1.1 Three explanatory approaches in case study research

	Co-Variational Analysis (COV)	Causal-Process Tracing (CPT)	Congruence Analysis (CON)
Research questions and research goals	**Does variable X make a difference?** Testing whether different values of X lead to different outcomes	**What makes the outcome (Y) possible?** Revealing the temporal interplay among conditions or mechanisms that lead to specific outcomes	**Which explanatory approach provides more/new insights?** Comparing the descriptive and explanatory merits of different theories
Focus	**Independent variables** as factors that have an autonomous influence	**Causal configurations** as sequential and situational combinations of causal conditions or social mechanisms	**Theories** understood as comprehensive interpretative and explanatory frameworks that compete with or complement each other
Selection of cases and theories	Select **multiple cases** according to: – strong **differences** in respect to the independent **variable of interest**, AND – high **similarity** in respect to **control variables**	Select one or more cases according to: – their **accessibility**, AND – the practical or theoretical **relevance** of the outcome Selection of one or more cases **sequentially:** 1. 'positive' case(s) 2. 'possible' case(s)	Select **multiple *theories*** according to: – their place in the scientific discourse, AND – the researcher's theoretical aspiration Selection of one or more *cases* according to the ex-ante '**likeliness**' **of cases** in respect to the selected theories
Data generation	**Observations:** Information corresponding to the indicators specified for the variables	**Observations:** – Information on the temporal unfolding of the causal-process; – Information on spatial-temporal distance and proximity between causes and consequences; – Information on perceptions and motivations of important actors	**Observations:** Information corresponding to the expectations (propositions, hypotheses, predictions) deduced from theories

27

Data analysis = drawing causal inferences for the cases under investigation	**Resulting data:** Scores of each variable for all cases **Necessary content of data:** Co-variation among scores of the dependent variable (Y) and scores of the independent variable of interest (X) **Conclusion:** X has a causal effect on Y **Further necessary conditions for conclusions:** No theoretically plausible co-variation among scores of the dependent variable and scores of other independent (control) variables	**Resulting data:** – Comprehensive story line – Smoking gun observations – Confessions **Necessary content of data:** – Causal chains and conjunctions – Smoking gun observations – Confessions **Conclusions:** – The causal configuration consisting of the conditions A,B and C is sufficient for outcome Y – The causal mechanism consisting of the social mechanisms s, a and t is sufficient for outcome Y **Further tools for drawing conclusions** (in respect to the necessity of each element of a causal configuration/mechanism): Counterfactuals and/or coherent theoretical conceptualizations of mechanisms or process dynamics	**Resulting data:** Confirmations or contradictions for each expectation **Necessary content of data:** a full set of confirmations and contradictions for each theory **Conclusion:** Relative importance or specific role of selected theories in explaining the case(s) **Further possible conditions for drawing conclusions:** Ex-ante expectations about the 'likeliness' that the case is congruent with the expectations derived from different theories
Generalization = drawing conclusions beyond the cases under investigation	**Statistical generalization** Drawing conclusions about the causal effect of X on Y from the selected cases and generalizing to a population of cases that are similar in respect to all control variables	**Possibilistic generalization** Drawing conclusions from the identified causal configuration(s) and mechanisms to the set of potential configurations and mechanisms and/or to the set of proven causal configurations and mechanisms	**Theoretical generalization** Drawing conclusions from the explanatory power of theories in more or less 'crucial' cases to the relevance of theories in the scientific discourse

reason why the COV approach is often complemented by causal-process tracing which allows reducing indeterminacy.

1.7.3   Data generation and data analysis

While it is a defining characteristic of all case study approaches that a large number of (diverse) empirical observations are collected per case and that there is an intensive reflection on the relationship between concrete empirical observations and abstract theoretical concepts, there are strong differences in the ways in which observations are transformed into data and in the ways this data are analyzed to draw causal inferences. Despite these differences, all case study approaches share one feature: in case study research, it is the first step, data generation, that is most crucial; case study researchers invest much more time and intellectual energy in this first step than do large-N statistical analysts, and the cogency of case studies depends much more on this. In Table 1.1, we present the processes of data generation and data analysis separately to present clearly the functional equivalents in each approach. Whereas for the rather deductive approaches COV and CON, this neat separation represents the way we conduct case studies (or at least, it corresponds to the way we present the findings), that is not the case with the inductive CPT approach, in which the separation of data generation from data analysis is less clear-cut.

In the COV approach, indicators that scholars have selected for operationalizing variables into observable entities define which empirical information is seen as relevant and which information must be collected for each case. The relevant empirical information is used to determine the scores for each of the variables; therefore, we call the corresponding information 'variable-scoring observations' (see above). Researchers invest significantly in making sure that each score is valid, and they typically employ a large number of empirical observations for this task. As a result, a crucial step in this research approach is the process of transforming the information that we find 'out there' in the social world into scores for individual variables. Compared with large-N studies, the COV approach makes it much easier to apply indicators in a context-sensitive way, which means that nominally different states of the social world (for example, number of parties in a parliament) can be treated as functionally equivalent (for example, for the concept of 'competition'), and nominally equal states can be scored differently. Data analysis takes place in a second distinct step after we have transferred all scores of all cases for all variables into a rectangular data sheet. Through visual inspection, we discover whether there is co-variation among the scores of the dependent variable of interest (Y) and the scores of the independent variable (X). If so, we can conclude that X has a causal effect on Y. A necessary condition for this inference is that there exists no other theoretically plausible co-variation among scores of other independent variables and the dependent variable – which is what we try to guarantee through the careful selection of cases but which has to be controlled for in the process of data analysis.

In the CPT approach, the search for relevant empirical information proceeds in a much more inductive fashion. The researcher has to search for all kinds of information about the temporal unfolding of the causal-process that allows her to present a comprehensive storyline with a sequence of causal steps. For decisive situations and phases of transformation, the researcher searches for information that gives him a more detailed picture of the 'scene' and a denser description of the temporal unfolding of events during these critical times. Finally, she has to dig deeper and collect information about the perceptions and motivations of major actors. The data generation process in the CPT approach is not only more inductive in comparison to the COV approach, but the separation between data generation and data analysis is also less clear-cut. Nevertheless, the functional equivalents to scores for the variables in the COV approach are 'comprehensive storylines', 'smoking guns', and 'confessions'. From the comprehensive storylines, the scholars extract 'causal chains' and 'causal conjunctions'; detailed descriptions of critical situations lead to strong evidence for a dense connection between a cause and an effect (corresponding to the observation of a 'smoking gun'), and 'confessions' provide deep insights into the perceptions and motivations of major actors. These kinds of condensed empirical information have to be combined with counterfactual thought experiments and/or with theoretical reflection on the working of causal mechanisms and process dynamics to identify those configurations of conditions and/or mechanisms that are individually necessary and jointly sufficient for making the outcome possible.

In the CON approach, the sort of information required is delineated by expectations (propositions, hypotheses, and predictions) deduced from the theories that have been selected and specified ex-ante. This is to some extent similar to the COV approach. Nevertheless, in this approach, the information is not transformed into variable scores but is used to determine whether the formulated expectations are confirmed or contradicted. As a result, the investigator obtains a set of confirmations and/or contradictions for each of the theories. As a second analytical step, he uses the differences among the theories with respect to the level of congruence between expectations and observations either for drawing conclusions about the relative importance of the selected theories in explaining the case(s) or for combining the theories into a comprehensive explanation. If the researcher is interested in judging the relative merits of the selected theories, he has different options for doing so: he can compare the absolute levels of confirmations and/or contradictions or he can compare the results with what he was expecting on the basis of some prior knowledge about the case(s) and reflections on the 'likeliness' that the case(s) would be congruent with the selected theories. Whereas reflections on the ex-ante 'likeliness' are not necessary for drawing conclusions about the relative merits of different theories in explaining the case(s) under investigation, such reflections are necessary for drawing solid conclusions about the relevance of the theories in the wider scientific discourse.

Conclusions beyond the cases under investigation are usually discussed under the heading of 'generalization' – we follow this practice, although one of the main messages of this book is that 'generalization' means something quite different within the different case study approaches. We will briefly scrutinize the different meanings and directions of generalization in the final section of this overview.

1.7.4   Generalization

In principle, drawing conclusions within the COV approach is similar to the understanding of generalization in large-N studies; we therefore call it 'statistical generalization'. The researcher draws conclusions from the cases selected to a population of cases. Nevertheless, unlike the findings of large-N studies, which are broadly generalizable, the findings of COV studies can only be generalized to a relatively small population. It is reasonable to assume that the independent variable (X) has a particular effect on a specific outcome (Y) only in cases that are similar with respect to all control variables (assuming that such similarity exists in the cases selected).

It is important to realize that the CPT approach does not strive for this kind of generalization but for something that we call 'possibilistic generalization'. The findings of a CPT case study lead to knowledge about the causal configurations (combinations of causal conditions or social mechanisms) that make specific outcomes possible. The configurations of conditions and/or mechanisms that the researcher identifies as necessary and sufficient for an outcome within the cases under investigation are used to elucidate the set of potential configurations (all possible combinations of the identified conditions and mechanisms) and/or the set of proven causal configurations. The first set is helpful for developing 'typological theories' inductively; the second set includes all those configurations that have been shown to lead to the outcome of interest.

Within the CON approach, the researcher uses the insights gained in the case study for the debate on the relevance of theoretical approaches in the broader scientific discourse. The impact that the case study might have on this theoretical discourse depends on how 'crucial' the selected case is for the theories that 'populate' the scientific discourse. In Chapter 4, we will lay out the factors that determine the theoretical 'crucialness' of cases. One of these factors is the standing of the selected theories within the scientific discourse (central or peripheral) – which makes clear the importance of case *and* theory selection for the possibility of drawing conclusions beyond the cases under investigation.

Overall, we hope that this overview serves as a helpful orientation for those who seek advice on determining the most appropriate approach for a given research goal and question. Chapters 2–4 will present the approaches and their underlying methodological concepts in much more detail and with illustrative examples. Our typology helps to reveal differences between the different approaches and clarifies the internal connections among the various elements of each approach. Like all typologies, our typology does have disadvantages. It might overstate the differences between the approaches and the need for internal coherence. According to our aspiration for striking a balance between principled and pragmatic research, Chapter 5 concludes the book by showing how our three divergent approaches can be combined.

2
Co-Variational Analysis

We call the first research approach to small-N studies co-variational analysis (COV). This methodological approach presents empirical evidence of the existence of co-variation between an independent variable X and a dependent variable Y to infer causality. This approach has dominated the thinking about small-N research designs since the 1970s. We present it here as the first approach because it has been central to most of the methodological reflections on small-N research designs. Nevertheless, as we will see at the end of this chapter, because of its inherent limitations, it seems wise to complement this approach with other approaches, especially with elements from the causal-process tracing approach (CPT).

The chapter proceeds as follows. First, we argue that the COV approach has strong affinities to a distinctive research goal, namely to determine whether a certain factor has an effect, that is, whether it 'makes a difference'. We assemble a broad array of typical research questions that illustrate this goal (Section 2.1). Second, we discuss the ontological and epistemological foundations of this approach. In particular, we focus on the counterfactual concept of causation, the logic of experiments, and deterministic versus probabilistic causation (Section 2.2). In Section 2.3, we address the criteria for case selection, a step that is crucially important in this approach to case studies because the selection of cases strongly determines the possibilities of drawing logical conclusions. We also discuss different modes of comparisons ranging from cross-sectional comparison and intertemporal comparison to the cross-sectional–intertemporal comparison and the counterfactual comparison. Section 2.4 is concerned with the approach-specific functions of prior knowledge and theory. We argue that an overview of existing theories and knowledge in the field of research is necessary for a number of reasons, including the conceptualization of variables, arguments about the plausibility of the effect of the variable of interest on the dependent variable, and the determination of other variables that might have an effect and therefore must be controlled for. Section 2.5 discusses data analysis. We demonstrate the logic of drawing causal inferences for the cases under investigation and emphasize that reference to theory and/or the complementation of this approach by elements of causal-process tracing contributes to making these conclusions more convincing. The chapter then discusses measurement and data collection issues. In the actual research process, issues of measurement and data collection must be addressed prior to case selection and data analysis. However, we discuss them here after those themes to help the reader understand why some issues of measurement and data collection must be settled before cases can be selected and analyzed (Section 2.6). We show that, in principle, small-N research is better able to achieve concept validity than large-N research because focusing on a few cases allows variables to be conceptualized in complex and multidimensional ways. Indicators can be employed in context-sensitive forms, and the integration of all observations in a final score of a variable can and should be done reflectively. In Section 2.7, we address the question of generalization. First, we clarify that generalization in the COV approach means that the empirical findings of the cases studied (for example, that X makes a difference) are generalizable to a population of similar cases (similar in respect to the control variables). In accordance with Robert K. Yin (2009: 15), we call the corresponding logic of drawing conclusions beyond the cases under investigation 'statistical generalization'. We argue that while generalization is relatively limited, in many instances, this is not a problem. For instance, case studies applied in evaluation research are primarily used to determine whether a policy measure made a difference, for example, in a specific country or city. Furthermore, case studies are often the first step in a larger research program. Showing that a factor makes a difference in a small sample of cases is often seen as a plausibility probe that must be tested with large-N studies to determine whether and how much the factor matters generally. These and other combinations of small-N and large-N studies will be discussed in more detail in Chapter 5. Finally, we briefly discuss the typical research process and the appropriate style of presenting the findings, emphasizing that the presentation of findings should be more deductive and linear than the actual research process usually is (Section 2.8).

We illustrate the features of the co-variational approach by using best research practices from the areas of comparative politics, European studies/public administration and international relations/international political economy. These are instances of real-world research that have used this case study approach and have been published in leading international journals. Throughout the chapter, we use two examples. The study by Herbert Kitschelt (1986) looks at the strategies and the impact of the anti-nuclear movement in four countries, and the study by Markus Haverland (2000) focuses on the adaptation of member states of the European Union to EU obligations. These two running examples will be supplemented with references to other studies. The chapter concludes with an integrated discussion of a study by Bernhard Zangl (2008) that examines the impact of judicalization on international trade conflicts.

2.1 Research goals and research questions

Very often, social practitioners and social scientists are interested in finding out whether specific features of the social reality make a difference – whether they produce a significant effect in the social reality or not. The co-variational approach attempts to answer this question by comparing different cases and by systematically comparing the variation of these features (the scores/values of the independent variable, usually denoted as X) with the variation of relevant potential effects (the scores of the outcome or the dependent variable, usually denoted as Y) (Mahoney and Goertz 2006: 230–1).

There are various reasons why a researcher might be interested in the effects of a specific factor. A new policy or organizational innovation might have been introduced and those responsible or affected by these changes want to determine whether this change had the intended effect; whether it 'works'. This is the bread and butter of evaluation research. Typical research questions include the following:

- Does the shift toward a more active labor market policy lead to a higher degree of labor market participation?
- Does the introduction of a new information technology system increase organizational performance?
- Does consultation with stakeholders increase the legitimacy of the regional planning project?

In addition to these goals of applied research, the focus on the effect of a distinctive variable is also apparent in more theoretically oriented research projects. To take our running examples, Kitschelt (1986) studied the strategy and impact of anti-nuclear movements with the goal of investigating whether a country's political opportunity structure affects the strategies and impacts of anti-nuclear protest movements. His study aimed to contribute to 'a generalized understanding of the factors that determine the dynamics of social movements' (1986: 57). Haverland (2000) was interested in whether the number of institutional veto points made a difference for the degree to which member states adapted their policy goals and policy styles to EU requirements. Haverland's study related to a larger debate about factors that determine the impact of the EU on member states. This debate had been dominated by an emphasis on the importance of the fit between EU requirements and the national status quo to explain the degree of adaptation of member states to the EU (Haverland 2000: 84). These studies presented the following research questions:

–   Does a country's political opportunity structure affect the strategy and the impact of anti-nuclear movements (Kitschelt 1986)?
–   Do institutional veto points reduce the degree of adaptation of national policy goals and policy styles to EU requirements (Haverland 2000)?

The common thread in the research questions stated above is their interest in the effect of a certain factor or independent variable. This approach to case study research can be labeled X-centered,[1] where X in our running examples is the political opportunity structure and veto points.

This approach to research is compatible with practically oriented as well as theoretically oriented research interests. Regardless of the source of the research question, the investigator should (as in all research) be as explicit as possible about the relevance of answering the research question, for example, for those affected by a policy change or organizational innovation, or for the scientific community.

2.2   Ontological and epistemological foundations and affinities

To understand the logic that underlies the causal inferences of the co-variational approach to case studies, it is important to elaborate on the experimental template, on the counterfactual concept of causation and on the difference between deterministic and probabilistic causal relationships.

2.2.1 Experimental template and counterfactual concept of causation

The co-variational case study approach seeks to approximate the conditions of an experiment (Gerring 2007a: 152–72; see also Lijphart 1971). Experiments are also X-centered. Hence, by conducting experiments, researchers want to determine the effect of a specific factor, typically called an 'intervention', 'treatment', or 'stimulus'. To establish the effect of a factor, other conditions must be controlled for. The idea of control in experiments is based on a counterfactual conception of causation. According to a counterfactual understanding of causation, the causal effect of a factor on the outcome means that in the absence of this factor, the outcome would not have occurred *in that case*. In terms of variables, if the score of the variable had been different (lower/higher), the outcome would have been different (lower/higher) as well *in that case*. The size of the causal effect is defined as the difference in the outcome between the two situations (Holland 1986; Fearon 1991; King, Keohane, and Verba 1994: 76–82). Of course, we do not know what the outcome would have been if the factor had been absent *in that case*. We cannot rerun history. This is why some authors speak of the fundamental problem of causal inference. The experiment *approximates* the counterfactual situation by comparing cases where the factor is present (higher score/lower score) with *other* cases where the factor is absent (lower score/higher score). These other cases cannot be identical but should be as similar as possible to the initial cases.

The experimental design is particularly suited for approaching the counterfactual situation because the investigator has control over the treatment. Hence, the investigator is able to provide the treatment (a dose of the independent variable, so to speak) to some participants in the experiment (the experimental group) and withhold the treatment from others (the control group). If the participants in the experiment are distributed randomly in the experimental and control groups – so the logic goes – both groups are equivalent; that is, both groups have similar scores, on average, for all variables other than the treatment variable. Hence, any difference between the experimental group and the control group in the average score of the dependent variable after the treatment can be ascribed to the treatment and not to any other factor. Note that if groups are randomly assigned, the researcher controls not only for those factors that are expected to have an effect but also for all factors that the investigator is not aware of (Cook and Campbell 1979; Babbie 2001).

2.2.2   Experimental control versus control in observational studies

The co-variational approach to case study research has a point in common with correlation-based methods in large-N research and it is that a manipulation of the independent variables (treatment) is not possible. Therefore, it is not feasible to assign participants (or, rather, cases) randomly to an experimental group and the control group. Hence, equivalence between the experimental group and the control group for the purpose of control cannot be established this way. Experimental control must be replaced by control mechanisms based solely on observation.

There is a crucial difference between small-N and large-N studies when it comes to control. In large-N observational studies, control is achieved through statistical manipulation. All cases of a population are selected, or a random sample is chosen. The effect of each of the independent variables is established through a statistical procedure that manipulates the values of the variables in a way that makes it possible to estimate the effect of each of the independent variables. In multivariate regression, the regression coefficient, typically denoted as β, indicates the magnitude of the assumed causal effect – in other words, the difference that this variable makes to the dependent variable if the scores of the other variables of the equation are held constant.

Small-N studies following the co-variational approach are similar to experiments in that control is related to case selection. Whereas cases ('participants') in experiments are assigned randomly to the experimental group and the control group, control in the co-variational case study approach is achieved by deliberately choosing cases that vary in the score of the independent variable ('treatment') and have similar scores on the variables for which the researcher seeks control. Hence, careful case selection is of great importance for this approach to case study research (see next section).

2.2.3   Probabilistic versus deterministic causality

Another major difference between observational large-N studies (and experimental designs) and the co-variational *case study* concerns the underlying assumption about causality. Researchers applying the co-variational case study design must assume that the causal relationship between the independent and dependent variables is deterministic and invariant (Mahoney 2003: 340–1). More precisely, the investigator must assume that the factor of interest is both necessary and sufficient to produce the outcome. Necessity means that if the causal factor is absent, the outcome cannot occur; sufficiency means that if the factor is present, then the outcome must occur. Hence, the COV approach is based on the following type of hypothesis: if X has a specific score, then a specific score for variable Y will *always* occur.

For instance, Maurice Duverger (1969 [1954]) has argued that an election system that applies a proportional rule produces a multiparty system, whereas an election system with a plurality rule (first-past-the-post) produces a two-party system. Framing this claim as a deterministic relationship would imply that a country that has a proportional voting rule will *always* have a multiparty system.

In contrast, a probabilistic hypothesis is formulated as follows: if X has a specific score, then the probability that Y has a certain score is high. Hence, framing 'Duverger's law' as a probabilistic relationship, the claim would be that if a country has a proportional voting rule, the *chance* that it has a multiparty system is higher than if it has an electoral system based on majority rule. If the hypothesis is formulated as a 'law', it assumes a deterministic relationship, and it is riskier and therefore easier to corroborate or to falsify (see Gerring 2007a: 53–7). If the assumed relationship is not found in the few cases, the hypothesis is falsified. Hence, if a country has a proportional voting rule but a two-party system, Duverger's law can no longer hold (at least not in a deterministic fashion). If the hypothesis is probabilistic, it allows for exceptions. Consequently, the fact that the assumed relationship is not found in a few cases cannot be taken as conclusive evidence against the hypothesis. If many more cases are included, the assumed relationship may still hold in a majority of cases, or on average.

Take our example concerning member states' adaptations to the EU. Strictly speaking, Haverland must hypothesize that the existence of a veto point *always* lowers the degree of adaptation to EU obligations. If Haverland had hypothesized that the existence of a veto point *increases the chance* of a lower degree of adaptation, then it would not be possible to verify or falsify the hypothesis by comparing a few cases. If there is no variation in the degree of adaptation to EU obligations across these cases, then the hypothesis still stands because it can be argued that the cases were exceptions. That such exceptions exist is in line with a probabilistic hypothesis.

Some methodologists argue that the need to assume an invariant relationship is a weakness of the co-variational case study design (for example, Lieberson 1991, 1994; Goldthorpe 1997). We think that this feature indeed points to certain limitations of this approach. Nevertheless, we believe that a deterministic understanding of causality makes sense for specific research purposes and contexts.

First, researchers are often interested in determining whether X made a difference in a specific case (for example, in evaluation research) and not whether X makes a difference more generally. A fully deterministic understanding of causality is the only adequate way to pursue this goal. A co-variational analysis can provide first evidence for the claim that X made a difference in the case of interest by showing that a different value of X in other cases is co-existing with a different value of the dependent variable Y. In order to strengthen the claim, the researcher has to apply causal-process tracing in order to show how exactly a certain value of X influenced the value of Y (see Chapter 3).

Second, the presupposition that the causal effect of X on Y is invariant makes more sense in a population of cases that are very similar (as it is the case within the COV approach) in comparison to a large population of cases that are diverse in many respects (as it is the case within a statistical analysis). In fact, introducing probability in causal thinking is in part a reaction to the assumption that other factors also influence Y and in part to the assumption that the causal effect of X on Y is dependent on the value of other factors or context conditions (such 'configurational thinking' forms the bases for the CPT approach, see Chapter 3). Since we hold the other factors constant within a co-variational analysis, an observed difference in Y cannot be accounted for by another causal factor. Furthermore, within a co-variational approach, we do not claim that other factors do not have a causal influence on Y (control variables might be causes as well), but only that X has an influence – under specific circumstances that are described by the control variables that we hold constant. This reduces the scope for generalization, but makes the claim that the cause makes invariantly a difference within the population of very similar cases very plausible.

Third, even if we presuppose a probabilistic understanding of causality, a co-variational case study makes sense as a first 'plausibility probe' for the claim that X makes a difference. If the claim is theoretically substantiated and receives confirmation by a case study that applies co-variation (and possibly causal-process tracing), we have good reasons and helpful experience in respect to concept specification and operationalization of variables for conducting a large-N study in order to test whether X makes a difference more generally (see Chapter 5).

2.2.4 Autonomous versus configurational causality

We have stressed the fact that the co-variational approach is X-centered in the sense that it focuses on the effects of causes and not on the causes of effects. In other words, when conducting a COV approach, we are primarily interested in the 'independent variable' and not in the 'dependent variable'. The term 'independent variable' points to another important feature of the COV approach: it assumes that the causal effect of 'independent variables' is universal (within the population of comparable cases) and that variable produces the effect independently from other independent variables. In other words, the COV approach assumes that 'independent variables' have an autonomous causal power.

This presupposition has also been criticized by methodologists and the contrasting presupposition that assumes that causal effects are always a result of the combination or interaction of different causes is one of the core features of the CPT approach as a major alternative in case study research (see Chapter 3). Nevertheless, similar arguments as for the deterministic presupposition of the COV approach apply here: certain research goals make the assumption that factors have autonomous causal power a sensible starting point; the selection of comparable cases or most similar systems is geared to 'single out' the effect of a specific, single variable. And we can take 'configurational causation' into account by complementing the COV approach with causal-process tracing or with medium-N studies applying Boolean Algebra (see Chapter 5). We will come back to this point at the end of Section 2.5.

2.3 Selecting cases

As stated above, the selection of appropriate cases is a crucial (if not *the* crucial) element of this approach to case study research. The validity of the causal inference made by the investigator, or how compelling the claim is that the independent variable of interest, rather than another variable, caused the effect, is largely based on the properties of the cases selected. What are appropriate case selection criteria for this approach to case study research? First, as in all types of small-N research, cases should not be selected randomly (see also King, Keohane, and Verba 1994). Selecting a few cases randomly may result in the cases not varying in the independent variable of interest. This would mean that the first element of the counterfactual situation is not addressed, comparing the situation when the factor of interest is present and the situation where the factor is absent. In the language of the experimental design, without variation in the independent variable, the 'control group' would be lacking.

Moreover, random selection may result in a situation in which the cases vary on those variables for which control is sought. This would be contrary to the second element of the counterfactual situation, namely, that all other conditions need to remain constant. In other words, the experimental group and the control group would not be equivalent.

2.3.1   Criteria for case selection

These two problems of random selection point not only to the need to select cases deliberately but also to the two criteria that deliberate case selection should fulfill. The case selection rule for the COV approach can be formulated as follows: first, choose cases that vary (as much as possible) with regard to your independent variable of interest or, in the words of King, Keohane, and Verba, 'according to the categories of the key causal variable' (1994: 137). Second, these cases must be similar (or as similar as possible) with regard to the variables you seek to control. Lijphart has called this case selection strategy the 'comparable cases' strategy (1971: 687, 1975), and Przeworski and Teune speak of the 'most similar systems' design (1970). Note that our approach is identical to what Lijphart (1975) has called the 'the comparative method'.

> The comparative method can now be defined as the method of testing hypothesized causal relationships among variables on the basis of the same logic that guides the statistical method, but in which the cases are selected in such a way as to maximize the variance of the independent variables and to minimize the variance of the control variables.
>
> (Lijphart 1975: 164)

If cases are selected that meet the two criteria mentioned above, then causal inferences can be drawn on the basis of observed co-variation between the factor of interest (independent variable) and the effects (dependent variables). If there is covariance over time or space between the independent variable (X) and the dependent variable (Y), we can infer that X has caused Y. This logic of causal inference has been called the method of difference by Mill.

> If an instance in which the phenomenon under investigation occurs, and an instance in which it does not occur, have every circumstance

in common save one, that one occurring only in the former; the circumstance in which alone the two instances differ, is the effect, or the cause, or an indispensable part of the cause, of the phenomenon.

(Mill 1875: 452)

It is very important to note that in contrast to many comparative studies that use the method of difference, in the COV approach cases are selected based on the score of the *independent* variable and not based on the score of the *dependent* variable. Following the logic of this approach, selecting 'on the dependent variable' would introduce selection bias.[2] As in an experiment, the dependent variable or outcome must vary 'freely' to identify the causal effect (see Geddes 1990; King, Keohane, and Verba 1994; Haverland 2006; Leuffen 2007).

Let us illustrate our method of case selection with a hypothetical example (see Table 2.1). Imagine the researcher is interested in the effect of the introduction of performance-related pay in a regulatory agency. The hypothesis is that performance-related pay increases staff performance because employees are open to financial incentives. To study the effect of performance-related pay on staff performance, agencies that differ with regard to the variable of performance-related pay must be chosen. In the hypothetical example, one agency has introduced performance-related pay, and the other has not. Yet, other factors may also affect staff performance such as the financial resources an agency has at its disposal, the educational level of its staff, or the quality of its information technology. To control for their effects, agencies selected should have similar scores on these variables. Note that at this stage of the research, the score of the dependent variable is unknown.

Cases that exhibit certain properties regarding their similarities and differences should be selected. This approach can be applied most fruitfully if the researcher has great discretion about which cases to

Table 2.1   Criteria for case selection: A hypothetical example

Variable	Case	Agency 1	Agency 2
Control variable	*Resource endowment*	Generous	Generous
Control variable	*Education level of staff*	High	High
Control variable	*Information technology*	Advanced	Advanced
Independent variable of interest	*Performance-related pay*	Yes	No
Dependent variable	*Staff performance*	?	?

choose. Unfortunately, this situation does not resonate well with the common practice in which investigators know from the start that they want or need to study a specific case, for instance, their own country. For applied research, the case that must be studied might be given. Typically, the researcher has to study a specific case in which a policy reform, an organizational innovation, or another change has occurred, and the researcher must establish whether this change had the intended effect. If the investigator needs or wants to include a specific case in the research, the co-variational approach might still be appropriate. In the study the researcher can attempt to include additional cases for which the independent variable has a different score (for example, no new policy adopted, no organizational innovation) but that are similar with regard to other independent variables. If this is not feasible, the researcher can still apply an intertemporal comparison, comparing his or her case before and after the change in the independent variable (see below). Otherwise, the researcher must choose one of the other two approaches to case studies.

2.3.2 Modes of comparison

Having outlined the basic principles of case selection, we can now discuss the various modes of comparison that can be based on the COV approach. Variation in the independent variable can be spatial and/or temporal. These two dimensions yield a fourfold typology (Table 2.2).

The comparison that exploits spatial variation in the independent variable of interest, that is, variation across cases at the same time period, will be called cross-sectional design.[3] An intertemporal design exploits the temporal variation of the independent variable of interest. It compares the situation before and after a change in the score of that variable. The specific unit we study will be split into two cases,

Table 2.2 Modes of comparisons within the co-variational approach

Variation independent variable of interest		Spatial variation	
		Yes	No
Temporal variation	Yes	Cross-sectional–intertemporal comparison	Intertemporal comparison
	No	Cross-sectional comparison	*Counterfactual comparison*

a 'historical' case, capturing the situation prior to the change in the independent variable, and a '(more) current' case that captures the situation after the change has occurred. As will be outlined below, the cross-sectional design is the most frequently practiced design, followed by the intertemporal design. However, we emphasize that it may also be possible to select cases where both temporal and spatial variation can be observed: the cross-sectional–intertemporal design. Finally, our two-by-two table contains a situation where there is neither spatial nor temporal variation. Having emphasized that we need to select cases that vary in the independent variable, one may conclude that a situation where such variation is lacking is not worth addressing. However, we will discuss this situation because it has received considerable attention in various studies, including those in comparative politics and international relations (IR), under the label of counterfactual comparison. Furthermore, counterfactual thought experiments play an important role in the CPT approach (see Section 3.5). In this comparison, there is no variation in the independent variable; in fact, it focuses on a single case. Hence, there is no variation at all between two cases. The investigator engages in a thought experiment by imagining what the score of the dependent variable would have been if the score of the independent variable had been different. Let us discuss each of these four modes of comparison in turn.

2.3.3 Cross-sectional comparison

Cross-sectional comparisons involve comparisons across cases at the same time, exploiting spatial variation. This mode of comparison is probably the most often used in case studies following the COV approach. In fact, our two running examples involve cross-sectional comparisons. Haverland (2000) compares three countries in the 1990s and Kitschelt (1986) four countries in the late 1970s and early 1980s.

Cross-sectional comparisons are widespread for a number of reasons. First, cross-sectional comparisons can be usefully applied in studies that compare countries within a specific geographical area, such as Latin America, or Scandinavia or Southeast Asia. The likelihood of finding cases that have similar control variables is quite high because countries in a specific geographical area share certain historical, cultural, and – indeed – geographical characteristics (Lijphart 1971: 688–9).

Furthermore, a cross-sectional comparison is often chosen because an intertemporal comparison (see next section) might not be feasible. There might be two reasons for this. First, the variable of interest may not have changed over a very long time. Therefore, it is not possible to split a case into two cases. In Haverland's study, the independent variable is the institutional veto point. In Germany, the veto point denotes the *Bundesrat*, the 'upper' chamber of parliament, the representation of the German state governments. The study focuses on the adaptation to European integration. Throughout the period of European integration, this institutional veto point was present in Germany. Therefore, it is not possible to compare Germany's adaptation to European integration before and after the institutional point was established. Another reason why a cross-sectional comparison rather than an intertemporal comparison should be chosen has to do with data availability. Very often, societies and researchers only become interested in certain issues after a change has taken place. Accordingly, there are no reliable and valid data available from the period before the introduction of the change. A prominent example is the privatization of public services. It is often not possible to research whether private provision increases effectiveness, efficiency, or consumer satisfaction with an intertemporal comparison because data are missing from the period when these services were offered through public organizations.

2.3.4   Intertemporal comparison

Intertemporal comparisons exploit variation over time. The score of the dependent variable is compared before and after the score of the independent variable has changed. Consider a study by Ellen M. Immergut on health policy (1990). To be sure, the study engages a cross-sectional comparison between France, Sweden, and Switzerland. However, Immergut also exploits temporal variation (see Lieberman 2001 for a discussion of this example). Similar to Haverland, Immergut sought to make an argument about the effects of veto points on policy change. The constitutional change in France that demarcated the shift from the Fourth to the Fifth Republic reduced the number of veto points in some policy areas. In the Fourth Republic, the French government needed the agreement of the French parliament for certain changes in health policy. In the Fifth Republic, the executive was directly elected and gained greater responsibilities for direct executive action. Because the executive was 'effectively freed from Parliament' (Immergut 1990: 402), it was possible to adopt far-reaching health reforms against the will of powerful societal actors represented in the French parliament.

Intertemporal comparisons, particularly those that compare situations shortly before and shortly after the change in the independent variable, potentially yield compelling evidence. In the French case, plans by the executive that were blocked in 1954 and 1957 – prior to the abolition of the veto point – could be adopted in 1960 – shortly after the abolition of the veto point. Analyzing such a short time frame in a single country potentially allows many variables to be kept constant. In other words, there are potentially theoretically more relevant similarities between France in the mid-1950s and France in 1960 than between France, Switzerland, and Sweden in the 1960s or at any other point in time (see also Lijphart 1971: 689).[4]

Intertemporal comparisons have another advantage over cross-sectional comparisons. The method of difference used in cross-sectional comparisons cannot tell us which of the variables that varies is the cause and which variable is the effect because both variables are measured at approximately the same time. Here, the researcher depends on theory to argue why the causal path works in a certain direction, or he or she must add causal-process tracing. In an intertemporal comparison, it is obvious that the change in X preceded the change in Y, which rules out the possibility that Y caused X (see also Rueschemeyer and Stephens 1997; Lieberman 2001). In Section 2.9 we will discuss extensively a case study that exploits the advantages of intertemporal comparisons although it does not fully correspond to this research design. Finally, since longitudinal information has already been collected, an intertemporal comparison can efficiently be combined with causal-process tracing (see Chapter 5).

2.3.5 Cross-sectional–intertemporal comparison

Combining the cross-sectional and intertemporal comparison into a cross-sectional–intertemporal comparison very closely approaches the experimental template. Two cases that were equivalent in all relevant respects before the score of the independent variable of interest changed in one of the cases but not the other are chosen. In this situation, it is possible to first measure the scores of the dependent variables in both cases before the score of the independent variable changed in one of the cases and then to measure the dependent variable in both cases after the change in the score of the independent variable in one of these cases. This process is a combination of spatial comparisons and comparisons over time. Imagine, for instance, a study that attempts to investigate the effect of political violence on economic growth.[5] To study the question, one could focus on the Basque region in Spain and compare that region with another Spanish region. The investigator would seek to identify a region with similar scores for other variables that might be related to economic growth, such as infrastructure, education, or natural resources. If such a region is found, the investigator can compare growth levels in the two regions prior to the outbreak of political violence in the Basque region with growth levels in the two regions after the outbreak of violence in the Basque region. From all co-variational comparisons, this one provides the most leverage for causal inference, but, unfortunately, it is very difficult to find such situations. In fact, in the study on which this example is based, it was not possible to identify a region that was sufficiently similar to the Basque region (see Gerring 2007a: 157–60).

2.3.6   Counterfactual comparison

Without spatial and/or temporal variation in the independent variable of interest, it is not possible to compare scores of the dependent variable for real cases to draw causal inferences based on the co-variational logic. What is possible is counterfactual reasoning. This means that we engage in a thought experiment and assess what the score of the dependent variable would have been if the independent variable had another score. Hence, we compare a real case where a factor is either present or absent with an imaginary case where the opposite situation applies.

Counterfactual reasoning has been used in disciplines such as history, IR, and comparative politics to increase understanding of singular (important) events or critical junctures (see, for example, Fearon 1991; Tetlock and Belkin 1996a; Ned Lebow 2000; Capoccia and Kelemen 2007). A case in point is the Cuban missile crisis, during which to many observers the world seemed very close to a devastating nuclear war. One of the many counterfactuals advanced is that 'had Kennedy displayed greater resolve prior to the crisis, Khrushchev would not have sent missiles to Cuba' (Ned Lebow 2000). Other events or situations that have invited counterfactuals are the onset of World War I, the British attempt to appease Hitler in 1938 or the importance of Stalin for the shape of Soviet Communism (Fearon 1991; Tetlock and Belkin 1996b).

It is important to note that counterfactual reasoning should not lead to unlimited speculation, nor are all counterfactual claims equally compelling. Several authors have suggested criteria for the development of good counterfactuals, such as clarity, historical consistency, and theoretical consistency (see, for instance, Fearon 1991; Tetlock and Belkin 1996b; Ned Lebow 2000; see also the appendix to this chapter).

2.3.7 Excursus: The method of agreement and the most different systems design

This chapter discusses research designs that are based on the concept of counterfactual causation and the experimental template. We have discussed Mill's method of difference that is used in the most similar systems design because this method is compatible with our experimental template and counterfactual conception of causation. Note, however, that another method of Mill is often discussed in textbooks and articles on comparative politics and comparative sociology: the method of agreement. The method of agreement informs the most different systems design (Przeworski and Teune 1970). For reasons elaborated below, we do not regard this type of design as a proper example of our co-variational approach to case studies. However, given its widespread usage, we briefly elaborate on it.

The method of agreement reads as follows:

> If two or more instances of the phenomenon under investigation have only one circumstance in common, the circumstance in which alone all the instances agree, is the cause (or effect) of the given phenomenon.
>
> (Mill 1875: 451)

This design is typically used for Y-centered questions. The researcher is interested in explaining a particular outcome. He or she chooses cases that have a similar outcome, 'two or more instances of the phenomenon' (cf. quote above), and then tries to determine what 'circumstances' these cases have in common. If researchers choose cases that are most different from each other (for example, cases from different regions in the world), then it is unlikely that they will find many features that these cases have in common. Hence, in a hypothetical example, the researcher identifies two regulatory agencies with high staff performance in Sweden and the Ivory Coast. These are very different political systems that vary in regard to their levels of resources, education, and informational technology. The researcher aims to determine what factor or factors they have in common.

We mention this method of case selection studies for completeness, but we do not regard it as a proper example of the COV approach to case studies. Briefly, the problem with this method is that the independent variable of interest does not vary (see, for example, Gerring 2007a: 41). Consider the example above. If a factor that both agencies have in common is identified, it cannot be regarded as a causal factor because we do not know, even approximately, how well the staff would have performed in the absence of that factor. Hence, the most different system design cannot be based on the counterfactual conception of causation. In the language of experiments, there is no control group; no group that does not receive the treatment.

We do not suggest that this method is without merit. It allows certain potential causes to be eliminated because variables that vary cannot produce a common outcome. Hence, for the purposes of exploration, an investigator can select cases with a common outcome, thereby select the dependent variable and a specific score of this dependent variable. For instance, researchers can select cases where significant social policy retrenchment has occurred. Using the method of agreement, the investigator can search for commonalities between these cases, factors that can *potentially* have a causal effect. If in all of these cases, the economic situation radically worsened and a conservative government was in power, both factors *might* explain significant social policy retrenchment. Factors that the cases do not have in common can be ruled out.

Then, the researcher must consider whether one or more of these factors makes a difference, if one maintains the COV approach described in this chapter that implies that one need to choose the independent variable one is most interested in and cases that vary on this variable and have similar scores on the control variables. Hence, if one is interested in whether the economic situation has made a difference, one must select cases that vary in the economic situation while keeping other factors constant, including the ideological outlook of the government.[6] An alternative would be to complement the method of agreement with causal-process tracing.[7]

2.4 The functions of prior knowledge and theory

The preceding sections have outlined central methodological concepts and case selection criteria. This treatment has not yet addressed the functions of prior knowledge and theory (including hunches, prior assumptions, 'theories' held by practitioners, and middle-range or grand theories in the social sciences).[8] Irrespective of the research approach chosen, researchers who seek to make a relevant contribution to the scientific literature should be aware of the state of the art of the scientific debate and explicitly relate their own study to this debate. This is the way knowledge accumulates. However, prior knowledge and theory also have specific and somewhat distinctive functions in the co-variational approach to case study research. In this section, we will discuss three functions:

- Prior knowledge and theory help to specify the concepts that make up the main independent and dependent variables. Hence, they clarify the meaning of our main factor of interest, and they delineate the phenomenon or outcome on which the independent variable is expected to have an effect.
- Prior knowledge and theory also provide *a priori* plausibility for the expected relationships. In other words, they help to establish why the independent variable might influence the dependent variable and why it has a 'positive' effect or a 'negative' effect (the 'sign' of the relationship).
- With regard to other independent variables, prior knowledge and theory help to identify potential rival explanations, which need to be controlled for, and they help to specify the concepts that make up these variables and to provide plausibility for the expected 'signs' of the relationship between these variables and the dependent variable.

We will now discuss each of the three functions. Note, however, that a fourth function of theories can be distinguished: theories help to operationalize the dependent, independent, and control variables. We will discuss this function in Section 2.6.

2.4.1 Specifying the main independent and the dependent variable

The first function concerns the specification of the main independent variable and the dependent variable. Hypotheses do not appear out of the blue. Instead, they emerge as we begin to engage with the field of study and after we have invested in the state of the art in respect to the research topic. If we are interested in the difference a specific factor makes, such as the differences in performance of a federal political system in contrast to a unitary system, we must specify our understanding of a 'federal political system'. Furthermore, we must think about what specific phenomenon, outcome, effect, or consequence we want to consider. In our example, we could look at very different aspects of performance that might be influenced by the structure of the political system, such as economic growth, satisfaction with the functioning of democracy, or innovation in specific policy fields.

Consider Haverland's study (2000) on the importance of veto points for member states' adaptation to the EU. First, the term 'veto point' needs to be defined. He specifies that 'veto points' are stages in the policy process at which an actor must agree to adopt a policy. The need to agree is grounded in a legal obligation; hence, the concept is similar to what Immergut (1990) labels constitutional veto points. Second, member states' adaptation is a broad phenomenon, and it is unclear which aspect should be studied. The author decides to focus on policy adaptation: changes in policy goals and policy styles to make member states compatible and in compliance with EU requirements. The decision to focus on policy adaptation rather than, for instance, adaptation of political processes is informed by the state of the art in the area of Europeanization research. Other studies have used policy adaptation as well, and the study was intended to speak to these studies (for example, Knill and Lenschow 1998).

2.4.2   Substantiating the research hypothesis

Investigators who hypothesize that a certain variable has an effect on another variable should consider why they expect the independent variable to have *an* effect and why the researcher expects a *specific* effect (the direction of the effect, in other words, whether the effect is 'positive' or 'negative'). For example, after deciding to study the political structure as the independent variable of interest and policy innovation as the dependent variable, the author needs to argue why political structure should have an effect on policy innovation or, more specifically, why a federal structure leads to *more* policy innovation. Here, the argument could be based on ideas of policy learning. In a federal system, lower-tier governments have more authority, which allows for more discretion in policy experimentation. The results of these experiments can diffuse to other (higher) levels of the polity, leading to more policy innovation than in unitary systems.

Within a COV approach and in contrast to the CPT approach, we do not try to determine empirically whether the assumptions formulated about the causal pathways and causal mechanisms that presumably lead from the independent to the dependent variable actually hold. While we argue that traces of the causal pathways and mechanisms do *not* need to be observed, we nevertheless argue that the assumed causal paths or mechanism should be plausible. Hence, our position is not as extreme as that of Milton Friedman, who argues that assumptions do not need to be realistic as long as the predictive power is sufficient (Friedman 1966: 41).

What are the sources for the assumed plausibility? For theoretically oriented research, the source should be fully developed theories that can be found in the scientific literature or developed deductively based on more general paradigms (see also Chapter 4). In applied research, such as evaluation research, the researcher may also draw on the 'theory' that informed the initiation of a policy change or an organizational innovation in the first place. In other words, the researcher can draw on the arguments made by those who propose or advocate such a change.

Let us consider our running examples. Kitschelt uses Institutional Theory when he argues, 'Political opportunity structures are comprised of specific configurations of resources, institutional arrangements and historical precedents for mobilization, which facilitate the development of protest movements in some instances and constrain them in others' (Kitschelt 1986: 58). He goes on to explain how and in what direction opportunity structures facilitate or constrain the capacity of social movements to engage in protest activities. He develops two hypotheses, one related to social movement strategy and the other related to social movement impact. Only the hypothesis concerning strategy will be discussed here:

> When political systems are open and weak, they invite assimilative strategies [...] when political systems are close and have considerable capacities to ward off threats to the implementation of public policy, movements are likely to adopt confrontational, disruptive strategies...
>
> (Kitschelt 1986: 66)

In this example, the direction of the effect is made explicit: open and weak political systems lead to *assimilative* strategies. The hypothesis is based on Institutional Theory focusing on a configuration of factors that enable or constrain actors. Nevertheless, the social and causal mechanisms that lead from the structures of the system to the strategies of social movements are not made explicit.

In his study on the EU and its member states, Haverland hypothesizes that the existence of institutional veto points matters for the degree to which member states adapt their policies and structures to EU requirements. These requirements are formulated or implied by EU legislation. As stated above, veto points are defined as stages in the political process at which an actor must agree to adopt legislation. Why is it plausible that veto points result in weak implementation or a low degree of adaption to EU requirements? When central governments face other political actors who control a veto point and who oppose the EU legislation, central governments need to bargain with the other actors to find a compromise. This bargaining process threatens the EU requirement to implement legislation on time. Moreover, striking a compromise with actors that oppose the EU legislation leads to a deviation from EU requirements (Haverland 2000: 85–6).

2.4.3 Identifying control variables

The COV approach requires that other independent variables that may have an effect on the dependent variable are 'controlled' for. This is achieved by deliberately choosing cases that have similar scores on these variables. As stated above, this kind of research has often been used in studies that focus on specific areas, such as studies focusing on Europe or Latin America. These are most-similar systems, so authors often *assume* that they are similar with regard to other potentially influential variables given a similar cultural, historical, or other context.

We suggest that researchers do not simply assume these similarities but actually demonstrate them. To do so, however, the researcher must identify the variables. There are potentially many factors that may explain variation in the dependent variable. The more independent variables that are included in the analysis for control, the more difficult it is to find cases that have similar scores on (all) these variables. 'All' variables cannot be included, but one should include the relevant ones. Excluding variables that would have a causal effect leads to what is called omitted variable bias (King, Keohane, and Verba 1994: 168–82). If a plausible explanation has been left out, the co-variation between the independent variable of interest and the dependent variable may be a spurious relationship rather than a causal relationship.

Therefore, a careful selection of variables is of paramount importance. The researcher should consider causal factors from the major theoretical approaches concerned with explaining the dependent variable. Hence, theories provide guidelines as to which variables are 'key variables' (Lijphart 1971: 690) that must be included for control and which variables can be excluded (see also Moses and Knutsen 2007: 111). Furthermore, prior knowledge and theories help to specify the concepts that make up these variables and to provide arguments for their plausibility.

2.5 Drawing causal inferences for the cases under investigation

After having selected adequate cases according to the principles that we have laid out in the previous section and with the help of some prior knowledge of the cases, the researcher digs deeper into the cases and collects the information that is useful for scoring each case in respect to the selected variables.

As laid out in Chapter 1, we can distinguish two steps within the process of drawing causal inferences in a co-variational approach:

- The interpretation of the collected information, the transformation and integration of this information into specific scores of variables, and the presentation of the scores of all variables for each case in a column or row of a rectangular data sheet (data generation).
- The inspection of the resulting rectangular data sets and the drawing of conclusions based on formal logic and theoretical arguments (data analysis).

We present the second formal step of data analysis first within this section and the first step of data generation in the next section, in order to highlight the dependency of drawing causal inferences within a COV approach on specific features of the data sets.

Typically, cases are selected on the basis of a preliminary classification with respect to the independent variable of interest and the control variables. Ideally, the main task of the case study proper is to find out what the scores of the dependent variables are (as implied by Table 2.1). Nevertheless, the ex-ante classification of the independent and control variables may be found to be incorrect after additional information has been collected and transformed into scores for these variables. In the following we show how to deal with a number of potential results of the data generation process.

2.5.1 Data set results and conclusions

Table 2.3 displays the scores of a hypothetical study that examines the effect of the introduction of performance-related pay in a regulatory agency. The hypothesis is that performance-related pay increases staff

Table 2.3 Supporting evidence based on method of difference

Variable	Case	Agency 1	Agency 2
Control variable	*Resource endowment*	Generous	Generous
Control variable	*Education level of staff*	High	High
Control variable	*Information technology*	Advanced	Advanced
Independent variable of interest	*Performance-related pay*	Yes	No
Dependent variable	*Staff performance*	**High**	**Low**

performance because employees are open to financial incentives (*a priori* plausibility based on Rational Choice Theory). Visual inspection of the table shows that both agencies have similar scores on the control variables and vary on the independent and the dependent variables. Applying Mill's method of difference (introduced above), this mechanical process of analysis provides some confidence that performance-related pay has *an* effect on staff performance. In one situation, the phenomenon occurs (high performance); in the other situation, the phenomenon does not occur. Both situations have every circumstance in common except one: the introduction of performance-related pay.

Also note that co-variation takes the 'direction' that is hypothesized. Performance-related pay leads to *better* staff performance. The factor had *the* effect we expected. This provides us with additional confidence that our explanation is correct.

In the situation displayed in Table 2.4, the dependent variable, performance-related pay, does not vary; the staff of both agencies perform at a similar level. Whether performance-related pay had been introduced does not seem to matter for staff performance. Performance-related pay does not make a difference; therefore, we infer that it had no causal effect.

Let us consider other potential results of the agency comparison. In the hypothetical result displayed in Table 2.5, the cases are not as similar as assumed at the stage of case selection. The staff of the second agency has a lower level of education, as the preliminary analysis prior to case selection suggested. We now have a situation in which the agencies vary on two independent variables. Performance-related pay has been introduced, but not everything else is the same. Hence, the visual inspection of the table does not allow us to infer that performance-related pay had a causal effect. We do not know whether performance-related pay or the level of education made the difference. The empirical evidence does not allow us to discriminate between

Table 2.4   Disconfirming evidence: No variation of the dependent variable

Variable	Case	Agency 1	Agency 2
Control variable	*Resource endowment*	Generous	Generous
Control variable	*Education level of staff*	High	High
Control variable	*Information technology*	Advanced	Advanced
Independent variable of interest	*Performance-related pay*	Yes	No
Dependent variable	*Staff performance*	**Medium**	**Medium**

Table 2.5 Inconclusive evidence: Variation in one of the control variables

Variable	Case	Agency 1	Agency 2
Control variable	*Resource endowment*	Generous	Generous
Control variable	*Education level of staff*	**High**	Low
Control variable	*Information technology*	Advanced	Advanced
Independent variable of interest	*Performance-related pay*	Yes	No
Dependent variable	*Staff performance*	**High**	Low

different explanations. In statistical terms, the result is 'indeterminate' (King, Keohane, and Verba 1994: 118–9).

Yet, as Gerring argues, a lack of similarity with regard to a control variable 'is tolerable if the deviation runs counter to the predicted hypothesis' (Gerring 2007a: 133). Hence, we need assistance from theoretical reasoning. As outlined above, we argue that investigators should begin with a hypothesis that is substantiated by *a priori* plausibility. This plausibility should point to the 'direction' of the causal effect. In other words, there is co-variation between the independent variables and the dependent variable that has a direction that is in line with what can be expected from a given theory, and there is co-variation that has a direction that goes against the theory.

Adding theoretical reasoning to the logic of comparison, as we propose to do, does not help to discriminate between the two variables that vary. This is because there are also good theoretical arguments, based on human resource theories, to expect that better-educated agency staff perform better. Note that the situation would be different if the staff of Agency 1 had a lower level of education and if there were no theoretical reasons to expect that lower-educated staff perform better (see Table 2.6). Then, additional theoretical reasoning, not visual

Table 2.6 Supporting evidence based on method of difference in combination with theoretical reasoning

Variable	Case	Agency 1	Agency 2
Control variable	*Resource endowment*	Generous	Generous
Control variable	*Education level of staff*	Low	**High**
Control variable	*Information technology*	Advanced	Advanced
Independent variable of interest	*Performance-related pay*	Yes	No
Dependent variable	*Staff performance*	**High**	Low

inspection, would lead us to infer that performance-related pay increases staff performance.[9]

Let us now turn to our running examples of real world research and consider their methods of case selection and data analysis.

2.5.2   Examples

Kitschelt's *Political Opportunity Structures and Political Protest*

Kitschelt's study (1986) was a cross-sectional comparison, and he used the appropriate case selection criteria. He was interested in the effect of domestic opportunity structures on the strategy and impact of social movements. Therefore, he chose countries that varied with regard to this independent variable. His independent variable had two dimensions: open versus closed input structures, and strong versus weak output structures (or implementation capacity). For didactical purposes, we simplify his design by focusing on only one dimension: the input structure of the political system.

Kitschelt chose cases that varied with regard to their input structure. He selected Sweden and the United States (US), which both had an open input structure, and France and West Germany, which had a closed input structure (see Kitschelt 1986: 64). At the same time, these countries were selected because they displayed similarities in a number of variables that may also affect the strategies and impact of the anti-nuclear movements. For clarity of presentation, we focus on three control variables: (1) the objectives of social movements, (2) the objective threat of nuclear power, and (3) the social base of the movement (see Kitschelt 1986: 60–1). By keeping these factors constant, Kitschelt can control for the effect of these variables.

A visual inspection of Table 2.7 indicates that only the independent variable of interest and the dependent variable vary, providing confidence that the relationship is causal. As discussed above (Section 2.4.2), the author also presented an argument why the relationship should exist and why a certain score of the dependent variable should be expected (the 'direction' of the relationship). In Sweden, for example, an open input structure of the political system is associated with an emphasis on *assimilative* strategies by the anti-nuclear movement.

A situation in which the dependent variable varied may have occurred, but this variation would not have made sense theoretically. Hence, if an open input structure had been associated with a confrontational strategy, the visual inspection of the table would lead to the conclusion that the opportunity structure would have made a

Table 2.7 Example: Kitschelt's *Political Opportunity Structures and Political Protest*

		SWE	France	US	Germany
Control variable	*Movements objective*	Shutting down nuclear sites	Shutting down nuclear sites	Shutting down nuclear sites	Shutting down nuclear sites
Control variable	*Objective threat*	1–2 gigawatts/million inhabitants	1–2 gigawatts/million inhabitants	1–2 gigawatts/ million inhabitants	1–2 gigawatts/ million inhabitants
Control variable	*Social base*	Middle-class	Middle-class	Middle-class	Middle-class
Independent variable of interest	*Opportunity structure*	Open	Closed	Open	Closed
Dependent variable	*Movement's strategy*	Emphasis on assimilative strategies	Emphasis on confrontational strategies	Emphasis on assimilative strategies	Emphasis on confrontational strategies

difference, but the explanation would still need to be rejected because the causal pathway or mechanism underlying the hypothesis could not have worked.

Note that the Kitschelt himself did not construct such a table in his article. However, we strongly recommend visualizing the analysis in a table, which helps to clarify and systematize the argument to readers and, as our experience with supervising students shows, to the authors of the respective study as well.

Haverland's *National Adaptation to the European Union*

Haverland's study (2000) concerned the adaptation of member states to the requirements of the EU. Cases that had the most similar scores with regard to variables that also affected the domestic adaptation to EU requirements in the area of environmental policy were selected. Haverland chose Germany, the Netherlands (NL), and the United Kingdom (UK), three countries that displayed similarities in economic capacities, the level of technological development, and the strength of the environmental movement.

At the same time, these cases varied on two independent variables rather than one variable. One of these variables captured the dominant approach in the studies on national adaptation to the EU requirement: the goodness-of-fit approach. According to this approach, those countries whose national policies, styles, and structure are most compatible with the EU requirements are more likely to adapt to the EU requirements. The other variable captures Haverland's argument that the structure of the decision-making process is important. Countries in which the decision-making process offers opportunities to veto the adaptation to the EU are less likely to adapt (Table 2.8).

Table 2.8 Example: Haverland's *National Adaptation to the European Union*

		Germany	NL	UK
Control variable	*Technological development*	Advanced	Advanced	Advanced
Control variable	*Economic capacities*	High	High	High
Control variable	*Strength environmental groups*	High	High	High
Control variable	*Goodness of fit*	High	Medium	Low
Independent variable of interest	*Veto points*	2	1	1
Dependent variable	*Successful adaptation*	No	Yes	Yes

Through visual inspection of the dataset observations and the application of Mill's method of difference, the economic capacities, technological development, and strength of the environmental movements can be eliminated as explanations. They are similar across cases; following Mill, similarities cannot explain differences; hence they cannot explain the difference in member states' degree of adaptation to EU requirements. This way of reasoning does not allow us to discriminate between the goodness-of-fit explanation and the veto point explanation. However, theoretical reasoning helps to discriminate between the two rival explanations. Regarding the goodness-of-fit explanation, Germany had the best goodness of fit, the UK the weakest goodness of fit, and the Netherlands held a position in between. With regard to the number of formal veto points, the UK and the Netherlands had one veto point, and Germany had the additional veto point of the 2nd chamber of the legislature (the *Bundesrat*, representing the state governments).

According to the goodness-of-fit approach, the country with the *best* goodness of fit, Germany, should adapt *most* successfully, whereas the Netherlands and the UK should adopt *less* successfully. In fact, the UK and the Netherlands adapted successfully to the EU. Hence, the veto point hypothesis could be corroborated, whereas the goodness-of-fit hypothesis received no empirical support for the case studied.

This example highlights an important point about the relationship between the different approaches to case studies that we discuss. Although we have introduced the COV approach in an ideal-typical way as an approach that attempts to answer the question 'does X make a difference?' with the help of theoretical knowledge and by carefully selecting cases, it can also be used to contribute to theoretical debates. In this example, the co-variational case study provided leverage for the rationalist theory, from which the veto point hypothesis was extracted, against the theory of Sociological Institutionalism, from which the goodness-of-fit hypothesis is drawn.

2.5.3 Concluding remarks

The example just discussed demonstrates that Mill's method of difference contributes to identifying a causal effect if cases are selected carefully, but it also points to the need for theory. Patterns of similarities and differences are often not sufficiently conclusive, and they do not allow for discrimination between all explanations. Theoretical reasoning provides plausibility for whether assumed relationships should be negative or positive and thus provides additional explanatory power.

The use of prior knowledge and theory also helps with the issue that the effect might be produced by the interaction of various variables. It has been argued, perhaps most forcefully by Stanley Lieberson (1991), that Mill's methods assume that variables produce the causal effect independently from each other, in the absence of an interaction effect between variables. Two independent variables interact when the strength of the causal effect of one variable depends on the score of another independent variable. Lieberson gives the example of explaining a car accident (1991: 312–5). Two drivers are drunk and ride through a red light. One driver unexpectedly faces a car from the right, and the other does not. The driver who faces the car from the right causes an accident, and the other does not. Lieberson argues that Mill's method of difference implies that (only) the unexpected car from the right was the cause of the accident. Being drunk and driving through a red light did not contribute to the accident because it applies to both drivers, and only one committed the accident. Hence, a variable that is plausibly part of the explanation is eliminated: a 'false negative' (George and Bennett 2005: 156; Leuffen 2007: 151). To be sure, if we apply the method of difference in a mechanical way, Lieberson is right. However, considering prior knowledge and theory significantly reduces the risk of false inferences. Furthermore, if there are reasons to expect interaction effects, researchers can combine the co-variational approach with causal-process tracing (see Chapters 3 and 5).

In Chapter 5, we introduce Qualitative Comparative Analysis (QCA). In QCA, as in the CPT case study approach, the starting assumption is that variables (termed 'conditions') do not act independently from each other but constitute causal configurations. With this assumption, we can reinterpret our data analysis in that each column in the table actually provides for a causal configuration: the presence and the absence of conditions that lead to an outcome. For example, the inconclusive result presented in Table 2.5 would be interpreted differently: the presence of generous resource endowments, in conjunction with the high level of education, advanced information technology, and performance-related pay produces high staff performance. In contrast, generous education levels in conjunction with low levels of staff education and the lack of performance-related pay produces low staff performance. Which of these conditions is (almost) necessary and/or (almost) sufficient to produce the high (or low) staff performance would be established by comparing a medium number of cases, typically around 20–50 cases. Chapter 3 introduces the terminology for configurational thinking, and Chapter 5 briefly elaborates on QCA.

2.6 Measurement and data collection

The co-variational approach, in its ideal-typical form, relies only on scores of the independent and the dependent variable for its data analysis. Hence, the COV approach considers only variable-scoring observations, not causal-process observations as the CPT and the CON approaches do. Consequently, the adequate transfer and integration of the empirical information into scores for the variables are of crucial importance for the COV approach.

In the COV approach, investigators should begin thinking about measurement and data collection issues not only before they engage in data analysis but also before the selection of cases. However, we discuss these issues after case selection and data analysis to help the reader understand why measurement and data generation issues are important for these other elements of this approach.

Measurement issues should be considered prior to case selection because case selection is deliberate and not random. Ideally, cases that vary in their score of the independent variable of interest and are similar with regard to the scores of other relevant independent variables should be selected. To facilitate this case selection, some effort should be made to arrive at valid measures of the independent variable and the control variables prior to case selection.

2.6.1 Conceptualization and measurement in large-N versus small-N research

In principle, there is no difference between large-N research and the co-variational approach to case study research in terms of conceptualization and measurement. We follow Robert Adcock and David Collier's treatment of this stage of the research process (Adcock and Collier 2001: 531). First, from a 'background concept' (Adcock and Collier 2001: 531), that is, the broad and potentially diverse set of meanings associated with a concept, a 'systematized concept' (Adcock and Collier 2001: 531) must be defined in accordance with the goal of the research project. This process is called conceptualization. Then, indicators (or measures) that reflect this concept must be derived. This process of linking abstract concepts to concrete (potential) observations is called operationalization. In the last step, the indicators must be applied to the case studied to score the cases (see also Buttolph Johnson, Reynolds, and Mycoff 2008). Case study research, by definition, focuses only on one or a few cases, whereas large-N research focuses on dozens, hundreds, or even thousands of cases. Therefore, case study researchers can, *ceteris paribus*, reflect more intensively on the indicators they use to score the cases. This applies to all three approaches to case studies we present in this book. It is easier to ensure that the measure approximates the true meaning of a concept for a few cases than it is for many cases. In other words, small-N research typically outperforms large-N research in terms of the concept validity of measurement. In particular, the intensive study of a few cases makes a high degree of contextual specificity feasible, devising indicators that are sensitive to the context of each of the cases (see Adcock and Collier 2001: 534–6; see also Przeworski and Teune 1970: 106–10; Locke and Thelen 1995, 1998).

Ideas about contextual specificity have been primarily developed by scholars working on cross-national comparisons. Countries differ regarding their histories, cultures, institutional configurations, and so on. Thus, the same observations may mean different things, whereas different observations might be functionally equivalent. Consider, for example, the research by James D. Fearon and David D. Laitin (2008) on the causes of civil war. One of the hypotheses is that the stronger the coercive capabilities of the central state, the less likely it is that civil war will occur. Studying dozens of countries, Fearon and Laitin needed to find an easily measurable indicator; so they took per capita income as an indicator of the strength of the central state bureaucracy and its coercive power. Given the low score of Algeria on this indicator, they expected this country to have a weak state bureaucracy and a lack of coercive power. However, when conducting a case study of Algeria, they found a motivated, well-trained, experienced, and resourceful army. This information led them to conclude that 'Algeria's moderately low per capita income (versus the regional or world averages) is in this case a poor measure of state coercive capabilities' (Fearon and Laitin 2008: 771). Prior to the knowledge they gained from the case study, they based their variable score for state power in Algeria on an observation of capital income. This operationalization led to a comparatively low score for state power and a relatively high chance that a civil war would occur. Using the more valid, context-sensitive, indicator (presence of a strong army) led to a higher score on state power. Given this high score on state power, the outbreak of civil war was puzzling: 'Civil war occurred despite relatively strong coercive capabilities' (Fearon and Laitin 2008: 771). Hence, the way a concept is operationalized can have significant consequences for the results of the study. Algeria turned out to be an anomalous case. How does the focus on a few cases benefit concept validity in our running examples? In Haverland's study of the adaptation of member states to EU requirements, the concept of veto points was very important. Arguing that more veto points in a political system leads to more problems in adaptation makes it crucial to adequately define and measure veto points. As stated above, in the literature, veto points are defined as those stages of a decision-making process at which an actor must agree to a policy. Does the required reading of an EU implementation measure in the German *Bundesrat*, the German upper house representing state governments, constitute a veto point? This cannot be determined from the outset. One must delve into the legal situation where, on the one hand, the central government is legally responsible for implementing EU laws, but, on the other hand, the German constitution demands the agreement of the Upper House when the competencies of the German States are involved. In the German system of cooperative federalism, the lower-tier states have important competencies in policy implementation. For this reason, it was decided that the *Bundesrat* has a veto. Contrast this situation with the Netherlands, a corporatist system. One might argue that the agreement of employer and employee organizations is needed for a policy change, amounting to a de facto veto point. Hence, a functional equivalent to the constitutional veto point in Germany might be found in the empirical domain of socio-economic policy making. Yet, closer inspection of the corporatist system and the type of policies discussed at corporatist venues suggests that corporatism does not lead to an additional veto point for the central governments.

In sum, focusing on a few cases allows for intensive study and deep knowledge of these cases and thus the operationalization of variables, and the measured scores for the cases are more valid than is typically the case in large-N research.

2.6.2 Determination of classifications and cut-off points

The intensive study of a few cases allows for measures that are typically more valid than those in large-N research. For case studies that follow the co-variation approach, a high level of validity is not only possible but also necessary. Case analysis is very sensitive to the way investigators conceptualize variables and classify cases into categories

(Lieberson 1991). Mill's method of difference only 'works' if the independent variables controlled for really have similar scores and fall into the same category, and if the independent variable of interest really has a different score and falls into a different category. Moreover, a 'positive' result, a corroboration of the hypothesis, only occurs when the scores for the dependent variable are different and fall into different categories. But are the observations that result in similar scores really similar and the observations that result in different scores really different? For the control variables, the reader might wonder whether the boundaries of the categories of the control variables are not set too broadly, allowing different observations to be labeled as similar. For instance, considering Kitschelt's study, the reader might wonder whether one gigawatt of nuclear energy per million inhabitants really poses a similar objective threat as two gigawatts per million inhabitants. In Kitschelt's study, both observations result in the same score. The reader might also wonder whether the categories of the independent variable and the dependent variable are not set too narrowly to allow roughly similar observations to be translated into different scores. How different do opportunity structures or the strategies of social movements need to be to warrant their assignment to different categories?

Whether arguing for similarity or differences, the researcher must explicitly reflect on why the cut-off point is set where it has been set because a 'positive' result crucially depends on the 'right' mix of differences and similarities.

Kitschelt is careful to motivate his scores. With regard to his independent variable, he states the following:

> Differences in the openness and capacity of political regimes are continuous rather than discrete variables. Given the number of variables on each dimension, many combinations of openness and implementation capacity may occur. Nevertheless, for comparative purposes, one may roughly dichotomize each of these variables...
>
> (Kitschelt 1986: 64)

He goes on to state, 'Some classifications [...] are likely to be contested and therefore deserve a brief discussion' (Kitschelt 1986: 64). He explains why, for instance, he classifies the French political system as closed, Sweden's political implementation capacity as high, and West Germany's implementation capacity as weak. The latter might be particularly controversial because he, as he states, 'breaks with the efficiency myth with which German politics has been falsely associated' (Kitschelt 1986: 64).

Kitschelt is aware of the fact that investigators need to convince readers that their classifications are correct, and they need to provide the necessary evidence. Everyone who conducts a case study informed by the COV approach should do so.

2.6.3 Replicability and measurement error

The focus on a few cases allows for context-sensitive measurement, which increases the validity of the measure and simultaneously makes valid measurements particularly important. The way cases are classified is significant for the results of the analysis. While the merit of small-N research for concept validity is widely accepted, many argue that measurement in small-N research is less reliable. The process of measurement, scoring cases according to pre-defined indicators, is said to be an opaque and somewhat subjective process. If another researcher measured the same concepts in the same cases, he or she might arrive at a different result. Therefore, case study research is not replicable and is prone to measurement error. Regarding replicability, it is important to restate the point made in the previous section that the researcher should be as transparent as possible about his or her indicators and the rationale for scoring the variables in a certain case.

The issue of measurement error deserves some more attention. Large-N research is typically more reliable because measurement errors, at least when they are distributed randomly, cancel each other out. In small-N research that follows the COV approach, measurement errors have decisive consequences. Consider again the example of Kitschelt. Assume that a measurement error has been made somewhere in the process of providing information about the capacity of nuclear power plants, from those who build them, to those who put the data in official documents, to the investigator who reads the documents and transcribes the figures. For instance, somewhere in the process, 'megawatt' has been conflated with 'gigawatt' for some of the installations, or the ratio to the number of inhabitants has been wrongly calculated as a hundred thousand instead of a million. As a result, a country does not, in fact, have 1–2 gigawatts per million inhabitants, but 10 gigawatts. In that country, the objective threat is much higher than in the other country. If the score of one variable is erroneous, the method of difference leads to inconclusive results. In this example, one of the control variables is not constant; therefore, variation in the movements' strategy or impact might have been caused by variation in this factor rather than the variation in the political opportunity structure, as concluded in the study.

It is understandable why the problem of measurement error for this kind of research is particularly voiced by researchers who usually do survey research (for example, Lieberson 1994: 1232–3; Goldthorpe 1997: 6). When studying hundreds or thousands of citizens, measurement error is likely to be undetected. For instance, the respondent may fill in the gross wage even though the question asked for the net wage. The investigator would not be aware of this error because he or she does not know the respondents. Case study research, in contrast, is intensive. Researchers know their cases. To put it bluntly, they would not make the error of classifying the US as a unitary state even though it is a federal state (see also Mahoney 2003: 352).

2.6.4   Data triangulation

The intensive focus on a few cases also allows for data triangulation, 'using multiple sources or data types to measure the same concept for a single unit' (Leuffen, Shikano, and Walter 2010). Take the example of 'objective nuclear threat'. Drawing on different sources of evidence, such as documents from the owners of the nuclear facilities, governments, and research institutes as well as expert interviews, should eliminate measurement error. In a small-N setting, cross-checking of evidence is less time consuming than it is in large-N research.

Data triangulation should also at least partly correct for any systematic bias in measurement. For example, interviews may lead to socially desirable answers; what is measured is not only the concept that was intended to be measured but also 'social desirability' or certain societal norms. Such systematic measurement errors affect measurement validity. By triangulating interviews with other evidence, such as documents by international organizations, this bias can at least be partly corrected. In this way, data triangulation also contributes to measurement validity (Yin 2009: 114–8; for an excellent treatment of data triangulation, see Leuffen, Shikano, and Walter 2010).

In conclusion, issues of operationalization and measurement are very important. Data analysis is sensitive to the way variables have been categorized and to measurement error. At the same time, the possibility of the intensive study of cases allows for a careful, context-specific operationalization and makes measurement error unlikely.

2.7   Direction of generalization

In the preceding sections, we have shown that it is possible to determine whether the independent variable of interest has an effect on a dependent variable when studying only a few cases. Is it possible to generalize this finding from the cases under study to further cases? After all, our research goal might be to find out whether X makes a difference more generally, not only whether X makes a difference for the cases we have studied. In fact, John Gerring, an important proponent of the co-variational approach, defines a case study as 'the intensive study of a single case where the purpose of the study is – at least in part – to shed light on a larger class of cases' (Gerring 2007a: 20).

As this statement makes clear, the type of generalization is the same as in the case of large-N research, generalizing from a selection of cases to a population. Thus, it makes sense to speak of 'statistical generalization' (Yin 2009: 38–40). At the same time, and in comparison to large-N research, the population to which findings from a few cases can be generalized is rather small. Large-N research is typically based on a random sample; hence, generalization is possible to a relatively large population. Studies following the co-variational approach to case study research, however, can only be generalized to the population of cases that display the same scores on all the control and independent variables as the cases that have been studied.

Haverland's conclusion, that institutional veto points matter for the pace and degree of national adaptation to EU obligations, can only be generalized to rich, technologically advanced democracies with a similar level of environmental consciousness. Because these factors have been held constant, the research is unable to speak to the question of whether institutional veto points would make a difference in cases of, for instance, poor member states or member states with weak technological capacities. The same holds true for Kitschelt's study on the impact of domestic opportunity structures on the strategies and effectiveness of social movements, which holds only for unstudied countries whose anti-nuclear movement has similar objectives, where the timing and nature of the conflict are the same, where the objective threat of nuclear power has a similar level, and where the social base of the movement is similar. Political opportunity structures 'can [only, JB and MH] explain a good deal about the variations among social movements [...] if other determinants are held constant' (Kitschelt 1986: 58).

However, this limitation is not always as relevant as it initially seems. Investigators conducting applied research are often not interested in statistical generalization. They have an intrinsic interest in a specific case. They want to know whether a policy change or an organizational innovation has worked in *their* cases. They compare *their* cases with similar cases to control for other variables, not to generalize to other similar cases.

Investigators who are theoretically oriented sometimes do not regard their study as the definite answer to the debate over whether a factor matters or not. They might see their work as a plausibility probe: a demonstration that there are at least some cases where a specific variable has made a difference and it is worthwhile to conduct a large-N study. The co-variational approach is therefore well placed as a first step in a combined design or a sequence of research projects within a research program (see Chapter 5).

2.8 Presenting findings and conclusions

The treatment of the co-variational case study approach in this chapter has followed a sequence that facilitates a good understanding of the issues involved. The actual research process follows a different sequence. As with all social science research, the actual research process is not linear but is characterized by iteration between different steps. For example, the measurement of variables might be adapted in light of more knowledge about specific cases. Nevertheless, the presentation of findings should ideal-typically follow a linear-analytical form of documentation.

First, the documentation should start with an introduction in which the research question and its relevance are outlined. This introduction should be followed by a clearly separated theoretical section with a clear-cut hypothesis about the presence and direction of co-variation for the variable of interest, including a specification of the dependent variable (outcome) and the *a priori* plausibility of the outcome. In this section, the potential control variables and arguments for their inclusion or exclusion must be discussed as well. In the next part, measures for the dependent, the independent, and the control variables must be devised. Based on a preliminary measurement of the independent variable and the control variable, cases that (seem) to differ in the score of the independent variable and (seem) to have similar scores for the control variables can be identified. In the following empirical chapter(s), the cases are presented, and the definite measurement of all variables is conducted for each case. This presentation is followed by a chapter in which data analysis is performed based on the presented logic of the method of difference. Nevertheless, as we have highlighted, data analysis is not a purely mechanical or logical exercise; instead, the scholar must take into account the arguments presented in the theoretical chapter. Usually, only the combination of empirical co-variation and plausible arguments allows causal inferences to be drawn within the COV approach. What follows is a discussion of the results, including the scope of generalization as well as the theoretical, societal, and practical implications of the results.

2.9 Example of best practice: Zangl's *Judicialization Matters!*

We will now discuss an example of best practice in an integrated way. We have chosen a study by Bernhard Zangl (2008) on international trade policy. The title of his article is *Judicialization Matters! A Comparison of Dispute Settlement under GATT and the WTO.* The title already indicates that the research is X-centered. The goal is to find out whether a certain variable, in this example 'institutionalization' or, more specifically, 'judicialization', makes a difference for state behavior. The study concerns US behavior. Zangl is explicit about his X-centered goal:

> The aim of the comparison is not that the institutionalist conjecture offers the best explanation possible for the behaviour of the United States, but to show that the judicialization of GATT/WTO procedure has affected the ways the US deals with the EU.
>
> (Zangl 2008: 831)

Hence, rather than the best explanation for the outcome, US government behavior, he seeks to demonstrate that a specific independent variable, the one that captures Institutionalist Theory, had an effect. This variable is judicialization. The presence of judicialization is defined in this study as the presence of those international dispute settlement procedures that are 'designed to adjudicate whether state actors comply with their international commitments' (Zangl 2008: 826). These procedures, as they are provided by the WTO, for instance, differ from *diplomatic* dispute settlement procedure known from the predecessor of the WTO, the GATT.

Having clarified the meaning of his central variable of interest, 'judicialization', Zangl continues by elaborating on the relevance of answering the question. According to the author, the study is theoretically relevant because the major theories of IR – Idealism, Constructivism, and Institutionalism, on the one hand, and Realism and Neo-Realism, on the other hand – provide different answers to the question of whether judicialization matters. Institutionalism and related approaches argue that judicialized dispute settlement procedures lead to a greater use and a larger acceptance of this dispute settlement, thereby contribute to the establishment of an international rule of law, whereas realists and neorealists maintain that 'irrespective whether [international dispute settlement procedures] are judicial or diplomatic, powerful states can always act as they please while less powerful states have to suffer what they must' (Zangl 2008: 826).

The author then moves to the theory supporting his hypothesis. He identifies and elaborates on four causal mechanisms that, according to Institutionalism, cause dispute settlement procedures to affect member state behavior and two reasons why these mechanisms are better activated by judicial dispute settlement procedures than by the diplomatic dispute settlement procedures (Zangl 2008: 827–30). Note that in comparison to many other studies using the co-variational approach, Zangl's theoretical arguments are particularly elaborated, corresponding to the implicit goal of the study (stated as 'relevance' above) and in line with research practices within the sub-discipline of IR, which is better structured along major theoretical lines in comparison to most other sub-disciplines.

Having elaborated on how the GATT/WTO system has been judicialized, the author focuses on case selection. He compares 'US behavior in pairwise similar disputes it had with the EU/EC under the GATT and WTO dispute settlement systems' (Zangl 2008: 831). Hence, he compares cases where the judicialized procedure was present (WTO cases) with cases where the judicialized procedure was absent and only diplomatic procedures were in place (GATT cases). In other words, in line with the first case-selection criterion of the co-variational approaches, Zangl selected cases that varied on the independent variable of interest.

In addition, he followed the second case-selection criterion and chose similar cases to control for confounding factors:

> Pairwise similar disputes were selected to keep the matter of dispute constant, thereby controlling for confounding factors. This helps in particular to rule out the possibility that differences in behaviour were caused by differences in the matters of dispute.
>
> (Zangl 2008: 832)

Note that both the matter of dispute and the parties of the dispute are held constant: it is always the US against the EU/EC.

Zangl then presents the largest part of his study, the case comparisons. In fact, Zangl does not make only one comparison; he makes four pairwise comparisons, for a total of eight cases. Each of the pairwise comparisons juxtaposes an instance where the US and the EU/EC were involved in a trade dispute under GATT and further there was also a similar trade dispute under the WTO. Prior to each comparison, Zangl explains why the cases can be regarded as similar. We will return to the benefit of making four comparisons rather than one comparison when we discuss the generalization element of his study.

Zangl convincingly demonstrates that neither the content of the trade dispute nor the identity of the counterpart can make a difference because both remained constant. He concludes with a section that discusses in a more cursory way three alternative potential explanations for US dispute settlement behavior under GATT and the WTO (Zangl 2008: 847–8). He mentions the realist claim that dispute settlement is shaped by the distribution of power between the involved states and dismisses the claim because power relations have hardly changed. Zangl also discusses an explanation focusing on domestic sources of international politics. He acknowledges that domestic interest groups and domestic politics are important, but, 'as this holds true for both GATT and the WTO alike, this can hardly explain the *shift* [italics in original] in US behavior' (Zangl 2008: 848). Again, here is Mill's method of difference at work: similarities cannot explain difference; constant factors cannot explain variation. A clear-cut rejection of the third explanation is not possible, however. This explanation stems from the idealist approach and claims that fundamental foreign policy beliefs of US presidents also matter. 'Multilateralists' are more likely to follow international dispute settlement procedures than 'unilateralists'. 'Unfortunately' for Zangl, the share of years with multilaterally minded presidents was higher under WTO then under GATT. Hence, the factor was not constant and the causal relationship could not be ruled out due to theoretical arguments. We would expect more compliance with international procedure in a period with more years of multilateralist presidents, and that is what has taken place. To be sure, Zangl can refer to some instances where the US did comply under unilateralist presidents and did not comply under multilateralist presidents, but he needs to conclude that differences between foreign policy beliefs are important as well. Hence, Zangl could not unequivocally claim that judicialization has made the difference. That his research has nevertheless been accepted in a major academic journal and is considered by us as an example of best practice of the co-variational approach demonstrates that real-world research is often not as 'clean' as textbooks sometimes suggest. This should serve as encouragement, certainly for beginning researchers.

What about generalization? Zangl is aware of the limitations of the co-variational approach to case study research. This is made explicit when he defends why he always chooses the EU/EC as a counterpart of the US:

> The focus on the EU certainly limits the ability to generalize from these disputes among powerful actors to disputes between power-ful and less powerful countries, but the EU is the only contender with whom the United States had disputes that allowed pairwise comparisons of similar cases.
>
> (Zangl 2008: 832)

The quote makes it clear that Zangl found the possibility of pairwise comparisons of overriding importance. Hence, Zangl traded general-ization for control for alternative explanations, and hence internal validity.

Nevertheless, Zangl does not forgo any aspirations for generalization. The fact that Zangl designed four pairwise comparisons rather than one allows him to generalize further than studies only engaging in one com-parison. The pairwise comparisons varied from *each other* according to the role of the US. In two pairwise comparisons, it was the US that complained about EU/EC trade practices, and in the other two pairwise comparisons, it was the EU/EC that complained about US practices. This design allows Zangl to show that the shift toward more rule-following behavior of the US under a judicialized dispute settlement procedure holds for two different roles of the US and can therefore be generalized to more cases (those where the US has either of these roles).

Second, Zangl argues as follows:

> [T]he focus on the United States was chosen because if the judicialization of GATT/WTO procedures can impact the behaviour of the most powerful state, then one can assume that it will have similar effects on the behaviour of less powerful states as well.
>
> (Zangl 2008: 832)

Zangl generalizes the finding that judicialization has an impact on state behavior from the studied cases involving the most powerful state to all other states of the world, including less powerful states. This assumption is very plausible. Nevertheless, it does not follow the logic that we have laid out for statistical generalization, which allows the transfer of the finding only to very similar cases.[10]

It is important to realize that Zangl's main interest is not statistical generalization but theoretical generalization – in other words, drawing conclusions from the cases studied to the theoretical discourse. As we have indicated, his main goal is to contribute to the theoretical debate on whether institutions or judicialization matters (in this example it becomes very clear that the struggles among competing theories and paradigms can have a very practical impact). This goal and the corresponding type of generalization have more affinity with the congruence approach to case study research and will therefore be discussed in Chapter 4. However, it is appropriate to reflect on it here because it serves as an appetizer for that chapter and as a reminder that elements of different approaches to case study research can be combined (see Chapter 5).

In the context of theoretical generalization, Zangl has selected 'very likely cases' for Realism as the dominant theory in the field of research (at least in the Anglo-Saxon literature). For these cases, we would have expected the hypothesis derived from Realism to be confirmed. The results of the co-variational analysis provide evidence against Realism and provide leverage for the contender theory, Institutionalism. Because Zangl has shown that judicialization matters even under the most difficult conditions (involving the most powerful state), the conclusion that judicialization matters should have a strong impact on the theoretical discourse. If Zangl had selected cases that were 'very unlikely cases' for the Institutionalist Theory, they would have been even more crucial for the theoretical struggle. Nevertheless, the fact that the US is the most powerful state in the world says nothing about the probability that it will act in accordance with Institutionalist Theory. If we reflect on the likelihood of the cases to confirm Institutionalism, we would do well to consider how strongly a state abides internally to the rule of law, resulting in the insight that the cases involving the US are far from being very unlikely cases for Institutionalism.

2.10   Summary and conclusions

Our first approach to case studies discussed in this book exploits the co-variation between an independent variable of interest and a dependent variable to infer causality. We call this the co-variational approach (COV). The COV approach is appropriate for investigators who are interested in the effect of a specific factor, or X-centered research. Does X

make a difference? For instance, does the national opportunity structure have an effect on the strategy and the impact of social movements?
Deliberate case selection is a crucial element of this approach. Based on
the experimental template, cases that have different scores on the independent variable of interest and similar scores on other independent
variables to control for their potential effect on the dependent variable
should be selected. Because case analysis is sensitive to operationalization, including the setting of 'cut-off' points, careful conceptualization
and measurement are also important. However, indicators *are* typically
more valid and measurement error *is* less likely as compared to large-N
research. Prior knowledge and theoretical considerations have a number
of important functions: they help in specifying variables, substantiating
hypotheses, identifying control variables, and discriminating between
explanations when patterns of variation are not sufficient to do so.
Yet, the analysis of data set scores and additional theoretical knowledge
might not be sufficient to achieve conclusive results. It might often be
fruitful to combine co-variational analysis with causal-process tracing
or congruence analysis. Given the focus on a few cases and the need to
keep control variables constant, generalization is necessarily limited to
the most similar cases. Researchers interested in broader statistical generalization may turn to a large-N study to test whether the relationship
identified for these most similar cases also holds for a larger and more
varied sample.

2.11   Appendix: How to make counterfactual analysis more compelling

In our overview of modes of comparison that are based on the
COV approach, we have briefly mentioned the counterfactual mode.[11]
Because there is no co-variation in the scores of the independent variable between real world cases, we have not addressed it in detail in the
main text. In this appendix, however, we will elaborate on and illustrate
three criteria that can be used to make counterfactuals more compelling:
clarity, historical consistency and theoretical consistency. We will discuss these criteria in turn and use a case study on policy making in the
EU as an illustration. In that study, the claim is made that the EU was
causally important for a strong legal codification of the Dutch packaging waste policy. The policy shifted from a voluntary agreement between
parts of industry and government, to a generally binding statutory act,
a ministerial regulation. The argument is that in the absence of the

European packaging directive, there would not have been a strong legal codification of the policy (Haverland 1999).[12]

Clarity

Clarity, the first criterion, demands that the independent variables and the dependent variable are clearly specified and delimited. In other words, the researcher must explicitly state which variables changed in her mental thought experiment and which remain unchanged (see, for example, Emmenegger 2011b: 369). The packaging waste study specifies that the relatively informal Dutch packaging agreement would not have been supplemented with a statutory act (change in the dependent variable) without the emerging adaptation pressure induced by the EU packaging waste directive (change in the independent variable). Hence, the study explores whether the absence of the EU packaging directive, a hypothetical change of the independent variable, would have changed the score of the dependent variable (degree of legal codification of national policy).

Historical consistency

Historical consistency demands that independent variables be specified in a way that requires few changes to historical facts. In other words, counterfactuals should rewrite history as little as possible (see, for example, Tetlock and Belkin 1996b: 23). Hence, the packaging waste study merely explores what would have happened in the absence of the European packaging directive. The researcher could have gone much further by exploring what would have happened without the existence of the EU, or at least without the Netherlands' membership in it. Then, however, one would have to rewrite history much more profoundly, and the story would become more speculative and therefore less compelling because, by implication, many more phenomena would be different. For instance, one could argue the following: Dutch-based multinationals, such as Unilever, Philips or Shell, are crucial players in Dutch packaging waste politics. Without the EU and its single market, their threat of exit (that is, shifting investments to other countries) would be less credible and their political power therefore weaker, which would have substantial consequences on the shape of Dutch packaging waste policies. Generally speaking, the more changes we make, the greater the number of consequences and the lower their predictability. However, if the investigator wants to use counterfactual reasoning to explore the extent to which a member state, a macro-political institution or an entire policy sector rather than a specific policy has been impacted by another comprehensive phenomenon such as the EU, he has to move in the direction of far-reaching and tricky scenarios.

Consistency with (well-established) theoretical laws

The third and last criterion requires that the hypothesized linkages between variables be consistent with well-established theoretical generalizations. In addition to historical constraints, we must constrain our counterfactuals in theoretical terms. Theoretically informed counterfactuals are generally more compelling than a-theoretical accounts; at a minimum, they will provide the reader with a more explicit perspective from which to evaluate the plausibility of the counterfactual (Ned Lebow 2000: 583). In the case of packaging waste, the author based the counterfactual in a Rational Choice approach. He argued that the government did not have sufficient incentives to formalize the packaging waste policy in the absence of the EU. The costs were higher than the benefits. The benefits decreased due to the declining public support for environmental measures, whereas the political costs were high because the Dutch policy would be binding for tens of thousands of companies, including many small- and medium-sized companies, rather than only for those 300 companies that participated voluntarily in the covenant (Haverland 1999).

3
Causal-Process Tracing

In most small-N studies, the tracing of causal processes plays an important role. Very often, causal-process tracing (CPT) is used as a complementary technique to co-variational analysis (COV). Tracing the process that leads from a causal factor to an outcome makes it possible to enhance the internal validity of a causal claim that 'x matters' (Gerring 2007a: 173–84). This 'added value' is especially warranted when the compared cases are not as similar as they should be (to be 'controlled'), when the co-variatonal analysis is indeterminate (because more than one independent variable co-varies with the dependent variable in a theoretically meaningful way), or when the measurement and classification of variables is not as clear-cut as it should be. We will provide examples for the combination of COV and CPT in Section 5.2, wherein we address overlaps and combinations of the three approaches to case study research.

However, in this chapter, we delineate the main features of causal-process tracing as a distinct approach to case study research. It will become clear that the CPT approach has affinities to specific research questions. Those questions, in turn, imply different ways to select cases in comparison with the COV approach, and they pursue different aims to draw conclusions beyond the investigated cases. Furthermore, the CPT approach begins with ontological assumptions different from those of the COV approach, the epistemological basis for drawing causal inferences is very different, and the CPT approach has its own terminology. Identifying CPT merely as an addendum to COV seriously underestimates the potential of this approach and, probably even more importantly, misrepresents the major goals and fundaments of this approach. Recognizing the distinct features of CPT does not inhibit the combination of causal-process tracing techniques with other techniques and approaches to causal analysis, but it makes us more aware that there are trade-offs and problems involved (which we also address in Section 5.2).

The first step to describing the distinct goal of the CPT approach is to argue that it is much less X-centered compared to the COV approach. In a first approximation, it can be argued that the CPT approach is Y-centered, which means that the researcher is interested in the many and complex causes of a specific outcome (Y) and not so much in the effects of a specific cause (X). 'How come?' and/or 'How was this (Y) possible?' are the pro-typical questions of this explanatory approach, not 'Does it (X) matter?' or 'Does it (X) make a difference?' Nevertheless, in contrast to historians, for social scientists, most often the research goal is not to explain only a single important social event (Gerring 2007a: 187–210 calls this a single-outcome study). Instead, social scientists also want to identify and explain more general and/or more abstract aspects of the social world, without losing sight of the diversity in outcomes and preconditions. As a consequence, they apply CPT to the search for necessary and sufficient conditions that lead to a specific type of outcome, or they use CPT to more closely understand the theory-based 'mechanisms' that actually link causal factors to outcomes. The pro-typical questions for these tasks are: 'Which (combination of) conditions make this kind of outcome possible?' and 'Which underlying mechanisms effectively make the cause creating the outcome?'

What unites all of these goals and pro-typical questions is the fact that the search for solutions and answers is based on 'configurational thinking' (Ragin 2008: 109–46). In contrast to the COV approach, which focuses on the effects of individual causes (independent variables), approaches based on configurational thinking begin with the following assumptions:

– almost all social outcomes are the results of a combination of causal factors;
– there are divergent pathways to similar social outcomes (equifinality); and
– the effects of the same causal factor can be different in different contexts and combinations (causal heterogeneity).

Configurational thinking dramatically impacts the way scholars perform comparative analysis. The set-theoretic logics and techniques that Charles Ragin and his followers developed to draw systematic causal inferences from the study of a medium number of cases (crisp set and fuzzy set Qualitative Comparative Analysis (QCA)) have complemented the research designs and techniques that study a small number of comparable cases on the basis of co-variational thinking (Ragin 2000, 2008; Schneider and Wagemann 2007; Rihoux 2008; Caramani 2009). Hence, QCA and the co-variational analysis of comparable cases differ with respect to the number of cases they investigate and the initial assumption regarding whether causal factors function autonomously or in combination. Nevertheless, both draw causal inferences on the basis of cross-case comparisons. In contrast, the CPT approach applies configurational thinking as the basis for within-case analysis.

Configurational thinking, especially the assumption that explanations should begin with the assumption that a plurality of causal factors work together to create an outcome, is the first basic characteristic of the causal-process tracing approach. The second basic feature is that CPT as a technique of drawing causal inference takes advantage of the fact that causality plays out in time and space. In contrast to many others, we take seriously the term 'process' and include only those methodological concepts and techniques under the heading of causal-process tracing that draw on the fact that causality plays out in time and space.[1] As a consequence, we will stress the importance of observations that allow for determining the temporal order by which the causal process unfolds ('comprehensive storylines'), the empirical observations that provide certainty and density with respect to the pathway leading from cause to effect ('smoking guns'), and empirical information that allows us to specify the underlying action-formation mechanisms that link causes and effects ('confessions'). These kinds of empirical information are not compiled into scores or values of variables and transferred into rectangular datasets that contain values for all variables and cases (as in the COV approach). They do not have to be standardized to draw a logical conclusion through cross-case comparisons, but they contribute to causal inference on the basis of temporal order, spatiotemporal density and analytic depth. On the basis of these kinds of 'causal-process observations', we draw conclusions on the status and role of causal conditions in the process of producing the outcome (not only necessity versus sufficiency but also which factor has been a 'precondition' for other factors in causal chains).

The result of a study that is based on CPT is a full-fledged 'recipe' for making an outcome of interest possible. In contrast to cross-case techniques (QCA), CPT reveals not only the necessary and sufficient ingredients but also when and how the ingredients have to be brought together to create the outcome of interest. Not only those who cook for themselves will immediately recognize what a difference this kind of knowledge makes for drawing practical conclusions from empirical studies!

The price for this great advantage in comparison to cross-case approaches is that we cannot easily generalize the results of a study based on CPT to the population of cases with similar outcomes. Causal-process tracing is a within-case technique of causal inference. As a consequence, the status of causal factors as 'necessary conditions' and the status of the combination of factors that lead to the outcome as 'sufficient' are strictly confined to the case(s) under study. For example, when we have identified a cause as necessary for the outcome in our case, this does not imply that this cause has the status of a necessary condition within a population of cases with similar outcomes because configurational thinking stresses the possibilities of equifinality and causal heterogeneity. If we want to know whether a causal condition is always necessary or always sufficient for producing a specific kind of outcome, we have to look at further 'possible cases' (Mahoney and Goertz 2004) or complement a small-N study with a medium-N study based on the fuzzy set Qualitative Comparative Analysis (fsQCA) technique (see Chapter 5).

Nevertheless, most researchers who apply CPT do not really strive for this kind of generalization, which is still very close to the X-centered way of thinking that characterizes the COV approach, with the focus on the effects of individual, independent variables. Much more in line with the diversity-oriented way of thinking that accompanies approaches based on configurational causation is what can be called 'possibilistic generalization': drawing conclusions toward the set of causal configurations that make a specific kind of outcome (Y) possible.

This chapter is set up as follows. First, we specify the different research goals that can be pursued with CPT and illustrate these research goals with typical research questions (Section 3.1). Next, we introduce the ontological and epistemological foundations of this approach: contingency, causal conditions, and configurations, and finally causal and social mechanisms (Section 3.2). In Section 3.3, we will provide an overview of the diverse logics of selecting cases. Because inferring causality is not based on cross-case comparisons, we do not necessarily have to select more than one case. Accessibility is the overarching criteria for selecting cases because the cogency of CPT relies on the ability of the researcher to assemble many empirical details, to have a profound knowledge and understanding of the development of structural factors, and/or to attain deep insights into the perceptions and motivation of major actors. Section 3.4 addresses the kind of empirical information that is necessary for process tracing and the ways and instruments that are most helpful in collecting the necessary information.

In Section 3.5, we will lay out how inferences can be drawn within a CPT approach. First, we illustrate the added value of 'causal-process observations' in comparison to 'variable-scoring observations' with a fictional example. Second, we define and illustrate three kinds of information that provide the empirical fundaments for drawing causal inferences within a CPT approach: 'comprehensive storylines', 'smoking guns', and 'confessions'. Finally, we demonstrate how these empirical findings should be combined with counterfactual reasoning and/or with theory-based concepts of social mechanisms in order to reflect carefully on the status of causal factors as necessary and sufficient conditions for an outcome or for the next step within a causal chain.

These features of CPT will be described and illuminated in Section 3.6 with the help of three examples. Henry Brady's analysis (2004) of the electoral consequences of TV stations' early declaration of Al Gore as winner of the presidential election in Florida in 2000 will be recapitulated because it shows best that the observations that form the basis of drawing causal inferences within a CPT approach are not isolated; instead, they either focus on the temporal succession of the process or they provide the empirical specifications of social mechanisms within a multilevel model of causation. The famous study of Theda Skocpol on social revolutions (1979) shows how configurational thinking is applied by describing causal chains and conjunctions. We will focus in this chapter on her methods for drawing causal inferences within her cases, something that she herself did not emphasize but has been most clearly revealed and visualized by James Mahoney (1999). The study by Nina Tannenwald (1999, 2007) on the sources of the nuclear taboo serves as a mechanism-centered example of CPT.

In Section 3.7, we scrutinize the ways in which conclusions beyond the cases under investigation are drawn. In contrast to the COV approach, generalizing conclusions drawn are not for the population of cases with similar values for the independent variables. Instead, generalizing conclusions are made in respect to sets of 'possible' causal configurations. Once again, it will become clear that CPT can be used for a wide range of scientific goals: from the detailed explanation of single important cases over building middle-range typological and configurational theories to the construction of multilevel models of causation. Before concluding with a summary (Section 3.9), we offer some suggestions for how the findings and conclusions should be presented within the various CPT approaches (Section 3.8).

3.1 Research goals and research questions

3.1.1 Starting points and research goals

Very often, social science research is stimulated by rare events, such as social revolutions, or by extreme examples, as the European Union (EU) is with respect to supra-national political institution building. Another typical starting point are puzzles (Grofman 2001). For example, decisions of social or political actors that apparently do not make sense (for example, the calling of a vote of confidence that a political leader does not need and which will seriously harm his party's future prospects if he loses) or results of a social or political process that are difficult to explain, such as the intervention of states in other countries in situations when the 'national interest' does not demand such a risky and costly effort. We are interested in discovering how exactly this specific result has been possible.

Another typical starting point for case study research is the desire to know how a specific social or political community (for example, a country or region) is able to be successful in a certain respect. For example: How is it possible that Switzerland or the Netherlands have successfully managed economic globalization? What are the preconditions that made Finland so successful in education? The result of causal analysis serves as a recipe from which others can learn – although sometimes the lesson might be that the same outcome cannot be achieved because some of the recipe's ingredients are unavailable in other settings. Of course, the interest in specific kinds of outcomes is not restricted to positive outcomes. We can also be interested in questions such as the following: Why do countries such as Greece and Portugal face a serious debt crisis? The insights gained by causal-process tracing help to identify many possible steps for intervention to prevent the same outcome from occurring again.

In general, there is a clear affinity of the CPT approach to Y-centered research questions because causal-process tracing is especially suited to tracing the combination and interaction of divergent causal factors in the process that leads to an outcome. The outcome can be a single important event, for example, World War I or a specific kind of outcome (for example, social revolutions). Nevertheless, we have to stress the fact that it is only an affinity, and CPT can also be used to complement or challenge a co-variational analysis in the search for the consequences of a specific causal factor (X). We provide examples that demonstrate how CPT can complement COV in Chapter 5. In this chapter, we provide an example of a study in which CPT was used to challenge an analysis based on co-variational techniques. Henry Brady used CPT techniques to challenge the claim that the premature declaration of Al Gore as the winner in Florida by TV networks in the presidential election of the year 2000 had massive consequences for voting results (Brady 2004).

We have already stressed the fact that the CPT approach has strong affinities to the presuppositions that are aligned with 'configurational thinking' – especially the assumption that a social outcome is usually the result of a combination of causal factors. As a consequence, the CPT approach not only uses the terminology that corresponds to these presuppositions (by talking about necessary and sufficient conditions) but the CPT approach is an especially adequate analytical approach to develop and test configurational theories and hypotheses.

As Gary Goertz (2003b) has shown, many social scientists specify their theoretical propositions in the language of necessary conditions. Furthermore, very often, these propositions have an explicit or implicit temporal dimension. It is either argued that a specific temporal order of causal conditions and events is crucial for reaching an outcome (causal chains) or that the conditions have to be present at the same time to be causally effective (causal conjunctions).

For example, the notion of 'windows of opportunity' points to the configurational assumption that policy entrepreneurs have to present their policy solutions during those periods of time in which the wider political conditions are helpful and the specific policy problem is recognized in order to be successful:

> If one of the three streams is missing – if a solution is not available, a problem cannot be found or is not sufficiently compelling, or support is not forthcoming from the political stream – then the subject's place on the decision agenda is fleeting.
>
> (Kingdon 1984: 187)

Finally, causal-process tracing is required if we want to know not only whether something mattered or made a difference but also how exactly it influenced the outcome. The search for empirical traces of the links or steps that lead from the cause to an effect through causal-process tracing can perform a complementary function. It can be used to strengthen or weaken the results of co-variational analysis to answer the pro-typical question of this approach: does it (X) makes a difference? Nevertheless, it can also be a crucial element of the theory-oriented congruence analysis approach (CON), which we lay out in detail in Chapter 4. If the links and steps that lead from X to Y are specified as generic social mechanisms with reference to basic social theories, CPT can contribute to the debates and struggles among competing theories and paradigms. In the latter case (and only in this case!), we refer to tracing 'causal mechanisms'. Providing empirical evidence that specific mechanisms actually lead to the outcome and not others is crucially important for theoretical developments and struggles for intellectual hegemony. Furthermore, mechanism-based explanations lay the groundwork for linking case study research to experimental research.

To illustrate the difference in focus between the research goal that accompanies a COV approach and an interest in revealing causal mechanism, we return to the study of Zangl (2008) on international dispute settlement that we presented as a best-practice example for the COV approach (Section 2.9). In his theoretical section, Zangl specified four mechanisms that potentially translate international dispute settlement procedures into compliant state practices. Two of the mechanisms are based on social constructivist theories (commitment and reputation), and two are based on rationalist accounts (credibility and sanctions). Zangl does not trace these mechanisms systematically in his empirical sections (however, he does sometimes mention the working of a specific mechanism) because he is basically interested in showing that judicialization makes a difference rather than clarifying which mechanisms actually make the judicialization of international dispute settlement procedures more effective in comparison to diplomatic dispute settlement procedures. Nevertheless, in his concluding chapter, he uses some of the collected information to make the following claims:

> The cases demonstrate that where the diplomatic GATT procedures were at all effective, this could be attributed to one mechanism, namely that of shaming and the potential loss of reputation. [...] The WTO procedure, by contrast, was not only able to rely on reputational concerns, but also on the other three mechanisms specified above.
>
> (Zangl 2008: 845–6)

He illustrates this claim with examples but does not apply a systematic CPT approach to clarify the workings of mechanisms for each case and phase of the dispute settlements. Such a systematic application of CPT would indeed make his claim that 'judicialization matters' even more convincing. Nevertheless, it would be even more interesting to those engaged in the theoretical debate between Rationalism and Constructivism in international relations (IR). For them, the systematic search for traces of mechanisms is not only warranted to strengthen Zangl's claim, but also would provide helpful insights for questions such as the following:

- Do we really need social constructivist accounts to explain international relations, or is it possible to explain all seemingly norm-based action on the basis of rational and interest-based behavior?
- How do social mechanisms based on rationalist theories and social mechanism aligned with social constructivist theories work together to influence state behavior?

3.1.2 Research goals and functions of causal-process tracing

All case studies that follow the CPT approach are grounded in configurational thinking and use the fact that causation plays out in time and space as a 'natural basis' for drawing causal inferences. These are the main distinct features of the CPT approach. Nevertheless, as indicated, the corresponding logics and techniques can be used for different goals. Table 3.1 provides an overview of the various goals, pro-typical research questions, and the major corresponding function of causal-process tracing. Being clear about the goal and function of CPT is important because it leads to different suggestions for case selection and influences whether and in which direction conclusions beyond the investigated cases can be drawn (see Sections 3.3 and 3.6).

Table 3.1 also makes clear why the chapter on causal-process tracing is located in the middle of our book on case study design: the techniques for tracing causal-processes are very often applied as complementary within the COV approach, and they also play an important role in implementing the theory-oriented CON approach. Nevertheless, as a stand-alone research design within the social sciences, the CPT approach is most closely aligned with the goals and functions that correspond to the pro-typical question of which conditions make Y possible (third point in table 3.1).

Table 3.1   Different research goals and the corresponding functions of causal-process tracing

Goals and pro-typical research questions	Major functions of causal-process tracing
• Providing rather comprehensive explanations of single, important events/outcomes: What and who made it possible that this (Y) occurred?	• Clarifying historical truth • Assigning responsibility
• Revealing and evaluating the effect of a cause: Does X make a difference?	• Increasing the internal validity of causal inference by identifying links between X and Y • Complementing co-variational analysis
• Revealing and evaluating the preconditions for specific kinds of outcomes: Which (sequential and situational combinations of) conditions make Y possible?	• Developing and testing middle-range or typological theories (configurational hypotheses) for specific kinds of outcomes • Complementing Qualitative Comparative Analysis as a static, cross-case analytical approach with a dynamic, process-centered within-case analytical approach
• Revealing and evaluating the effectiveness of theoretically specified mechanisms: Which (combination of) social mechanisms make X effectively cause Y?	• Testing and developing theoretically specified causal mechanisms (configurations of social mechanisms) • Major part of a congruence analysis

3.1.3   Research questions

We can illustrate these different goals with the following typical research questions:

(1) What led to World War I (Levy 2007)?
(2) Why has there been no use of nuclear weapons after World War II (Tannenwald 2007)?
(3) Why is Switzerland not a member of the EU?
(4) What caused the explosion of the oil rig 'Deepwater Horizon' in the Gulf of Mexico?[2]
(5) What were the electoral consequences of the fact that TV networks prematurely declared Al Gore the winner of the presidential election in Florida in the year 2000 (Brady 2004)?

(6) Which configurations of causal conditions led to social revolutions (Skocpol 1979)?
(7) Which conditions are necessary and sufficient to make humanitarian interventions possible (Junk and Blatter 2010)?
(8) Which conditions led allies to make specific contributions to burden sharing in the Persian Gulf War (Bennett, Lepgold, and Unger 1994)?
(9) Under which configurations of societal-structural and political-institutional conditions do young democracies in Latin America and Europe consolidate their democratic systems and under which configurations do they not consolidate (Schneider 2009)?
(10) How exactly do international institutions shape the identities and interests of state actors (Checkel 2006, 2008)?
(11) Which causal mechanisms and pathways made the 'nuclear taboo' effective in the United States (US) after World War II (Tannenwald 2007)?

The first five questions lead to case studies that primarily seek to shed light on single important events/outcomes, although the third and the fourth questions make clear that a case can also be worthwhile to investigate if it is only important to some people. Whereas the first four questions are Y-centered, the Brady study is X-centered. Questions six through nine point to configurational assumptions as the starting point for empirical investigations in the preconditions for specific kinds of outcomes. The studies by Skocpol and by Junk and Blatter are based on specified middle-range theories that assume certain pathways and conjunctions as necessary and sufficient preconditions for outcomes that occur(ed) rather seldom. The Bennett, Lepgold, and Unger study addresses equifinality. The study begins with the assumption that very different conditions can stimulate allied states to contribute to burden sharing in the Gulf War.[3] Schneider's study starts with an underlying assumption of causal heterogeneity. He assumes that certain political institutions facilitate the consolidation of democracy under specific conditions within the society and that the same political institutions undermine the consolidation process if the social conditions do not fit to these political institutions. The latter two questions indicate a primary interest in the underlying mechanisms that link causal factors with outcomes.

The questions also make clear that a concrete research project can pursue more than one of the goals that we have distinguished for analytic purposes. The revolutions in France, Russia, and China are certainly important events in themselves, but Theda Skocpol's aim was to show that the preconditions that led to these revolutions have similar basic causal configurations. The second and last questions actually both refer to the same study (Tannenwald 2007), which illustrates that smart scholars can use the study of important social events (or non-events in this case) for both practical and theory-oriented goals.

3.2 Ontological and epistemological foundations

Although – or maybe because of the fact that – there has been a lively methodological debate about the causal-process tracing approach, there exists no consensus with respect to the underlying ontological and epistemological foundations of this approach, which, in turn, leads to very different definitions of major concepts and terms. The term 'causal mechanism' is an especially highly contested concept (for an overview, see, for example, Mahoney 2003; Gerring 2007b, 2008; Falleti and Lynch 2009). In the following, we provide specific definitions of the most important methodological terms and concepts. We arrived at our definitions by taking into account two principles. First, the definitions have 'resonance' within the scientific debate and are similar to the use of the term in colloquial language (Gerring 2001: 52). Second, each concept is defined considering other methodological concepts within case study methodology and especially within the CPT approach. In other words, the CPT methodology is the most important systemic context for specifying the meaning of a methodological concept.[4]

We begin with reflections on 'contingency' as a notion from the philosophy of science that contains the major ontological and epistemological foundations for the CPT approach. Next, we define two major terms – necessary conditions and sufficient conditions – as basic building blocks for 'configurational thinking'. Furthermore, we reflect on the difference between 'additive causality' and 'interactive causality' and introduce the terms 'causal chains' and 'causal conjunctions' as important distinctions for an analytical approach in which timing and temporal sequences play important roles in drawing causal inference. Subsequently, we specify our theory-oriented understanding of 'causal mechanism' as a configuration of three kinds of social mechanisms: situational mechanisms, action-formation mechanisms, and transformational mechanisms. Finally, we discuss the term 'context', which is often invoked in the methodological debate on causal mechanisms, and argue that it does not make sense to see 'context' or 'context-sensitivity' as something specific for mechanism-based explanations. Instead, the ability to take into account much contextual information for the analysis of each case is a basic feature of all small-N approaches.

3.2.1 Contingency

'Contingency' is a key term used by proponents of causal-process tracing to point to their basic assumption that the effects of causal conditions and the workings of causal mechanisms are dependent on other factors and mechanisms and that CPT is especially suited to reveal these (inter)dependencies and configurations. Sandra Mitchell (2002: 183–7) provides an overview of different understandings and sources of contingency, based on insights gained from examining how biologists address causal complexity and generalization. First, she clarifies that 'contingency comes in degrees so that the difference between generalizations in biology and in physics is not one of a lawless and lawful science, but rather a difference in the degree the causal dependencies described depend on prior conditions' (2002: 180).

According to Mitchell, four main sources and forms of contingency can be differentiated:

– space-time contingency,
– evolutionary contingency,
– multicomponent contingency, and
– multilevel contingency.

These forms of contingency correspond to the major epistemological and methodological concepts of the CPT approach, as will become clear in the following sections and chapters. First, the assumption that causality plays out differently depending on the spatial and temporal setting provides the ontological fundament for one of the central epistemological features of the CPT approach: causal inferences are drawn on the basis of temporal and spatial contiguity (see Section 3.5). In contrast to this first type of contingency, which focuses on the current structural environment (in crucial moments) as the source of conditionalizing factors, the second type of contingency locates these conditions in the past. Evolutionary contingency is considered in CPT methodology through the reflections on 'causal chains' and 'process dynamics'.

Multicomponent contingency points to the insight that the interaction of multiple causal factors is often not based on simple rules such as additivity. Instead, the interaction between multiple causal factors alters the very functioning of one or more of these factors. The interaction can dampen or amplify the causal power of individual factors and potentially even nullify their effects or reverse their causal direction (Mitchell 2002: 186). The ontological assumption of multicomponent contingency forms the basis for the search for causal combinations or configurations, which is an important characteristic of the CPT approach. Finally, multilevel contingency refers to the fact that the operation and effects of causes on a lower level of analysis depend on their embeddedness in material, ideational, or institutional structures on a higher level of analysis. This form of contingency provides the basis for our understanding of causal and social mechanisms and for the assumption that a full-fledged mechanism-based explanation is based on a multilevel model that includes structural conditions and actors as well as situational mechanisms, action-formation mechanisms, and transformational mechanisms.

3.2.2   Causal conditions and configurations

Similar to Qualitative Comparative Analysis (Ragin 2000), causal-process tracing is an analytical approach based on 'configurational thinking' (Ragin 2008). In consequence, in both approaches, it is most adequate to consider causes or causal factors as (potential) causal conditions and to focus our analysis on the question of which causal conditions and/or causal configurations are 'necessary' and/or 'sufficient' for the outcome of interest. At this stage, we briefly want to introduce the basic definitions and discuss the differences in their meanings in within-case and cross-case analyses. We begin with the definitions as they have been introduced in cross-case analysis.

Necessary condition

A causal factor (X) is a necessary condition if the outcome (Y) occurs only if X exists. Nevertheless, Y does not always have to occur if X exists. In other words, Y is not possible without X, but X does not always lead to Y.

Sufficient condition

A causal factor (X) is a sufficient condition if the outcome (Y) always occurs when X exists. Nevertheless, Y can also occur when X does not exist. In other words, X always leads to Y, but Y is also possible without X.

The status of necessity and sufficiency can also be attributed to causal configurations (combinations of causal factors):

Necessary configuration

A causal configuration (W = X AND Z) is a necessary condition if the outcome (Y) occurs only if W exists.

Sufficient configuration

A causal configuration (W = X AND Z) is a sufficient condition if the outcome (Y) always occurs when W exists.

The main difference to the way we conceptualize deterministic causation in the COV approach (Chapter 2) is the fact that within the CPT approach we do not assume that X is a necessary AND sufficient condition for the outcome, but we begin with the assumption that a plurality of causal conditions is necessary to be jointly sufficient for the outcome.

In contrast to cross-case analysis (QCA), CPT is always searching for causal conditions that are individually necessary and, in combination with other causal conditions, sufficient for the outcome. As previously highlighted in the introduction to the CPT approach, this means that we have to strictly distinguish between the status of a causal condition or configuration within a specific case and the status of a causal condition or configuration in a larger population of cases. We might have been able to provide strong evidence (through causal-process tracing) that a causal factor was necessary for producing the outcome in a specific case, but it might very well be that this factor is not necessary in another case. Recognizing and accepting this fact has a major influence on the way we draw further conclusions beyond the investigated case(s) (see Section 3.7).

3.2.3 Additive and interactive configurations

Beginning with the assumption that a plurality of causal conditions is necessary to be jointly sufficient to create a specific outcome does not yet imply a specific assumption regarding how the causal conditions work together. To obtain a more precise understanding of what we are searching for when we examine 'causal configurations', we can differentiate between:

– the additive effect of a configuration of causal factors and
– the interaction effect of a configuration of causal factors.

In the first meaning of 'configuration', it is assumed that each causal factor has a specific amount of causal power. In a specific situation, more than one causal factor is necessary to overcome a certain threshold to produce the causal effect. Nevertheless, in principle, it would also be possible to reach the effect if one causal factor were to have a stronger expression or a larger amount of causal power (in correlational terminology: if the factor were to reach a higher score on a scale that measures the existence and strength of a causal variable). In contrast, the second meaning of 'combination' suggests that the causal power of each individual causal factor depends on the existence (or on a specific strength) of the other causal factor and that each of the causal factors is a necessary condition for the causal effect. One single causal factor can be very strong. Nevertheless, it would never be able to cause the outcome alone. An additive understanding of causal factors assumes that each factor is, in principle, substitutable for the other factor, whereas the notion of causal interaction implies that each causal factor is a necessary condition and, together, they are sufficient for the outcome.

3.2.4 Causal conjunctions and causal chains

Combining configurational thinking with the other core feature of CPT – the importance that timing and temporal sequences play in inferring causality – leads us to another important distinction. We can differentiate between the following two types of causal configurations:

- A 'causal conjunction' is a causal configuration in which multiple causal conditions work together (in additive or interactive ways) at a specific point of time or over a short period of time to produce the outcome of interest. In other words, the causal conditions work together in a specific situation.
- A 'causal chain' is a causal configuration in which specific causal conditions form the necessary and (usually together with other conditions) sufficient preconditions for triggering other necessary and sufficient causal conditions or configurations at a later point in time, and this causal chain leads at the end of the process to the outcome of interest. In other words, the causal conditions work together in a specific sequence. Causal chains imply an interactive configuration because each factor in a causal chain is non-substitutable. Furthermore, the 'interaction' is asymmetric because each precondition influences the next factor in a causal chain but the reverse is not true (otherwise the causal chain turns into a causal spiral, something that we address in the section on 'process dynamics').

One of the main advantages of CPT in comparison to the cross-case techniques based on configurational thinking (QCA) is the fact that CPT is able to clearly identify in which temporal order the elements of a causal configuration concatenate to produce the outcome.

3.2.5 Social and causal mechanisms

We propose to use the term 'causal mechanism' to refer to those causal configurations that link generic social mechanisms in a multi-level model of causation. In accordance with theory-oriented adherents of a mechanism-based social science, we view causal mechanisms as configurational entities combining three different types of social mechanisms: 'situational mechanisms', 'action-formation mechanisms', and 'transformational mechanisms' (Esser 1993, 1999–2001; Elster 1998; Hedstroem and Swedberg 1998: 22; Hedstroem and Ylikoski 2010; see Figure 3.1 and the following examples).

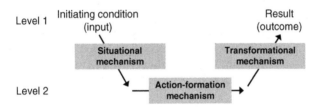

Figure 3.1 Different types of social mechanisms that together form a causal mechanism

The action-formation mechanisms are based on theoretical micro-foundations, general assumptions about the behavior of individuals. Rational Choice Theory has developed the most sophisticated specifications of the action-formation mechanism, but there are additional theories that provide micro-foundations, such as Symbolic Interactionism (Goffman 1967), the Theory of Communicative Action (Habermas 1981a, 1981b), and others (Turner 2003 [1974]). The situational and transformational mechanisms link different levels of analysis. In the social sciences, there already exist a broad range of analytical models that include a coherent set of social mechanisms, for example, models of strategic interaction within Game Theory, models of diffusion, and models of network effects (Esser 2002: 140).

Such a narrow and therefore clearly delineated definition has the following advantages and consequences:

– It is the only consistent way to distinguish the term 'mechanism' from other kinds or conceptualizations of causal factors (variables or conditions). A mechanism is neither an intervening variable nor a necessary or sufficient condition on the same level of analysis. If we trace those kinds of causal factors, we do not need an extra term. In order to avoid ambiguity (two terms for the same thing), we should talk about causal mechanisms only when we mean something different than variables, and something more specific than causal conditions.

- Introducing the term 'mechanism' highlights the ambition of the researcher to integrate empirical analysis with basic social theory. Viewed from the perspective of empirical research, mechanism-based explanations are more closely linked to basic social theory than variable- or condition-based explanations, which have a stronger affinity to applied research interests. From the perspective of social theory, using the term 'mechanism' implies an affinity for actor-centered explanations and micro-foundations (not necessarily a commitment to a strong version of methodological individualism; see Hedstroem and Ylikoski 2010: 59–60).
- Defining causal mechanisms as configurations of generic social mechanisms points to the fact that mechanism-based explanations stimulate the combination of case study research with abstract modelling and experimental research.

Illustrating the configurational logic of causal mechanisms

We can illustrate the various social mechanisms and the consequences of various configurations with stylized versions of theories in IR. Rationalist approaches share the assumption that state governments are the major actors and that they attempt to pursue the interests of their countries. In other words, the action-formation mechanism is based on the Rational Choice Theory. Nevertheless, the same action-formation mechanism leads to different results depending on the definition of the situation. If the actors perceive the situation to be 'anarchic', a state in which the states are in a constant struggle for power and survival (as assumed in the realist tradition), then it is logical that countries attempt to reach solutions in which they profit more than their competitors (the logic of relative gains). If the actors perceive a liberal community, in which each actor tries to enhance its utility without caring much about the consequences for the others, the states can accept many more solutions, based on the logic of absolute gains, as a Liberal Theory of IR would have it. In other words, the same action-formation mechanism leads to different state actions depending on the situational mechanism. The overall result of state interactions furthermore depends on the institutional environment, which contains the major transformational mechanism within such an approach. Even if all states follow the absolute-gains logic, the result will be different when the involved community of states accepts the majority rule as a decision-making rule (as increasingly is the case in the EU) in comparison to a situation when the agreements depend on unanimity.

Similar configurations of social mechanisms can be envisioned based on other behavioral theories, which function as the conceptual anchor point within such a multilevel approach to define causal mechanisms (for example, norm-based action, symbolic interaction, communicative action, rhetorical action). A full-fledged mechanism-based explanation comprises a multilevel model based on generic social mechanisms at the micro level and the links between the micro and macro levels of analysis and the specification of these three types of social mechanisms for the cases under investigation. Within such a multilevel model, each specified social mechanism has the status of a necessary condition for the outcome, and the combination of the different mechanisms is viewed as a sufficient condition for the outcome.

3.2.6 Summary

Table 3.2 provides an overview and summary of the main concepts that are relevant for applying configurational thinking in a causal-process tracing approach.

The divergent types of causal configurations in each column have a strong affinity for each other, but there exists no one-to-one connection. Causal chains and causal mechanisms imply an interactive

Table 3.2 Types of causal configurations

	Configuration based on additive causality: Substitutable causal conditions	**Configuration based on interactive causality:** Non-substitutable causal conditions
Different types according to **mutual substitutability**		
Different types according to **temporal order**	**Causal conjunction:** Situational combination of causal conditions	**Causal chain:** Sequential combination of causal conditions
Different types according to **theoretical ambition**	**Causal combination:** A configuration of (all kinds of) causal conditions	**Causal mechanism:** Multilevel model of causation based on the configuration of three types of social mechanisms

understanding of causality. Causal combinations of individually necessary and jointly sufficient conditions, in contrast, can be based on
additive or interactive causality and can contain causal conjunctions
and causal chains.[5]

3.2.7   Appendix: Contexts

Some scholars perceive context to be the necessary complement to
causal mechanisms within Social Science explanations. Falleti and
Lynch (2009: 1152), for example, define context 'as the relevant aspects
of a setting (analytical, temporal, spatial or institutional) in which a set
of initial conditions leads (probabilistically) to an outcome of a defined
scope and meaning via a specified causal mechanism or set of causal
mechanisms'. From our point of view, we should clearly differentiate
between those factors of influence that we are primarily interested in
(because of theoretical or practical reasons) and additional features of
a case that help us to reach a more thorough understanding of a case
and lead, in consequence, to an adequate interpretation of empirical
information and a more valid classification of causal factors and outcomes. Whereas the former are potential causal conditions, the latter
form the context for causal conditions, causal mechanisms, and outcomes. For example, if a specific institutional setting has been identified
as being of crucial importance for the implementation of a new policy
paradigm, we should not call this a 'contextual factor'; instead, it is a
necessary condition within a causal configuration that (perhaps, in combination with other conditions) has been shown to be sufficient for the
outcome. For the major factors of interest, the terminology of necessary
and sufficient conditions, together with the principles of configurational
thinking, allows for a much more precise description of the status and
function of causal factors than the term 'context'.

Furthermore, if we avoid to use the 'context' when we mean another
condition that is necessary in order to make a condition sufficient it
is possible to use the term 'context' in a specific and, therefore, more
precise way. Within a COV approach, contextual information allows us
to select indicators and to assign scores on the measurement scale in a
much more differentiated and reflective way, in comparison to large-N
studies, where the indicators are uniform and the assignment of scores
is usually conducted in a rather mechanical way. In other words, contextual information enhances the internal and conceptual validity of
our measurement (see Section 2.6). Within a CPT approach, contextual information is important for providing comprehensive storyline,
especially for gauging the certainty and reliability of the most important

pieces of empirical evidence: 'smoking guns' and 'confessions' (see Section 3.5). Within a CON approach, context information fulfills a similar function insofar as it can be employed to thoroughly reflect on the congruence between concrete observations and abstract propositions (see Section 4.7).

Concluding remarks

These definitions of major methodological concepts based on a configurational ontology and a critical-realist epistemology allow researchers to specify more clearly what they are searching for when they indulge in causal-process tracing. It is probably an illusion to assume that there will ever be a consensus among the social scientists with respect to these terms and concepts, and perhaps it makes sense to define core concepts differently in different research contexts and fields (as causal mechanisms are defined differently by those who are strongly involved in macro-historical analysis, for example, Mayntz 2002; Tilly 2008). Nevertheless, we hope that in the future there will be no case studies that exclude a section on research design and the specifics of the applied methods. Those who stipulate that they do causal-process tracing should specify their understanding and usage of core elements of this approach, such as 'causal configuration' or 'causal mechanism'. This leads to more transparent and reflective case studies and stimulates methodological debate and progress in small-N research.

3.3 Selecting cases

The selection of cases is not as crucial within a CPT approach as it is in a COV approach because causal inference is not based on comparison between cases. Nevertheless, the case selection has to be justified and considered carefully. First and foremost, when we want to apply CPT, the cases have to be 'accessible' to identify the kind of empirical information that is necessary to make convincing causal claims. Secondly, the logic of case selection depends on the specific goals that we want to pursue. We will address the different logics according to the four different goals that we have laid out in Section 3.2 below. First, however, we must address some misleading advice and trade-offs.

3.3.1 Misleading advice and trade-offs

Small-N research with an emphasis on causal-process tracing does not rely on the co-variation of variables across cases to draw causal inferences. Therefore, the logic of case selection is very different within the

CPT approach in comparison to the COV approach. Methodologists rooted in the tradition of large-N studies do not take this into account and provide misleading advice (for example, King, Keohane, and Verba 1994: 130; Pappi 2003: 95). Four assumptions for case selection are especially misleading (arguments for our position can be found in Dion 2003; Collier, Mahoney, and Seawright 2004; Bennett and Elman 2006):

- it is necessary to select more than one case;
- the more cases examined, the better;
- selection should not be based on the dependent variable (outcome); and
- selection must include not just 'positive cases' (with respect to the outcome).

We address the first two points in the following paragraph and the latter two afterwards.

The more the better?

There are good reasons for small-N researchers to examine more than one case, but there is no methodological necessity for it for drawing causal inferences, and there are trade-offs for increasing the number of cases examined. We have to dig deep into the individual cases to find convincing and comprehensive evidence (as many 'smoking guns' and 'confessions' as possible; see next section) as the empirical bases for drawing causal inferences. With a given amount of resources, increasing the number of cases reduces the possibilities and probability of finding sufficient empirical evidence to provide a convincing narrative and explanation for each individual case. We face a strong trade-off because, on the other hand, examining a plurality of cases might not only stimulate and guide the search for empirical information within each case but also is helpful for drawing conclusions in respect to the status of causal factors as necessary and/or sufficient conditions. For example, important findings in one case stimulate the search for similar aspects in the other case. Furthermore, applying CPT in two very similar cases helps to focus the process-tracing endeavor and the counterfactual thought experiments (Emmenegger 2010).

Why it makes sense to select positive cases on the dependent variable (outcome)

It is quite common in small-N research to select cases on the basis of the outcome (dependent variable) and to select only cases with a positive outcome. For example, the major explanations for the creation and development of the EU focus on the historical process in Europe and are not based on a comparison between Europe and other continents (for example, Moravcsik 1998). Selecting one or a few positive cases is methodologically acceptable because the causal inferences that we draw are based on the epistemology and techniques of causal-process tracing and not on comparing cases and accounting for the co-variation of variables between cases.

The other major argument against selecting based on the dependent variable and selecting only positive cases focuses on problems of generalization and not on the possibility of drawing causal inferences. Insights from large-N studies are applied to small-N studies, and it is argued that selecting only positive cases leads to biased results. This argument does not consider that most research designs that apply the CPT technique do not strive to make generalizable conclusions on the effect of a specific cause within a population of cases with similar conditions. We will discuss the types of conclusion that are possible within a CPT in Section 3.6 and will observe that those goals are fully in line with selecting 'positive cases' with respect to the dependent variable (outcome).

At this point, it might be worthwhile to mention the initial argument for why we do not need variance in the dependent variable when drawing causal inferences on the basis of causal-process tracing, even when we are interested in the effect of a causal factor: if we want to determine whether a causal factor is a 'necessary condition' for an outcome, only the investigation into 'positive cases' (cases in which the outcome exists) makes sense. We do not learn anything from negative cases for the necessary condition hypothesis. If we find out that a condition exists in cases in which the outcome is negative, this means that the condition is not sufficient, but we cannot conclude that the condition is not necessary.

Nevertheless, if we want to know whether a factor that we have identified as being necessary for the outcome within one case has the same status within the wider population of cases with similar outcomes, the study of a 'positive case' is only the first step and must be complemented by an examination of additional cases. If we want to know whether a causal condition must be viewed in general as a necessary condition for producing a certain kind of outcome, we have to complement the study of positive cases with the study of 'possible cases' – cases that possess almost all causal factors of the positive cases but not the outcome. It must be stressed, however, that the definition of 'possible cases' depends on the prior study of positive cases that reveal the relevant causal factors (Gerring 2004: 351; Mahoney and Goertz 2004; Ragin 2004: 128–33).

3.3.2   General criteria for selecting cases

These clarifications and the justifications for selecting 'positive cases' are important because it is still a contested terrain in case study methodology. Nevertheless, we now turn toward more hands-on advice for selecting cases. There is one overarching methodological principle that should guide the selection of cases if the major technique for drawing descriptive and causal inferences is process tracing: accessibility. To reveal the dense succession of causes and effects, but especially to reach deeper insights into subjective perceptions and motivations of important actors, the scholar must have access to many sources of information. Ideally, the researcher should have access to background information, such as internal documents and protocols, and should be able to talk to major actors in an open and trustful atmosphere. One of the most difficult aspects of causal-process tracing is balancing the need to build up a trusting relationship with major actors, based on empathy and sympathy, and the need to maintain a distance to reflect and analyze their statements critically. Whereas our method teachers taught us 'don't go native' we would argue, 'go native but come back'. The warning referred to two dangers that case study researchers experience. First, they might get lost in the myriad of details that real cases exhibit, and they might lose focus on the conceptually and theoretically relevant factors. Second, they might become too closely affiliated to the actors they investigate and take their statements at face value. Nevertheless, for convincing case studies, especially for those that rely heavily on CPT, the researcher cannot avoid these risks but should be aware of them.

3.3.3   Specific criteria for selecting cases according to different research goals

In addition to 'accessibility' as the general criterion for case selection, we can specify additional criteria in accordance with the specific goals for which causal-process tracing can be used (see Section 3.2, Table 3.1):

– One of the most plausible justifications for selecting cases is to refer to their practical relevance and social importance. For these case studies, the goal is to reach a rather comprehensive understanding of important events/outcomes, and internal validity of the findings is absolutely paramount because very often these explanatory studies are the basis for assigning responsibility to social actors (individuals or groups). Small-N studies very often investigate very important historical events and phenomena, as our pro-typical research questions and examples demonstrate: world wars, revolutions, the use and non-use of nuclear weapons, and important elections. Nevertheless, 'social importance' is a relative concept – it can only be specified with reference to the specific audience of a research project. The non-membership of Switzerland in the EU is a very important topic for the Swiss – it is less important for the citizens of the EU and even more less important for other people in the world (although this might be viewed differently by very wealthy people all over the world). Furthermore, adherents of causal-process tracing argue that case study research makes it possible to generate 'useful' knowledge because the focus on necessary and sufficient conditions or causal mechanisms provides insights that allow actors to identify specific points and times of intervention in social processes (for example, George and Bennett 2005: 263–85). For example, a case study that provides strong evidence that a positive general mood for international cooperation has been a necessary precondition for a break-through in international negotiations in specific policy fields (see Blatter 2009) conveys the message that negotiators should wait for these 'windows of opportunity' and minimize their efforts in times when these windows are closed. 'Useful knowledge' is also a concept that can only be specified in relation to specific actors. Overall, selecting important cases and focusing on useful knowledge for specific actors reveal the pragmatic roots of the CPT approach (see Chapter 1).

- If causal-process tracing is used to complement co-variational analysis in the search for the effect of a specific causal factor, case selection follows the logic of the COV approach, which means that we have to select more than one case and that the cases should be as similar as possible in all respects except with respect to the causal factor of interest, for which we need strong variance (see Chapter 2). Whereas such a complementation of co-variational analysis with causal-process tracing has many advantages, we should be aware of the trade-offs with respect to case selection. Case selection according to the imperatives of the COV approach neither guarantees 'accessibility' nor is it the adequate approach when we attempt to reveal causal conditions and configurations for a specific (kind of) outcome.
- As we will lay out in more detail in Section 3.6, those case studies that attempt to identify the (combinations of) causal factors that form

the necessary and sufficient conditions for specific kinds of outcomes have a more or less explicit goal of drawing conclusions beyond the case(s) under investigation. They seek to make a contribution to the debate on which pathways are possible for reaching an outcome of interest; in other words, CPT-based case studies contribute to specifying the set of proven causal configurations for a kind of outcome (leading to typological theories). The goal is not to draw generalizing conclusions on the effect of a specific causal factor (independent variable) in a specific set of cases that are similar with respect to all other potential causal factors (most similar systems). Therefore, case selection in the CPT approach does not follow the *sampling* logic of large-N studies, and it is also not based on *similarity with respect to potential alternative causal factors*, which is adequate advice for the COV approach. Instead, case selection in a small-N study that attempts to reveal causal configurations is based on *similarity with respect to the outcome* and on a *sequential* logic of case selection. For example, if we were interested in the preconditions for adapting to economic globalization and preserving low unemployment rates, in an initial study, we would select only successful countries/cases (for example, Switzerland, the Netherlands, and Scandinavian countries). Furthermore, we would select countries where we expect different pathways to successful adaptation to economic globalization (for example, a 'liberal' pathway and a 'corporatist' pathway). The goal of such an initial study, including two to four cases/countries, is to identify the specific causal configurations that make a successful adaptation possible. Note that in contrast to the 'most different system design', which we briefly mentioned in Chapter 2, the goal is not to find the one common causal factor that explains a similar outcome in different contexts.

The second step in the research process can be another small-N study focusing on 'negative but possible cases' (Mahoney and Goertz 2004) or the complementation of the small-N study with medium- or large-N studies. Whereas the latter is especially warranted if we want to determine whether specific configurations are generally producing a positive outcome in a population of similar countries, the former is appropriate when we want to determine whether it is really the combination of causal factors that make the outcome possible. We can test this assumption by selecting countries that have clearly been less successful ('negative cases' with respect to the outcome). Mahoney and Goertz (2004: 662) describe the 'possibility principle' in the selection of 'negative cases' with the following example. Research on the preconditions of the economic success of Asian 'tigers' since the 1960s has led to the following argument: the ability of countries to move from import-substitution industrialization (ISI) policies to export-oriented industrialization (EOI) policies before heavy industry was established was a necessary precondition for economic success. In other words, the formula for economic success is the following causal chain: ISI policies are necessary for achieving light industrialization, which is a necessary but insufficient precondition for heavy industrialization and economic success. Only with a transformation to EOI policies could a successful heavy industry be established, which made enormous growth rates possible. All those conditions together, as well as their temporal order, are viewed as sufficient for producing large growth rates. To test whether the switch in economic policy from ISI to EOI was really a necessary condition for economic success, it is appropriate to choose only those countries as 'negative cases' that had the first preconditions (ISI policies and light industrialization). As a consequence, James Mahoney and Gary Goertz defend those researchers who examined South and Central American countries such as Brazil or Mexico but ignored countries in Africa, which were characterized in the first half of the twentieth century by non-industrial forms of commodity exportation.

In Chapter 5, we address another basis for case selection. Case studies, especially those that focus primarily on CPT, can be embedded in (explicitly formulated or implicitly existing) larger research programs. If large-N studies using statistical techniques of analysis or medium-N studies based on Qualitative Comparative Analysis have been conducted as a first step, their results can be used for selecting specific cases for in-depth studies. One goal of these case studies is to test the results of the large-N or medium-N studies; nevertheless, there are further goals as we will lay out in Chapter 5.

3.4 Collecting empirical information

In all empirical studies, much effort must be put into the collection of empirical information. Even more than in other research designs, the cogency of CPT-based case studies depends on the quality and trustworthiness of the empirical evidence. A thorough 'soaking and poking' is necessary to become familiar with the selected case(s). Social scientists who focus on causal-process tracing apply information-gathering techniques that have been developed by historians and ethnographers, and they think very much like detectives and less like statisticians.

As always in the social sciences, the search for information begins with a review of the relevant academic and non-academic literature. In comparison to other approaches, the CPT approach demands a more case- and less theory-centered search for relevant literature. A review of existing studies from various disciplines provides the researcher with a broad spectrum of potentially important factors of influence. Depending on the literature, the researcher may need to narrow her focus in the next step, when she is collecting and analyzing further primary data. For example, the literature may suggest causal configurations of macro structural factors and accordingly the focus may be on selecting information that allows for plotting the historical development of structural factors, such as economic growth, strength of interest groups or hegemonic paradigms in a policy field or public discourse. As in all other approaches, this means that the researcher must find the relevant statistics to select media reports and gather documents and statements from important organizations and actors. In comparison to the COV and CON approaches, the CPT approach demands that a rather broad spectrum of factors be taken into account and that the development of these factors over time be documented as completely as possible. Therefore, archival work is paramount, and social scientists can learn from historians how to work with archival sources (for example, Howell and Prevenier 2001). Those who are especially interested in tracing causal mechanisms must collect information that reveals the perceptions and motivations of individual, collective or corporate actors. As a consequence, they turn to adequate sources, such as biographies, or conduct narrative interviews with relevant actors. From ethnographers they can learn how to take into account the cultural contexts in which actors are embedded to reach a better understanding of the perceptions and motivations of these actors (for example, Hammersley and Atkinson 2007).

3.5   Drawing causal inferences for the case(s) under investigation

The core characteristic of the CPT approach is the fact that 'causal-process observations' and not 'variable-scoring observations' or 'data-set observations' form the main empirical basis for drawing causal inferences (for the definition of these terms, see Chapter 1). The analyst attempts to reveal the various steps that lead to an outcome; he reflects on the role that causal factors played in each sequence within the identified causal pathways and focuses on those situations when a plurality of causal factors come together and shape further pathways in decisive ways. The corresponding empirical information complements the information that has been collected to determine the scoring or classification of the independent variables (starting conditions) and the dependent variable (outcome). As a consequence, causal-process tracing can be used to complement a COV approach (see Chapter 5). Nevertheless, the use of 'causal-process observation' also makes it possible to draw causal inferences without any comparison across different cases. Within a CPT approach as an ideal-type, stand-alone research design, the information on the starting conditions and the outcome are no longer transferred into scores or aggregated to classify a case with respect to a specific variable. Instead, they are used to determine the temporal order between causal conditions and effects/outcomes. Furthermore, we use the terms 'causal conditions', 'causal configurations', and 'causal mechanisms' instead of 'variables'. Finally, causal-process observations make it possible to draw causal inference in cases in which variable-scoring observations and datasets would not allow any logical conclusion. These major differences and the added value of causal-process observations will be illustrated first with the help of a fictitious example before we dig deeper into the logic and features of causal-process tracing.

3.5.1 The added value of causal-process observations

Figure 3.2 illustrates two cases with the same outcome: the destruction of villages in a wildlife habitat. We want to discover what has caused the destruction of the two villages. Prior experience point to two potential causal factors: (a) a stampede of elephants or (b) a firestorm, facilitated by dry weather and heavy winds. Causal-process tracing allows us to reach a better understanding of the relevance and roles of these two factors within the two cases.

We have collected the following variable-scoring observations for the independent variables by consulting the wildlife administration and meteorologists. Both villages are within areas where elephants live, and both areas experienced dry weather and heavy winds during the time when the two villages were destroyed. Both villages were fully destroyed. As a consequence, we cannot draw inferences from the resulting dataset alone. Simply coding the dependent and independent variables as either 1 or 0 results in only scores of 1 for all variables in all cases. On this basis, we cannot draw any conclusion based on the logics of co-variation.

Instead of searching for further cases in which one of the two explanatory factors or the outcome was not given, applying a CPT approach

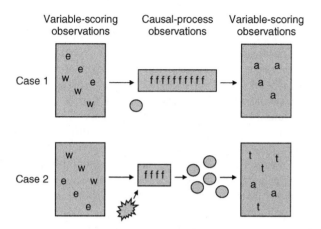

Figure 3.2 Causal-process observations in addition to variable-scoring observations
Note: e = elephants; w = wind; f = firestorm; OOO = stampede; a = ashes; t = traces of trampling.

means searching for further evidence within the cases to draw causal conclusions.

A first step is to more closely examine the outcome. Typically, a large-N study can differentiate only between destroyed villages and villages that are not destroyed because the only way to receive information about many villages is to survey the relevant area by airplane. In a small-N study, the researcher collects her data on the ground and visits some villages (only destroyed ones = 'positive cases') and their surroundings to find evidence that point toward specific causes of the destruction. In our example, the social scientist has found the following evidence in the destroyed villages. In village one, there are a lot of ashes and no evidence that the houses were trampled down; in village two, we found some ashes and much evidence that indicates that the destruction occurred by trampling. Given this evidence with respect to the outcome (illustrated in the boxes on the right-hand side in Figure 3.2), she draws the conclusions that village one was destroyed by a firestorm and village two was destroyed by elephants (the existence of some ashes in this case can be 'explained away' by the use of fireplaces by the inhabitants). Nevertheless, only if the researcher adds causal-process observations is she able to produce convincing and complete explanations. If she finds a path of burned land that leads toward the village, the causal inference that a firestorm has caused the destruction is much more convincing than finding only ashes in the village.

Furthermore, our second case illustrates that causal inference that is drawn only on the basis of value-scoring observations might be incomplete and, therefore, misleading. The causal-process observations in case two indicate that the destruction of the village has been the result of a causal chain in which both causal conditions were necessary and, in their temporal succession, sufficient to destroy the second village. The empirical evidence points to the following causal process. First, at some distance to the village, fire broke out because tourists took insufficient precautions when using a fire pit. In combination with strong winds, the careless use of the fire pit then led to a firestorm. The firestorm actually never reached the village, but it triggered a stampede of elephants, and the herd of elephants turned toward the village and trampled it down.

Process tracing in case two brought two major insights that would have not been possible by a research design that only observed the scores of (ex-ante determined) variables. First, there is another causal factor that is a necessary condition for the destruction of the village in this case: careless use of a fire pit outside the villages. Case two shows that in combination with strong winds, it is sufficient to create a firestorm that can lead to the destruction of villages. This insight is especially valuable for adherents to CPT because it produces knowledge that can be easily used to develop measurements for preventing the destruction of villages in the future. The second insight from CPT in case two is that fire also played a role in the destruction of this village and that the existence of elephants alone was not a sufficient causal factor. Again, this finding, which would not have been possible with a COV approach alone, might be quite important when practical conclusions are drawn from the case studies. In comparison to the results that would have been created with case studies based only on a COV approach and variable-scoring observations, the additional insights from a CPT approach will reduce the political pressure to reduce the number of elephants as an evidence-based policy measure for the protection of villages.

3.5.2 Major features of causal-process tracing

Drawing causal inferences with the help of causal-process tracing is grounded in the fact that causality plays out in time and space. 'Causal narratives', which provide comprehensive and continuous storylines regarding the causal process, have always played a major role in case study research (Levy 2002). In recent years, a flurry of methodological reflections has ensued on the 'logics of history' (Sewell 2005) and on 'temporality' (for example, Büthe 2002).

Most of these reflections brought the rigor of formal logic to the analysis of causal processes, especially when we attempt to reach a more precise understanding of causal pathways by differentiating causal chains according to the question of whether they are based on necessary or sufficient causal conditions (Goertz and Levy 2007; Mahoney, Kimball and Koivu 2009) and by reflecting on the possible process dynamics (for example, Bennett and Elman 2006).

Nevertheless, it must be stressed that one of the core advantages of small-N studies is the fact that the researcher is able to invest heavily in the search for many pieces of empirical evidence. When the empirical bits and pieces form a coherent picture, they can provide a high level of certainty that a causal-process has occurred as described. In other words, drawing causal inferences on the basis of CPT relies not only on the cogency of formal logic but also on the density and depths of the empirical evidence that the case study research is able to assemble. Crucially important for 'dense' descriptions are 'smoking guns' – core observations within a coherent cluster of observations that closely link cause and effect in time and space. 'Deeper' insights into the perceptions, motivations, and anticipations of important actors in crucial moments are gained through 'observations' that we call 'confessions'. This terminology points to the fact that scholars applying CPT should primarily think like detectives and attorneys, who must convince juries, and not so much like statisticians.

Furthermore, we want to emphasize the fact that the new interest in case study methodology and especially in CPT has been triggered by theoretical developments in which temporality plays a major role (see Chapter 1). This, in turn, allows empirical case study research to draw on a flurry of theoretical concepts that focus on causal conditions and causal mechanisms that influence the unfolding of social processes over time (for example, Mahoney 2000a, 2006; Pierson 2000a, 2000b, 2004; Grzymala-Busse 2011). In order words, CPT does not only rely on formal logics and empirical evidence but also on general theoretical concepts.

3.5.3   Empirical fundaments of CPT: Storylines, smoking guns, and confessions

A full-fledged explanation based on the fact that causality plays out in time takes into account a longer period of time through which the overall causal process evolves, and much shorter periods of time in which causal conditions add up and/or interact in decisive ways for the further development of the causal process. In the shorter periods, the causal process is placed 'under the microscope', and the longer period ensures that the 'bigger picture' is not lost (Checkel 2006).

First, a small-N study based on CPT provides a 'comprehensive storyline', in which the development of potentially relevant causal conditions is presented in a narrative style. Usually, this bigger picture concentrates on structural factors and not on micro-level aspects, such as the perceptions and motivations of actors. A major goal of these comprehensive storylines is to differentiate the major sequences of the overall process and identify the critical moments that further shape the process.

Second, the study provides more detailed insight into the causal processes that occur at critical moments. The most important goal is to find empirical evidence that provides a high level of certainty that a causal factor or a combination of causal factors actually led to the next step in the causal pathway or to the final outcome of interest. In other words, we attempt to find 'smoking-gun' observations embedded in a dense net of observations that show the temporal and spatial proximity of causes and effects. Furthermore, we attempt to reach 'deeper' insights into the perceptions, motivations, and anticipations of major actors; the observations that provide these deeper insights will be called 'confessions' because we want to highlight the complementary role of these 'observations' to the 'smoking-gun' observations.

These three types of causal-process observations build the empirical basis for a thorough reflection on the question of whether certain causes or configurations should be viewed as necessary or sufficient causal conditions for the outcome in the case under investigation. Before we introduce some logical foundations for these reflections, we describe the characteristics of the empirical information necessary to qualify it as 'comprehensive storylines', 'smoking guns', or 'confessions'.

Comprehensive storylines

The narratives, or storylines, that provide an overview of the overall process that has led to the outcome of interest have two functions:

- They describe the most important structural causal conditions that potentially have an influence on the outcome and the development of these factors over time.
- They identify the most important steps that have led to the outcome. In other words, the overall process is sectioned into different sequences that are separated by decisive situations and phases of transformation. The latter are rather short periods of time that have

the characteristics of 'critical (con)junctions' – their outcome strongly affects the further path of a causal process (for example, Pierson 2000b: 87–9, 2004).

Tracing the development of potentially relevant structural causal conditions and outcomes over time is an important step in the CPT approach. First, it allows for identifying 'turning points' and 'phases of transformation' for these conditions and outcomes. This, in turn, is the empirical basis of two additional steps:

– The temporal proximity and succession of turning points and phases of transformation of different conditions can be used as evidence for or against the claim that there are causal connections between these conditions.
– Turning points and phases of transformation can be viewed as 'critical moments', for which it makes sense to dig deeper into the empirical process to reveal the workings of causal conditions and mechanisms in detail.

This can be illustrated with a fictitious example, as presented in Figure 3.3. Let us assume that we are interested in the preconditions that make a strong increase in welfare possible. Let us further assume that we found three main theories for the explanation of rapid socio-economic growth in the literature: a socio-economic approach that focuses on urbanization; a culturalist approach that views the 'capitalist spirit' stimulated by the Reformation/Protestantism as the crucial

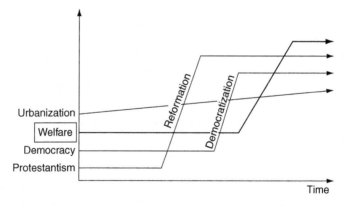

Figure 3.3 Development of potential causal conditions for increasing welfare over time

trigger, and a political-institutionalist approach that assumes that (the transformation toward) democracy is a precondition for socio-economic welfare expansion.

To trace the preconditions for rapid growth, we examine countries that experienced slow increases of welfare in earlier years and a dramatic increase in welfare in later years. In other words, we choose a 'positive case'. Some might argue that we have selected two cases according to the research design of a intertemporal comparison (which is one option within the COV approach that we laid out in Chapter 2). Nevertheless, that is not an accurate interpretation because the case is selected based on the value of the dependent variable and not based on the value of the independent variable of interest (as would be the case within a COV approach). Furthermore, we do not attempt to control all independent variables, only the one of interest. Finally, as will become clear shortly, tracing the development of causal conditions and outcomes over time within a CPT approach follows a different logic, uses different terminology, and leads to different suggestions to focus on during the analysis.

Figure 3.3 reveals the empirical results of our attempts to trace the developments of the outcome of interest (welfare) and the three potential causal conditions over time.[6] Please note that the presented results do not represent the state of the art in this field of research but are instead presented for purposes of illustrating the different ways to draw causal inferences within COV and CPT approaches. [7]

In Figure 3.3, we can identify 'turning points' and 'periods of transformations' for the outcome of interest (welfare) and for two of the three potential causal conditions. These turning points are moments in which the pace or the direction of developments change and can be used to differentiate social processes in different sequences. First and foremost, we can identify a close temporal contiguity between the period when the process of democratization occurred and the beginning of the phase of strong growth rates. This serves as important (but not sufficient) initial empirical evidence for the theoretical assumption that it is, indeed, the process of democratization that triggers a higher rate of socio-economic growth. There is no such temporal contiguity between the process of religious reformation and the turn toward higher growth rates. This serves as important (but not sufficient) empirical evidence that a new religious spirit did not trigger higher growth rates, at least not directly, because the empirical results allow for the possibility that reformation has triggered democratization, which, in turn, led to stronger increases in welfare. In fact, the presented empirical results of the long-term developments serve as initial empirical evidence for such a causal chain (see below). The fact that we find a steady process of urbanization without any turning points serves as initial evidence that this potential causal factor has not had a direct influence on accelerating growth rates. Furthermore, this is only one piece of evidence, and it is as of yet unclear whether or not urbanization played any role in the overall process toward stronger increases in welfare.

In principle, the empirical information that is presented in Figure 3.3 can be analyzed and interpreted in co-variational terms as well as in the configurational terminology of causal-process tracing. Within co-variational thinking,[8] we use the terms that are depicted on the left-hand side of the graphic as variables and interpret the lines as scores on a scale that measures the value of these variables. We must transform the information into 'variable-scoring observations' to draw logical conclusions within a intertemporal comparative case study design. The main challenge is identifying how to sequentialize the overall process into different cases. If the overall process is broken down into two cases, one covering the first half of the process, and the other one covering the second half of the process, and the values of the variables are measured in the middle of each time period, the researcher cannot draw any decisive conclusion because the dependent variable (welfare) is 'overdetermined' because two independent variables show corresponding co-variation: Democracy and Protestantism. Only if we break down the process into three cases, one before the Reformation occurred, one for the following period until the turn toward higher growth rates set in, and one for the period following the growth rate increase, can we discriminate between Democracy and Protestantism as causes for higher growth rates. This example shows how strongly the co-variational results drawn from an intertemporal comparison are dependent on how we slice the overall process into case-pieces.

Within a CPT approach, we do not refer to dependent and independent variables and do not focus on the co-variation of these variables. Instead, we use the terminology of 'causal conditions' and focus on the temporal contiguity and temporal order of 'turning points', and 'phases of transition' in the development of these conditions. The different way of thinking is also evident due to the fact that we use terms that refer to processes and not terms that point to concepts for which different values or levels can be measured, for example, 'democratization' instead of 'level of democracy'. The underlying assumption is that the transformational process of democratization has triggered causal mechanisms that stimulated socio-economic growth (for example, the 'creative destruction' that individuals experience during the transformation toward democracy stimulates similar innovative activities within the economic realm). A co-variational analysis would be more consistent with a different link between democracy and welfare. Here, the assumption would be that only when democracy became a stable form of political regime did it serve as a condition for increasing socio-economic welfare (for example, because the rule of law as an important dimension of a modern liberal democracy is a necessary condition for capitalists to invest). Within a CPT approach, the main challenge for the researcher is to find further empirical evidence that provides certitude that democratization has indeed triggered the higher growth rates. For this, he would attempt to more closely examine the period of time when the process of democratization occurred and when the growth rates accelerated. Furthermore, he would attempt to find empirical evidence for (and against) the different causal mechanisms invoked by the slightly different causal conditions 'democratization' and 'stable democracy'.

Smoking guns

This leads us to the second important concept that indicates the empirical fundament of causal-process tracing: 'smoking guns'. We use the term 'smoking gun' (or 'smoking-gun observation') for an observation that presents a central piece of evidence within a cluster of observations, which together provide a high level of certainty for a causal inference. We take terminology serious; in consequence we use this term slightly differently in comparison to others who write on causal-process tracing (see Chapter 1).

First, a smoking gun is an observation and not a test. A smoking-gun observation is connected to other observations, and together, the full cluster of observations can be used inductively to make strong causal claims. A smoking-gun observation receives its strength for making causal inferences by its dense temporal and spatial connection to other empirical observations and not by its connection to a specific theory or hypothesis. Such an observation can form the empirical basis of a test for a theory or hypothesis, but only when it is combined with counterfactual thought experiments or with a congruence analysis based on the ex-ante specification of causal mechanisms (see below).

Clearly, the metaphor highlights the fact that a gun is an especially important piece of evidence, if we observe it when it is still smoking following its use with a significant consequence (for example, killing somebody). In other words, the metaphor refers to temporal contiguity between the observation and the activity that caused the death of a person. The metaphor also reminds us that one observation alone, not even a smoking gun in the hands of a suspect, is never sufficient for creating a strong piece of evidence. This core observation must be complemented by further observations that provide further evidence for the causal claim on the basis of temporal and spatial contiguity.[9] The observation of a smoking gun is only a strong piece of evidence if we have further observations that provide certainty that the killed person has died or has been fatally wounded a few seconds prior. We need to complement the observation that serves as an indicator for the existence of a cause with at least one more observation that serves as evidence for the existence of the consequence or the effect. These two observations must be connected by temporal contiguity. In other words, the gun in the hands of a suspect is only a strong piece of evidence if we have at least two observations that provide certainty that two things occurred at the same time or in a short period of time: smoke as an indicator that the gun has been fired a moment before, and observations or medical indications that give us a high level of certainty that the person has died because of the bullet that hit him at this moment (for example, observing that the killed person fell on the floor at the same time when we saw the gun smoking). If the person who has been shot did not move when he was shot, a necessary piece of evidence would be that the autopsy would clarify that the person actually died during or after the moment when we observed the smoking gun. We have to make sure that the person did not die before to be able to claim that the shooting was not only sufficient but also necessary for the death of the person.

Spatial contiguity is another requirement for a smoking-gun observation becoming a strong empirical basis for making causal inferences. If we observe a smoking gun in Phoenix, Arizona, and have strong evidence that a person died in Amsterdam at the same time, we do not have a smoking-gun observation, despite the temporal contiguity. To make a smoking gun a decisive piece of evidence, we need additional observations, for example, evidence that shows that the suspect and the killed person were present in the same place at the same time and that the gun was directed at the person who died. Of course, in the social sciences, we need a broad understanding of 'spatial contiguity' that extends beyond a narrow geographic definition and includes notions such as 'social contiguity' (joint membership in a community), close ties, or intensive communication within a social network (something that appears as 'proximity' in social network analysis). Independently from our conceptualization of 'spatial contiguity', an observation arrives closer to the status of being a 'smoking-gun observation' the more we find further evidence that allows us to literally trace the 'pathway' between a cause and an effect.

Finally, the term smoking-gun observation has clear affinities for actor-centered elements of an explanation. In most cases, our major interest is in identifying the person who has shot the victim.[10] To shed light on the causal processes that have occurred at 'critical moments', we attempt to determine how individual, corporate, or collective actors behaved, why they acted as they did, and what the consequences of their actions and interactions were. In consequence, the behavior and the capabilities of actors usually take center stage in smoking-gun observations. They complement the focus on structural factors that dominate within the bigger picture that we draw when we scrutinize the comprehensive storylines.

Confessions

Smoking-gun observations usually do not reveal the motivations of the actors, but sometimes they can. Consider, for example, if we had found evidence that the wife of the suspect was sleeping next to the victim at the moment when we observed the smoking gun in the hand of the suspect. In general, a judge or a jury would find it very difficult to convict a suspect when they cannot imagine any motive for the deed, even if many pieces of evidence point to a suspect.

In principle, there are two ways to complement (a) the macro-structural features of a causal process that we establish in the comprehensive storylines and (b) the smoking-gun observations, which document actions, interactions, and consequences at critical moments on a meso level with explanatory features on the micro level (c):

– We can infer the motives by combining the empirical information on structural factors (for example, the 'objective' interest constellation, the dominant frame in the public discourse) and the empirical information on the actions of the involved actors with a behavioral theory that provides a clear and consistent conceptualization of an action-formation mechanism that works on the level of individual actors.
– We can attempt to find 'confessions', explicit statements of actors in which they reveal why they acted the way they did. These statements can contain information about all elements of a full-fledged mechanism-based explanation: information about how the actor perceived the situation (for example, the 'subjective interest constellation', his individual dominant frame or problem definition),

indications about driving motivations (maximizing power, security or wealth, following established norms, or receiving attention, for example), and reflections about the anticipated consequences of specific actions. The latter depends not only on the perceived situations – such as interest constellations – but also on the perceived transformational mechanisms, for example, voting rules or likeliness of diffusion processes.

Please note that 'confessions' are important pieces of evidence, but as in judicial trials, we should not take them at face value without critical reflection. We should carefully examine the contexts in which actors provide information about their perceptions, motivations, and anticipations. For example, when actors are interviewed by journalists or scholars, processes of ex-post rationalization often occur: actors justify their decisions by arguing that they pursued a specific goal, but in reality, the behavior was much less reflective and strategically oriented, or it was driven by other goals. On the other hand, statements that actors make within the social or political process often serve strategic purposes: they attempt to send signals to other actors to enhance their bargaining power or to strengthen their legitimacy to the wider audience. In other words, we should be aware of typical biases with respect to motivations when we interpret the statements of actors in specific contexts.

Nevertheless, confessions, traces of causal mechanisms that provide insight into the perceptions, motivations, and anticipations of major actors, are important complements to smoking guns because they reduce a problem of drawing causal inferences on the basis of temporal succession. Actors can anticipate certain developments or actions and react to these anticipated developments in advance. This undermines the logic of drawing causal inference on the basis of temporal succession because the 'consequence' lies ahead of the 'cause'. Nevertheless, with respect to logic, the problem can easily be solved because the 'real' sequence is as follows: (a) stimulus, which triggered the anticipation, (b) action in accordance with the anticipation, (c) adjustment to or avoidance of the anticipated situation. The real challenge lies at the empirical level, especially when the anticipated situation did not occur because of earlier adjustments. Nevertheless, in principle, it is possible to identify the first 'critical moment' at which the actor began to change his behavior in anticipation of a situation that he perceived to be possible or probable.

Ideally, a full-fledged explanation based on CPT should include all three kinds of empirical evidence: comprehensive storylines that provide the 'big picture' by tracing the historical development of structural factors; smoking-gun observations, which create certainty with respect to the dense link between a cause and an effect; and confessions, which reveal the perceptions, motivations and anticipations of important actors. These types of causal-process observations are the main foundations for drawing causal inferences within a CPT approach. Nevertheless, the causal inferences that we draw become more convincing the more we connect the causal-process observations to formal logic and social theory.

3.5.4 Logical foundations of CPT I: Causal chains

The discussions and reflections on 'path dependency' (for example, Mahoney 2000a, 2006; Pierson 2000a, 2000b, 2004; Bennett and Elman 2006) and 'causal chains' (Goertz and Levy 2007) have produced many insights about time and temporality in social processes that can be used to make causal-process tracing more systematic and reflective.

Many adherents to causal-process tracing demand the explication of the entire causal chain that leads to the outcome of interest. George and Bennett, for example, state:

> A satisfactory historical explanation of a particular case needs to address and explain each of the significant steps in the sequence that led to the outcome of that case. If even one step in the hypothesized casual process in a particular case is not as predicted, then the historical explanation needs to be modified.
>
> (George and Bennett 2005: 29–30)

Indeed, for the cogency of a full-fledged explanatory approach based on CPT, it is important that the causal chain contain no major gaps and that the researcher provide a continuous causal narrative. Nevertheless, each narrative has to reduce the complex reality to focus on those factors that seem to be the most important in explaining the outcome of interest. The selection of these important factors is, to a large extent, driven by prior knowledge and the debates in the field of research. Furthermore, we can also judge the 'importance' of causal factors, by reflecting on their role and status within causal chains. Gary Goertz and Jack Levy (2007) have introduced the terminology and logic of necessary and sufficient conditions to shed light on causal chains. These concepts allow us to be more aware of what it means to call (implicitly or explicitly) an element of a causal chain a necessary or sufficient condition.

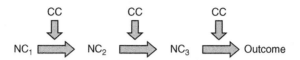

Figure 3.4   Chain of necessary conditions

SC_1 ⟹ SC_2 ⟹ SC_3 ⟹ Outcome

Figure 3.5   Chain of sufficient conditions

If a causal factor is called a necessary condition (NC), it implies that the outcome would not have occurred without this condition. Nevertheless, other factors have to be added to make the outcome actually occur. In other words, the existence of a necessary condition makes the outcome or the next step in a causal chain possible, but complementary or contextual conditions (CC) must be included to explain why it actually occurred (Goertz and Levy 2007: 26) (Figure 3.4).

If a causal factor is called a sufficient condition (SC), it implies that the factor has been able to produce the next step in the causal chain or the final outcome without further causal factors. Therefore, the causal strength of a sufficient condition is higher than the causal strength of a necessary condition within a causal chain (Figure 3.5).

Furthermore, Goertz and Levy (2007: 27) demonstrate that it makes sense to assume that the first condition in a sufficient condition causal chain is the most important one because such a chain implies that the first condition is the 'trigger' of the process, and the other elements of the causal chain are simply transporting the initial stimulus toward the outcome. As a consequence, the assumption that there is a causal chain of sufficient conditions makes it necessary that the researcher reflect thoroughly on when (at which point in time) and where (with which structural factors) to begin when tracing the empirical evidence of a causal chain.

Causal-process observations and conclusions on the status of causal conditions

How can we bolster the claim that a causal factor should be assigned the status of a necessary condition or the claim that a causal factor or a causal configuration has been sufficient for an outcome through within-case analysis? Different kinds of empirical observation and different techniques and theoretical concepts are necessary for these tasks.

The quest for necessary conditions is much more X-centric than the search for sufficient conditions. As Goertz and Levy (2007: 15) explain: 'To say that S is necessary for Y means simultaneously the counterfactual that without X, Y would not have occurred.' In consequence, if we want to make the claim that a factor has been a necessary condition, we have to apply counterfactual reasoning. We have established the principles of counterfactual reasoning in Section 2.3 as one specific research design of the X-centered co-variational approach. Nevertheless, counterfactual thought experiments are not restricted to independent variables. Within a CPT approach, they can be applied for all major steps within a causal chain. Crucially important is the insight that counterfactual reasoning requires a solid and comprehensive knowledge of the historical process that we want to 'rewrite' in our thought experiment.

In contrast, if we want to bolster the claim that a causal factor (or a configuration of causal factors) has been sufficient for an outcome (or for the next step in a causal chain), we should turn toward coherent theoretical models based on a consistent set of social mechanisms. These multilevel models of causation provide a logically consistent 'pathway' from a causal factor to an outcome. Furthermore, each element of these models – each social mechanism – is deterministic, but overall, the outcome is contingent on the specific configuration of social mechanisms (see Section 3.2). Therefore, we need empirical observations for each step to clarify which situational, action-formation, and transformational mechanisms have been operating. Smoking-gun observations and confessions are the most important observations for these kinds of information. Together, the multilevel models of causation, and the dense and deep insights that we achieve through smoking-gun observations and confessions provide the best foundation for making strong claims about sufficient conditions.

3.5.5 Logical foundations of CPT II: Process dynamics

Andrew Bennett and Colin Elman (2006: 259) have developed a typology of what can be called 'process dynamics' (see Table 3.3). Positive feedback loops represent the first type of process dynamics. They are certainly the most discussed process dynamic, and they are usually illustrated with the example of the QWERTY keyboard, which has been widely adopted, although it has no superior qualities in comparison to other keyboards. Those 'lock-in' effects have been explained by the following features from the production process and from the

Table 3.3   Process dynamics

Type of process dynamics	Sequences or causal chain	Example
Positive feedback loops	ER(p) → PS(p) → ER(p) → PS(p) ER(m) → PS(d) → ER(m) → PS(d)	Election rules (ER: proportional versus majoritarian) and party systems (PS: pluralistic versus dualistic)
Negative feedback loops	B → H$_1$ → B → H$_2$ → B	Westphalian state system, the attempts of different states to reach a hegemonic position (H) is countered by others and leads to a balance of power equilibrium (B)
Cyclical processes	A → a → A → a → A	Politics of abortion; mutual mobilization of proponents (A) and opponents (a) of abortion

Source: Bennett and Elman (2006: 259), with some major changes and additions.

usage of technologies: large set-up costs or fixed costs and economics of scale, learning effects, coordination effects, network externalities and adaptive expectations. Social scientists have shown that not only technological but also social and political processes follow the dynamics of path dependency, and they have identified typical mechanisms that explain the positive feedback loops on the basis of causal mechanisms rooted in important social science theories (Mahoney 2000a: 517).

One typical example of a positive feedback loop is the relationship between election rules and party systems. Rules for parliamentary elections based on the principle of proportional representation lead to a party system with many parties; election rules based on simple majority rules produce two-party systems. The parties in the two-party system have no interest in changing the rules because it would undermine their duopolistic position. In multiparty systems, larger parties, which might have an interest in changing the rules, usually rely on smaller parties for building a ruling coalition. The smaller parties block any attempt to change the election rules. In both systems, important parties, which have emerged because of specific election rules, will take care that these rules are not changed.

Nevertheless, positive feedback loops are not the only process dynamics common in social and political life. Negative feedback loops and cyclical processes are also very common. Bennett and Elman (2006: 258) illustrate these alternative dynamics with the balance-of-power dynamics in the Westphalian State System and with the politics of abortion (see Table 3.3): each success of the proponents of abortion resulted in an increased mobilization of the opponents, and vice versa. These alternative process dynamics are also driven by underlying causal mechanisms that can be aligned to basic social theories (see Mahoney 2000a).

This very brief overview makes it obvious that alternative process dynamics are possible. As a consequence, a researcher who uses the terminology of process dynamics should explicitly reflect not only on why a specific dynamic emerged but also on why the countervailing dynamics have not set in.

Causal-process observations and process dynamics

Furthermore, we can specify the roles that the different kinds of causal-process observations play to put empirical flesh on the logical bones of these process dynamics. The comprehensive storylines are necessary to identify which kind of dynamics has actually occurred. Once again, it becomes obvious how important it is within a CPT approach to justify the period of time that we take into account in our empirical study. It is possible that a process that exhibits strong features of path dependency, based on mechanisms that provide positive feedback loops in a shorter period of time, is much more accurately described as a cyclical process, if we take a more long-term perspective.

Identifying the process dynamics with the help of comprehensive storylines is only the first step in a causal explanation that focuses on these dynamics. The next step is to trace the causal mechanisms that lead to positive and/or negative feedback loops. For this task, we rely on the kind of empirical information that smoking-gun observations and confessions represent.

3.6 Examples

In the following, the basic features of CPT will be described and illuminated with the help of three examples. Henry Brady's analysis (2004) of the electoral consequences of TV stations' early declaration of Al Gore as winner of the 2000 presidential election in Florida will be recapitulated because it shows best that the observations that form the bases for drawing causal inferences within a CPT approach are not isolated. Instead, observations either focus on the temporal succession of the process or they provide the empirical specifications of social mechanisms within a multilevel model of causation. The famous study of Theda Skocpol on social revolutions (1979) shows how configurational thinking shows up in the description of causal chains and conjunctions. The study of Nina Tannenwald (1999, 2007) on the sources of the nuclear taboo serves as a mechanism-centered example of CPT.

3.6.1   Brady's *Data-Set Observations versus Causal-Process Observations*

Our first example is Henry Brady's analysis (2004) of *The 2000 U.S. Presidential Election* in Florida. Brady analyzes the consequences of the fact that on Election Day in the year 2000, TV networks prematurely declared Al Gore the presidential winner in Florida. The outcome of the presidential election in Florida has been very consequential for the US and the entire world, as it was crucially relevant to the fact that George W. Bush became 43rd President – not Al Gore. Furthermore, the voting in Florida produced major political, legal, and scholarly disputes. One of those disputes concerned the potential suppression of the Republican vote by the fact that the media prematurely declared Al Gore the winner shortly before polls had closed in Florida's conservative western Panhandle. John R. Lott contributed to this dispute by publishing a study that estimated the Republican losses at 10,000 votes. Lott (2000) reached this conclusion by employing a 'difference-in-difference' form of regression analysis, based on dataset observation. He collected turnout data on all 67 Florida counties for the presidential elections from 1988 to 2000 and estimated a time-series cross-sectional regression with fixed county and time effects, and a 'dummy variable' for the 10 Panhandle counties. Lott compared the set of counties that received 'treatment' in the year 2000 (the panhandle counties whose polls were still open when the election was 'called') with those that did not (the remaining 57 Florida counties in the eastern time zone), while controlling for differences reflected in the data from previous elections (Brady 2004: 268).

Brady turns to causal-process observations, recalculates the potential Republican losses, and concludes with a 'figure that is two orders of magnitude smaller than Lott's result' (Brady 2004: 270). Brady reaches his conclusion using several diverse pieces of evidence to clarify that an overwhelming majority of voters had already voted before the TV networks declared Gore to be the winner in Florida. First, Brady established that the media calls of the election were made 10 minutes before the polls closed in the panhandle counties. Brady calculates that during these last 10 minutes, only about 4,200 voters were still going to the polls. This calculation is based on the assumption that voters come to the polls uniformly during the day, or at least during the last hour. Brady invests heavily in bolstering this assumption, which is crucial for his conclusion: he examines Census data from 1996 that contains information about the time when voters go to the polls, interviews election officials in Florida, and reviews media reports. None of these observations and information has the status of a 'smoking-gun observation', but together they provide a solid empirical foundation for inferring that only 4,200 people voted after the media declared Gore the winner in Florida.

Next, he investigates how many of the 4,200 people who voted in the last 10 minutes might have been influenced by the media. To answer this question, Brady applies general knowledge beyond the case: based on research on media exposure, he calculates that about 20 percent of the voters heard the media call of the election. Furthermore, Brady reviews the literature on the impact of early calls and applies the findings of this literature – that about 10 percent of the voters might have decided not to vote after they were exposed to the media call of the election. In other words, Brady introduces general knowledge on causal mechanisms for making further causal inferences within the case. Finally, he applies another piece of empirical information that he gathers by examining the larger picture of his case: in the panhandle counties, the Bush vote was about two-thirds of the total. Therefore, Brady assumes the same proportion among those who were still to vote in the last 10 minutes.

Overall, Brady concludes with the following results: 'My detective work leads to the inference that the approximate upper bound for Bush's vote loss was 224 and that the actual vote loss was probably closer to somewhere between 28 and 56 votes' (Brady 2004: 270). In addition, Brady reflects on the reasons why Lott had reached such different results. One problem with Lott's calculation is that he did not take into account the specifics of the 2000 elections in comparison to earlier elections (for example, the strong mobilization efforts by organized labor). Brady's conclusion: 'Even after putting aside the practical problems of collecting suitable data, it would be hard to collect data that could rule out all the possible confounding effects. Consequently, rather than seeking additional data-set observations, in my judgment it would be more productive to do further in-depth analysis of causal-process observations...' (Brady 2004: 271).

It is worthwhile to further reflect on the types and quality of the causal-process observations that Brady used in his analysis because we think that these observations are still underestimated.[11] First, we restate Brady's arguments in terms of necessary and sufficient conditions; then, we have a closer look at the empirical information and the temporal and theoretical foundations that form the basis for drawing causal inferences.

Brady argues that only those people in the Florida Panhandle who were planning to vote during the last 10 minutes could have been influenced by the TV stations. In other words, having the right to vote in the Panhandle counties, having not voted until the last 10 minutes and having the intension to vote are necessary conditions for being influenced by the call of the election. Yet, these conditions are not yet sufficient for actually being influenced. Being exposed to the media and being open to external influence are further necessary conditions for determining the call of the election to be effective. All five conditions must have been fulfilled to be sufficient to determine that the voting behavior of individuals was affected.

Now, we turn to the ways in which Brady combined (implicitly) empirical information with temporal laws and mechanisms to make convincing calculations on the number of people who were actually swayed by the premature call of the election.

The first and most important step in Brady's line of argumentation is based on the assumption that those who had already voted could not have been influenced by the media reports. The conclusion is convincing because this assumption is based on the natural law of temporal succession. It is not merely improbable but rather impossible that the media influenced their voting behavior. Brady adds information about the overall voting process (the 'big picture' or 'comprehensive story') to draw a first important conclusion: only 4,200 people could have been influenced. In other words, a cluster of empirical information on the overall process and the laws of temporal succession are necessary and together sufficient bases for drawing strong causal inferences.

The second step in Brady's argumentation is convincing because the empirical information is not 'isolated', but rather his information addresses precisely the necessary steps within a multilevel model of causation. The various pieces of information are gaining explanatory power because they specify the social mechanisms that work together to make the media influence effective: the average media exposure rate can be interpreted as the relevant specification of a situational mechanism; the information about the average percentage of people who are swayed by the media call of the election does the same for the action-formation mechanism, and the assumption that the distribution between Bush and

Gore voters is the same among those who voted in the last 10 minutes as among those who had previously voted might be viewed as the relevant specification of the relevant transformation mechanism.

Overall, the Brady study should not only be recognized by case study researchers because of the explicit comparison between a CPT approach and a statistical analysis but also because it contains all the ingredients that are necessary to make a causal-process analysis compelling.

3.6.2 Skocpol's *States and Social Revolutions*

Theda Skocpol's study on social revolutions (1979) is not by accident the case study on which almost all case study methodologists exemplify their analytical approaches, as she uses many techniques to make her descriptions and explanations plausible – not merely cross-case comparisons (1979: 37–8). We will return to this example in Chapter 5, where we describe case studies that combine different analytical approaches. Here, we focus on the narrative analysis that she applies. For many observers, it is the crucial element that makes her book a compelling treatment of revolutionary processes (Mahoney 1999: 1157; Sewell 2005: 97). Mahoney's recapitulation of her argumentation reveals that she draws heavily on the logics of causal conjunctures and causal chains (Mahoney 1999: 1164–8). Skocpol's explanation of the three revolutions in France, Russia, and China is primarily based on a conjunctural argument. She claims that two general factors had to come together to lead to a social revolution: state breakdown and peasant revolts. Only the fact that both factors came together at the same time made social revolutions possible – in other words, state breakdown and peasant revolts are individually necessary and jointly sufficient conditions for social revolutions. To bolster this claim, Skocpol not only compares the three cases but also takes into account five 'possible cases' (cases in which some of the those conditions exist that were viewed as preconditions for social revolutions, for example, relative deprivation) that did not experience social revolutions (for example, England and Prussia). On the most aggregated level, Skocpol primarily applies Mill's method of agreement (first for the positive cases and then for the negative cases), but she treats the combination of the two causes as a single (configurational) factor for the purpose of using Mill's method (Mahoney 1999: 1158).

On a less aggregated level, Skocpol identifies the same set of further preconditions that lead to state breakdown and to peasant revolts in France, Russia, and China. To produce a state breakdown, the following factors are considered relevant: (a) agrarian backwardness, which reduces the competitiveness of the countries; (b) a non-autonomous state, which prevents government leaders from implementing modernizing reforms; and (c) international pressure, which promotes crises for regime actors. On this level, Skocpol argues not according to Mill's method but instead applies the techniques of causal narratives. Mahoney (1999: 1166-7) has revealed this fact most clearly. Figure 3.6 depicts one sequence of the overall causal narrative for the case of France. It shows that the factors that Skocpol uses to explain social revolutions are, in fact, causal chains and causal conjunctions that lead to state breakdown in France.

Equipped with the terminology of necessary and sufficient conditions, we can identify, for example, three individually necessary and jointly sufficient conditions for the backwardness of French agriculture: (a) property relations that prevent new agricultural techniques; (b) a tax system that discourages innovation; (c) and the fact that sustained growth discouraged innovation (Figure 3.6: nos. 1-3). These factors are considered independent, additive factors that contributed to the backwardness of French agriculture (4). For Skocpol, the backwardness in agriculture itself was not responsible for the inability to compete successfully with England. Nevertheless, it is responsible for the failure to achieve an industrial breakthrough (8) because it meant that there was a weak domestic market for industrial goods (5).

A comparison between Skocpol's original description and Mahoney's recapitulation in Figure 3.6 gives us an opportunity to reflect on the relationship between necessary and sufficient conditions. In Mahoney's recapitulation, points 4 and 5 represent a causal chain of sufficient conditions that lead to the failure to achieve the industrial breakthrough. Skocpol uses the following wording: 'At this stage in world history, the progress of industry necessarily rested mainly upon prosperity in agriculture. But French agriculture, though advanced by Continental standards, was "backward" relative both to English agriculture and to French commerce and industry' (Skocpol 1979: 55), providing many references to historical studies for this claim. Because prosperity in agriculture is considered a necessary precondition for industrial breakthroughs, the non-existence of agricultural prosperity in France is a sufficient condition for the failure of the industrial breakthrough.

In Figure 3.6, point 25 is an example of a causal conjunction. At a specific point in time, the financial problems of the French state culminated because four factors came together: (a) failure to sustain economic growth (9); (b) inability to compete successfully with England (10); repeated defeats in war (16); and obstacles of the state to generate loans (19). Skocpol argues that these factors were individually necessary and

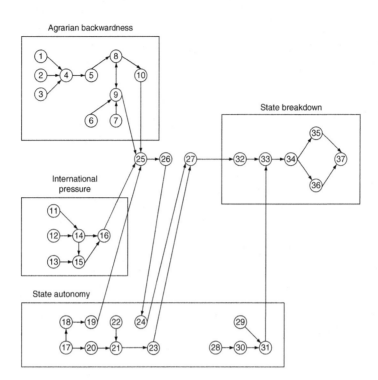

Figure 3.6 Causal chains and conjunctions in the process of state breakdown in France

Note: 1. Property relations prevent introduction of new agricultural techniques. 2. Tax system discourages agricultural innovation. 3. Sustained growth discourages agricultural innovation. 4. Backwardness of French agriculture (esp. vis-à-vis England). 5. Weak domestic market for industrial goods. 6. Internal transportation problems. 7. Population growth. 8. Failure to achieve industrial breakthroughs. 9. Failure to sustain economic growth. 10. Inability to successfully compete with England. 11. Initial military successes under Louis XIV. 12. Expansionist ambitions of state. 13. French geographical location vis-à-vis England. 14. Sustained warfare. 15. State needs to devote resources to both army and navy. 16. Repeated defeats in war. 17. Creation of absolutist monarchy; decentralized medieval institutions still persist. 18. Dominant class often exempted from taxes. 19. State faces obstacles generating loans. 20. Socially cohesive dominant class based on proprietary wealth. 21. Dominant class possesses legal right to delay royal legislation. 22. Dominant class exercises firm control over offices. 23. Dominant class is capable of blocking state reforms. 24. Dominant class resists financial reforms. 25. Major financial problems of state. 26. State attempts tax/financial reforms. 27. Financial reforms fail. 28. Recruitment of military officers from privileged classes. 29. Military officers hold grievances against the crown. 30. Military officers identify with the dominant class. 31. Military is unwilling to repress dominant class resistance. 32. Financial crisis deepens. 33. Pressures for creation of the Estates-General. 34. King summons the Estates-General. 35. Popular protests spread. 36. Conflict among dominant class members in the Estates-General; paralysis of old regime. 37. Municipal revolution; the old state collapses.
Source: Mahoney (1999: 1166),[12] extracting and visualizing Skocpol (1979).

jointly sufficient. Whereas point 4 (backwardness of French agriculture) represents a typical structural factor and is usually built up over long time periods, point 25 (major financial problems of the state) is a situational factor directly connected to the action of important actors. In this case, the financial problems triggered the state officials to attempt a reform of the tax system (26).

In general, Skocpol draws on a broad array of sources, mainly publications of historians, to buttress her many factual and causal claims. For example, she draws heavily on the work of J.F. Bosher as a source for her claim that the financial problems of the state could not be solved anymore because of the fact that a socially consolidated dominant class was capable of blocking tax reforms (Skocpol 1979: 63–4). Skocpol does not discuss every step in her causal narrative in methodologically reflective terminology.[13] What makes her stories compelling is the fact that she is able to combine cogent narratives within each case with the same overall theoretical framework for all three cases of social revolutions. This is a first hint that CPT is most convincing if it is embedded within an abstract theoretical framework. This is especially important for the causal mechanism-centered approach, for which we scrutinize an example in the following.

3.6.3   Tannenwald's *The Nuclear Taboo*

Our third example represents a mechanism-centered type of the causal-process tracing approach. Nina Tannenwald (1999, 2007) explains how the habit of not using nuclear weapons has become expected and required behavior in the US after World War II. She outlines how the taboo evolved and identifies not only its effects but also traces the causal mechanisms and various causal pathways through which ethical norms influence the behavior of the US administration.

Tannenwald begins by stressing the importance of the 'outcome' that she is investigating: 'The non-use of nuclear weapons [since the bombing of Hiroshima and Nagasaki] remains the single most important phenomenon of the nuclear age' (Tannenwald 1999: 433). Next, she makes clear that this outcome cannot easily be explained by the conventional account of the non-use of nuclear weapons: deterrence. There have been many wars in which states with nuclear weapons did not use nuclear weapons, although they did not fear nuclear retaliation because the adversary state had no nuclear weapons. She provides further 'empirical anomalies' with respect to deterrence theory: non-nuclear states have attacked nuclear states (for example, Argentina attacked Britain in the Falklands in 1982), and many states have not developed nuclear weapons, although realist deterrence theory would predict this as the only means for states to maintain security and autonomy in an anarchic international system. In other words, Tannenwald begins with observations that are 'puzzling' from the perspective that dominates the thinking of practitioners and theorists. Furthermore, she claims that these puzzles cannot be solved without taking into account the role of ethical norms that became habitualized and institutionalized as taboo.

In her book, Tannenwald traces the consequences as well as the sources of the taboo. In other words, the nuclear taboo is treated as a factor of influence (cause) as well as the outcome. For each major step in the causal chain – norm development and norm consequences – Tannenwald develops a specific explanatory framework. Furthermore, she dedicates specific chapters in her empirical story to the question of how the taboo mattered and other chapters to the questions of how it arose and how it developed into its specific from. Nevertheless, it is important to recognize that she assumes recursive causality and identifies positive feedback loops that lead from norm development through norm consequences toward the stabilization of the norm (Tannenwald 2007: 64). In consequence, the positive feedback loops transpose the causal chain into a causal spiral.

In addition, Tannenwald is able to show that, over time, other causal mechanisms became more prevalent in the working of the taboo. Whereas, at the beginning, the taboo worked primarily as an external restricting force for realist decision-makers, later on, the taboo was internalized and institutionalized and influenced the identity and perceived interests of the US administration. In consequence, Tannenwald's book is an excellent example of what we have proposed in our introductory chapter: case studies are able to include very different theoretical approaches and build bridges between Rationalism and Constructivism!

Let us more closely examine her explanatory approaches and the specific techniques that Tannenwald applies. The conceptual elements of Tannenwald's explanations are presented ex ante in separate sections (in her article) or chapters (in her book) before the full-fledged empirical storyline. Tannenwald (2007: 64–6) differentiates between five causal pathways that lead to the nuclear taboo[14]: societal pressure, normative power politics, the role of individual state decision-makers, iterated behavior of non-use over time, and institutionalization. Furthermore, she stresses the importance of 'historical contingency' – the relevance of temporal conjunctions and sequences – and applies counterfactual reasoning: 'If Eisenhower [who had not internalized the taboo; JB and MH] had been president before Truman [who had internalized the taboo; JB and MH], or if nuclear weapons had been used in the Korean War, the development of the nuclear taboo might have proceeded quite differently, or not at all' (Tannenwald 2007: 66–7).

In her description of these pathways, she refers to more theory-based mechanisms: instrumental adaptation of political leaders to public opinion; the boomerang effect of strategic social construction; moral persuasions, cognitive assumptions, and learning processes – mechanisms that all are elements of the behavioral assumptions that are traditionally associated with the 'homo sociologicus' and have been popularized as the 'logic of appropriateness' (March and Olson 1989) in the Anglo-Saxon literature; habitualization or customization; and institutionalization, which provides a system of formal rules and roles, compliance procedures, and standard operating procedures (Tannenwald 2007: 64–6). Quite typically for the less theory-oriented causal-process tracing approach (at least in comparison to congruence analysis), Tannenwald does not exert much effort in laying out the theoretical basis of her causal concepts and pragmatically uses very broad understandings of concepts such as 'institutionalization' (thereby following the tradition of the Historical Institutionalism in contrast to the more specific sociological and economic strands within the Neo-Institutionalism; see Hall and Taylor 1996).

Tannenwald differentiates the following effects of the nuclear taboo and specifies the theoretical bases and mechanisms that lead to these effects: (a) the 'regulative effect', which is based on a rationalist theory and assumes that norms constrain individual behavior; (b) the 'constitutive effect', which is based on constructivist theorizing and assumes that norms do not only shape the identities of actors and define their roles and appropriate behavior but also shape the perception and categorization of topics such as weapons; and (c) the 'permissive effect', which is conceptualized as a non-intended side effect of the cognitive processes by which norms focus the attention on specific issues and unavoidably divert attention from other issues (in this case, from the fact that the US military has developed non-nuclear weapons with similar destructive force and has used these weapons in the Gulf War of 1991). Next, she identifies three pathways and the corresponding mechanisms that lead to specific effects: (a) domestic public opinion constrained political leaders; (b) world opinion, which is also perceived as an external constraint and works through the behavioral mechanism that political leaders care about their reputations because they do not want to become isolated; and (c) the personal moral convictions of individual state decision-makers. There is a clear affinity of these pathways and mechanisms with the three dominant theoretical approaches in IR: Rationalism, Realism, and Constructivism. However, Tannenwald does not make this link explicit nor is it a point-to-point relationship. Especially in her description of the world opinion pathway, she oscillates between realist and constructivist reasoning (Tannenwald 2007: 49).

After having laid out the conceptual elements of her explanations, Tannenwald briefly describes her methods (Tannenwald 2007: 69–71) and subsequently presents the empirical information in chronological order. She examines domestic and international discourses in the media and in the diplomatic arena, statements, and decisions of US presidents and top advisers in the US military and administration as well as the process of institutionalization, mainly on the basis of other academic literature and also with the help of primary sources, such as protocols, letters, and diaries (very important sources for 'confessions').

The empirical storyline begins with the bombing of Hiroshima and Nagasaki as the crucial point of reference for the emerging taboo. In the following chapters, she covers the Korean, Vietnam, and 1991 Gulf Wars. Each war is treated as a 'case', but Tannenwald does not draw causal inferences by comparing the cases. Instead, she discusses intensively in each case how far the decision (not) to use nuclear weapons can be explained with reference to the realist deterrence theory and how far ethical norms played a role. Furthermore, she uses many sources to trace specific pathways and reflects intensively on the concrete working of specific mechanisms. Furthermore, in chapters alternating with the chapters that focus on the decisions in the four wars (showing the causal consequences of the taboo), Tannenwald focuses on the emergence and institutionalization of the taboo. The period from 1945 to 1962 is characterized by discursive struggles between taboo promoters (social movements, UN diplomacy, the Soviet Union, and Third World states) and those who wanted to conventionalize or normalize the use of nuclear weapons (the US administration and military). During this period, the taboo emerged as a dominant public opinion (domestically and internationally), but the US government considered it an external restriction and tried to fight it. That changed in the period from 1962 to 1989, when the taboo was not only institutionalized in international treaties but also internalized and accepted to a certain extent by the US administration. Tannenwald describes and explains these developments in a pro-typical way for the CPT approach: she points to four (slow-moving) structural and material changes that facilitated these developments (for example, the expanding 'club' of states with nuclear weapons) and complements this by highlighting the crucial role of the Cuban missile crisis in October 1962 as an 'important turning point in the development of the taboo' because it raised the awareness of the potential catastrophic consequences of nuclear weapons for the US (Tannenwald 2007: 253).

A mechanism-centered approach is clearly the most theory-oriented application of CPT and exhibits strong overlaps with the congruence analysis approach (see Chapter 4). Nevertheless, those who trace causal processes and, especially, causal mechanisms usually apply a less-broad spectrum of theoretical approaches than is the case in a small-N study that applies the method of congruence analysis. Their research goals are to further clarify the working of mechanisms within their specific field of research – not so much to contribute to the overall struggle between divergent theoretical paradigms for recognition or dominance. Therefore, they are usually taking into account only one paradigmatic approach. Prominent examples are the '*Analytic Narratives*', which combine historical narratives with the analytic models of Rational Choice and Game Theory (Bates *et al.* 1998), and Jeffrey T. Checkel's analysis of the socializing power of the EU, a project that aimed to provide stronger micro-foundations for social constructivist accounts in IR (Checkel 2006).

3.7 Direction of generalization

Some advocates of case study research argue that case studies should concentrate on the unique features of a case and believe that inferences beyond the investigated cases can only be drawn by the readers when they compare the findings and contexts of the case studies with their own experiences or cases – a process that is called 'natural generalization' (for example, Stake 1995). We will argue at the beginning of this section that it makes more sense to distinguish between implicit and explicit generalizations.

Nevertheless, most proponents of causal-process tracing argue that we can use case studies not only for revealing the specifics of a single historical event but also for drawing generalizing conclusions beyond the case under investigation. In contrast to the statistical understanding of generalization in large-N studies, the kind of generalization that is most appropriate for a CPT approach can be called 'configurational' or 'possibilistic' generalization.[15] In the remaining sections of this chapter, we will show how possibilistic generalizations can be drawn toward sets of causal configurations or toward sets of causal mechanisms.

3.7.1 Implicit and explicit generalizations

There are very valuable small-N research projects that are 'solely' interested in describing, interpreting, and explaining specific important events and outcomes. These 'single-outcome studies' (Gerring 2007a) do not want to generalize beyond the case under investigation, and therefore the researcher can focus her intellectual energy fully on generating a comprehensive storyline and in searching for smoking-gun observations and confessions to create a convincing explanation of the individual case. Nevertheless, every researcher is de facto embedded in a scientific community, and every study is influenced by scientific discourses that occur independent of specific research projects and goals. Therefore, it is very likely that even case-centered studies are influenced by theoretical concepts and frameworks, and it is possible and very common that other researchers subsequently use the detailed descriptions and explanations of single-outcome studies as empirical material for more theory-oriented interpretations and causal storylines. Theory-oriented reinterpretations of causal narratives usually intend to rise up the 'ladder of abstraction' and use analytic frameworks and concepts defined primarily with reference to a theoretical discourse. Whereas a good single outcome study is dependent on a very thorough and deep knowledge of the case, the major precondition for using a case study for making a contribution to the theoretical discourse is a solid knowledge of the scientific discourse, with all of its theoretical approaches and facets (see Chapter 4, wherein the theory-oriented congruence analysis approach is described in detail).

In contrast to those who embark on a single-outcome study, whereby the process of generalization occurs implicitly or only indirectly, those who are searching for the causal configurations that make a specific kind of outcome possible or those who want to contribute to mechanism-based theory development should be explicit in formulating the implications that their findings have beyond the cases under investigation.

3.7.2 'Possibilistic' generalization

It is important to realize that causal-process tracing does not strive for 'statistical generalization'. Correlational and co-variational analysis aims at drawing conclusions from a sample of cases to the wider population of cases that are similar with respect to the independent (and control) variables. The goal is to answer questions such as 'Does X make a difference?' (COV-oriented case studies) or 'How strong is the difference that X makes?' (statistical analysis in large-N studies) not only for the cases under study but also for the entire population of cases from which the selected cases are drawn. It is misleading to assume that a CPT approach has the same goals and is merely exchanging 'causal factors/variables' for 'causal configurations' or 'causal mechanisms'. Instead, the goals and directions of generalization are entirely different: the goal is to specify the set of causal configurations (based on a combination of necessary conditions or on a combination of different types of social mechanisms) that make specific outcomes 'possible'.

The term 'possible' has two meanings in this context:

– It can denote the set of 'potential' causal configurations, based on all logically possible combinations of causal factors, or the set of 'potential' causal mechanisms, based on all logically possible combinations of situational, action-formation, and transformational mechanisms. Together with theoretical reasoning, CPT helps to identify the set of relevant factors and the repertoire of social mechanisms that build the foundations for these sets of potential causal configurations. In other words, CPT can be used as an inductive element in the process of generating the 'property space' for typological theories (George and Bennett 2005: 240–51). The main advantage of having such a set of potential causal configurations is to guide the selection of cases for further in-depth studies based on CPT, or it can be the starting point for a medium-N study using the QCA technique (George and Bennett 2005: 251–3; Leuffen 2007). Furthermore, CPT can contribute to the development of basic social science through the identification of new social mechanisms, which in turn makes the conceptualization of new multilevel models of explanation possible.
– It can point to the set of 'proven' causal configurations (combinations of causal conditions or social mechanisms). This set is usually much smaller than the set of 'potential' causal configurations and contains those combinations of causal conditions or social mechanisms that have actually been confirmed in empirical studies as being effective for producing an outcome.

The ratio between the set of proven causal configurations and the set of potential causal configurations is an indicator of an important aspect of causal diversity: equifinality! The higher the ratio, the more we can conclude that there are quite different pathways or causal configurations that lead to the outcome of interest.

Each small-N study based on CPT can potentially enlarge these sets of possible causal configurations. For diversity-oriented social scientists, the discovery of new pathways and recipes that lead to certain results is, indeed, what they are striving for.

Nevertheless, these scrutinized ways of generalization tend to increase the complexity of causal explanations, and this tendency has to be checked by practical or theoretical considerations to focus the research on those causal conditions and causal mechanisms that are at the heart of scientific controversies or those that lead to useful practical advice. Whereas those research projects that begin with a non-integrated set of potential causal conditions have clear affinities to applied research and lead to middle-range theories for specific fields of research (George and Bennett 2005: 263–85), the causal mechanism-centered approach is usually used in scientific research programs and scientific discourses geared toward more generic explanatory models. These differences will show up in the following when we illustrate these kinds of possibilistic generalizations with two examples.

3.7.3 Drawing conclusions to the sets of causal conditions and configurations

George and Bennett (2005: 239–62) have scrutinized inductive and deductive means to employ insights gained through CPT within a few case studies for the development and for the testing of typological theories. In the following, we focus on an example that represents the most common method of possibilistic generalization because it inductively develops a set of causal combinations and configurations[16] that make a specific kind of outcome possible. Furthermore, we use Alexander George and Richard Smoke's study on deterrence because they explicitly reflected on the kinds of conclusions they were striving for in an extensive appendix (George and Smoke 1974: 616–42).

The main goal of George and Smoke was to challenge the then-dominant theory of deterrence, which was deductively derived on the premises of Game Theory and consisted of a set of generalizing propositions on how deterrence works. It focused primarily on the activities of the 'defender', leading to a problematic focus on military threats in its practical application (George and Smoke 1974: 58–87). The authors challenged this theory by differentiating deterrence theory according to the various sequences within a political crisis (initiation theory, commitment theory, and response theory) and by developing a typology that connects specific types of deterrence failures to specific combinations of causal conditions. They proceeded inductively and built their differentiated deterrence theory based on the 11 case studies, which were conducted according to a set of guiding research questions.

George and Smoke (1974: 519–33) first identify two major and six minor conditions that influence the deterrence outcome. Based on the two major conditions, they develop the following types of deterrence failure, which are characterized by specific configurations of two causal conditions and a specific type of calculated risk, as the next step in the causal chain, which leads to specific types of deterrence failures (George and Smoke 1974: 534–59; George and Bennett 2005: 323):

- The 'fait accompli' type of deterrence failure is characterized by the combination of the aggressor's belief that the action is controllable and his belief that the defender shows no commitment to the attacked ally – together, the two beliefs lead to the calculation that the best option is 'to get it over with quickly'.
- The second type, called 'limited probe', is characterized by the causal configuration that the aggressor believed that the action is controllable and that he thinks that the defender's commitment is uncertain – these beliefs lead the aggressor to think that the best option is controlled application of limited force.
- In the third type, labeled 'controlled pressure', the aggressor believes that the defender's commitment is unequivocal but soft and that the action is controllable – in consequence, he thinks that the best option is carefully applied pressure.

Implicitly, the authors first identified a set of causal conditions that are relevant for explaining a rather broad class of outcomes (deterrence failure). Next, they selected those conditions that were always necessary to explain the outcome, and finally, they developed a set of causal configurations whereby each causal configuration leads to a specific subclass of the outcome. In principle, further case studies might expand both the set of causal conditions and the set of major causal configurations.

According to the authors, the three types of deterrence failure represent a specific kind of generalization that is especially valuable for practitioners because it has diagnostic power. Each type represents a consistent pattern of causal factors and specific outcomes – the diagnostic power results from the fact that the defender can draw logical conclusions from the behavior of the aggressor on the conditions that lead to such an activity. This in turn allows for adequate adjustments of the behavior of the defender. Another crucial aspect of this kind of conclusion is the specification of different pathways that lead to a similar result. Nevertheless, we should recognize that this corresponds to the notion of 'equifinality' only if we apply this term in a loose sense because the outcomes that are aligned to specific causal configurations also differ (slightly). This is a quite common feature for diversity-oriented scholars who strive for useful typological theories (George and Bennett 2005: 232–62).

3.7.4 Drawing conclusions to the sets of social and causal mechanisms

In Section 3.2, we argued that a mechanism-based explanation is based on a causal model that combines a social mechanism at a lower level of analysis with social mechanisms that link this lower level of analysis with the level of analysis at which the causal conditions and outcomes reside. With reference to Peter Hedstroem and Richard Swedberg (1998: 22), we differentiated three generic causal mechanisms: 'situational mechanisms', 'action-formation mechanisms', and 'transformational mechanisms'. In consequence, the most consistent means of generalizing within a mechanism-centered CPT approach is to draw conclusions from the findings of the case study to the set of social mechanisms or to the set of causal mechanisms (multilevel models of causation) that are recognized within the social sciences. We find the first form of generalization in Nina Tannenwald's book on *The Nuclear Taboo* and the second form of generalization in Frank Schimmelfennig's book on the Eastern enlargement of the North Atlantic Treaty Organization (NATO) and the EU. Schimmelfennig's book is more theory-oriented – and it will be presented in detail in Chapter 4 as a showcase of the congruence analysis approach.[17]

Tannenwald (2007: 370–4) presents the first conclusions from her study under the heading 'implications for theory'. She claims that the study shows that norms have not only constraining but also constitutive and permissive effects, and that her study has revealed the corresponding mechanisms through which norms become effective (for example, instrumental adaptation to public opinion, changing perceptions of 'suitable targets', legitimizing non-nuclear weapons). In her final conclusions, she emphasizes that norms have been marginalized in the literature on deterrence and that she has been able to show that norms matter even in this hard-nosed topic. Furthermore, she stresses that norms work through a plurality of causal pathways and have different effects – not only the constraining effects that rationalists recognize and the positive constitutive effects that are central for most constructivists. In other words, the main theoretical message of the book is a plea for the recognition of the 'multiple ways that norms exert effects' (Tannenwald 2007: 371). Quite typical for a study that is primarily interested in making a contribution to the specific field of research and not so much to the theoretical or paradigmatic discourse in the social sciences, she does not develop full-fledged multilevel models of causation and remains rather vague with respect to the relationship between the various mechanisms. Although she has shown in the empirical parts of her study that the divergent mechanisms were predominant during the various phases of establishing and institutionalizing the taboo, the final conclusions remain rather fuzzy: she states that 'the nuclear taboo evolved out of, and is sustained by, a combination of strategic interests and moral opprobrium' (Tannenwald 2007: 25, 371) and argues that 'the analysis highlights the mutual shaping of norms, interests and identities' (Tannenwald 2007: 371).

Frank Schimmelfennig's conclusions (2003) represent the best practices with respect to how we can draw generalizing conclusions from causal-process tracing to the set of multilevel models of causation. He argues that his study indicates that the combinations of specific situational mechanisms and action-formation mechanisms dominant in IR are not the only possible ones, and offers a new possible combination of these mechanisms. The dominant combinations in IR are a materialist account of the factors that shape the preference formation with a rationalist theory of action-formation, on the one hand, and a culturalist approach to interest formation together with a sociological theory of action-formation, on the other hand. Schimmelfennig points to Jeffrey W. Legro (1996), who has challenged this exclusive combination and argued for a combination of a culturalist approach to preference formation and a rationalist account for explaining the (inter)action of the state actors. In his study on Eastern enlargement, Schimmelfennig found the following combinations of situational and action-formation mechanisms: the first step of state interest formation occurred in accordance with a rationalist/materialist approach to preference formation, followed by the second step of international interaction, which is in line with a social constructivist conceptualization of action-formation. Implicitly, the decision-making rule of unanimity forms the third causal mechanism for the full-fledged explanation (Schimmelfennig 2003: 281–7). In other words, Schimmelfennig draws conclusions from his case study to the set of multilevel models of causation that should be accepted as possible causal mechanisms in IR.

Schimmelfennig's study shows clearly that causal-process tracing and congruence analysis are not mutually exclusive approaches in small-N studies and that clever social scientists can use the insights they obtain from in-depth studies both for a configurational explanation of important political outcomes and for an innovative contribution to a major debate in the social sciences.

3.8 Presenting findings and conclusions

The presentation of findings and conclusions in a CPT approach depends very much on the goals of the research project and the specific functions that CPT fulfills within this project (see Section 3.2). Nevertheless, there are some general characteristics and suggestions that are useful for all studies applying causal-process tracing.

First, we want to stress the fact that case studies and especially CPT-based approaches are often interested not only in explaining the outcome (the causal analysis) but also in a precise and reflective presentation of the outcome of one or a few cases. Providing insights on what a democratic regime or a social revolution, for example, actually means in specific countries is an important goal itself (necessary not only for causal analysis but also for normative evaluations and conceptual innovations). In consequence, the detailed description and interpretation of the outcome is usually an important part of the presentation of the findings of case studies.

Second, CPT has an inductive flavor because the causal inferences are based on causal-process observations, such as smoking-gun observations, and not with respect to the co-variation of variables across cases (as in the COV approach), or the comparison between theoretical expectations and empirical observations (as in the CON approach). Nevertheless, CPT can be embedded in an inductive or deductive research design, and it is always advisable to present the state of the art before delving into the details of the cases under investigation. Even for single-outcome studies, it is absolutely necessary to become acquainted with the existing attempts to explain the outcome. The chapter that precedes the empirical chapters can be more case-centered (with an overview of the literature on the case), it can focus on the field of research (introducing the main explanatory approaches and hypotheses), or it can indicate an interest in basic social theory by reflecting on social and causal mechanisms. Anyhow, such an introductory chapter is always necessary to justify the focus of the empirical research. Although the CPT approach can take into account a larger number and wider range of causal factors (in comparison to the COV approach, at least) and is open to taking into account new surprising insights, it is clear that the study cannot and should not fully represent the entire causal process but rather must focus on specific aspects.

Third, because CPT represents a within-case analysis, the structure of the report reflects this case orientation. This means that the empirical section of the report is structured according to cases (if more than one case is analyzed) and/or according to sequences (for the presentation of the findings of each case) and not according to variables or theories.

Fourth, typically, the empirical information is presented first in a detailed and descriptive way, and subsequently (at the end of each empirical chapter and/or in a final chapter) this information is condensed and reflected upon with the goal of interpreting the findings in analytical terms (George and Bennett 2005: 92–4).

Fifth, because the combination and interaction of causal conditions and mechanisms as well as the temporal sequence of causal processes play such strong roles in the CPT approach, scholars are well advised to visualize their concepts and findings in flow diagrams. The translation of narratives and descriptions into flow charts forces the researcher to clarify the assumed and proven relationships between the various elements of the explanation. For example, diagrams reveal whether the combination of causal conditions is conceptualized as a causal chain or a causal conjunction, whether the scholar assumes that the elements of a causal configuration add up to the outcome or next step in the causal process or whether she argues that they interact with each other to produce the result (see Mahoney 2000b, whose diagrams have clarified Skocpol's line of argumentation substantially).

3.9 Summary

Causal-process tracing is an analytical approach that draws causal inferences based on causal-process observations with the goal of identifying the sequential and situational configurations of causal factors that lead to specific outcomes. Causal-process observations can be used to complement co-variational analysis in the quest to discover whether a specific cause made a difference, or it can be a major part of a congruence analysis, with the goal of determining which theoretical lens is more adequate to describe and explain certain social events. As a stand-alone research design, it is geared toward identifying the causal chains, causal conjunctions, and causal mechanisms that make specific kinds of outcomes possible.

In contrast to the other approaches, the CPT approach is not dependent on systematic comparisons – neither on the comparison of variables across cases (as is the case within the COV approach) nor on the comparison between ex-ante formulated theoretical expectations and empirical observations (as is the case within a CON approach). Therefore, the cogency of the causal inferences relies primarily on the quality and credibility of the causal-process observations. Three kinds of causal-process observations are especially important for this task: comprehensive storylines, which contain the major steps and sequences of the overall process; smoking-gun observations, which provide detailed descriptions of important moments and reveal close spatio-temporal connections between causes and effects; and confessions that include statements about the perceptions, motivations, and anticipations of major actors. In other words, these kinds of causal-process observations provide temporal order, density, and depth in the description of the causal process. They provide the empirical data for reflecting on the status of causal factors and mechanisms as necessary and sufficient conditions for specific steps in the process or for the outcome of interest.

The causal-process tracing approach is strongly aligned with the ontology and epistemology of 'configurational thinking' and represents the within-case complement to the cross-case analytic techniques that have been developed by Charles Ragin and his collaborators under the label of QCA. In consequence, the goal of CPT is not to generalize the findings to a population of cases that are similar with respect to independent variables (most similar systems) but rather to contribute to the specification of the set of causal configurations that make specific outcomes possible.

4
Congruence Analysis

The core features and major advantages of small-N research are the researcher's ability to collect a broad and diverse set of observations per case and the ability to reflect intensively on the relationship between empirical observation and abstract concepts. These features are used within the co-variation approach (COV) by operationalizing and scoring the dependent and independent variables in a context-sensitive way, by using diverse indicators for each variable and by applying diverse sources of empirical information for each indicator (triangulation). The causal-process tracing approach (CPT) takes further advantage of this feature by adding 'causal-process observations' to the 'variable-scoring observation' for drawing causal inferences. There is a further means of profiting from the multiplicity – and especially from the diversity – of observations per case in small-N research. The multiplicity and diversity of observations makes it possible to connect empirical cases to a rather large set of theories and these theories might be connected to different paradigmatic camps (see Chapter 1). This feature makes small-N research an appropriate approach for comparing and combining divergent theories and therefore an especially fruitful ground for theoretical innovation. In this chapter, we seek to present the foundations and major elements of such an endeavor.

A *congruence analysis* approach (CON) is a small-N research design in which the researcher uses case studies to provide empirical evidence for the explanatory relevance or relative strength of one theoretical approach in comparison to other theoretical approaches. She achieves this by deducing sets of specific propositions and observable implications from abstract theories in a first step and then by comparing a broad set of empirical observations with these implications drawn from diverse theories. A higher degree of congruence between deduced implications from one theory and the observed evidence within the case(s) in comparison to the degree of congruence between the expectations drawn from another theory and the empirical evidence is used to argue that the first theory has a stronger explanatory power.[1]

We can formulate two pro-typical questions that express the goals of the CON approach:

– Does theory A provide a better explanation in comparison to other theories?
– Does theory A provide relevant explanatory insights that no other theory has revealed?

The two pro-typical questions indicate two slightly different perspectives on the major goals of the social sciences and on how scientific progress occurs in these academic fields. Therefore, we distinguish between two subtypes of the congruence analysis:

– a competing theories approach; and
– a complementary theories approach.[2]

It seems important to stress that epistemologically both subtypes remain firmly in the 'middle ground', as we have laid out in Chapter 1 – although with slightly different leanings. The first subtype demonstrates a clear affinity to positivist and realist epistemologies but stops short of any strong epistemological assumption that we can actually verify or falsify theories through empirical testing. Instead, it presupposes that we can use empirical information to judge the explanatory power of a theory in relative terms by comparing these actual observations with expectations that are deduced from this theory and with the expectations that we deduced from another theory. It assumes that divergent theories lead to contradictory implications in the empirical world, that theories stand in stark opposition to each other, and that the goal is to identify the best or most important theory. These assumptions are relaxed in the case of the second subtype. This approach implies that theories lead to complementary implications in the real world and that a plurality of theories is not a source of confusion and uncertainty but rather provides the basis not only for more comprehensive explanations but also for conceptual and practical innovations. Furthermore, the assumptions of the second subtype legitimize the search for theories that are able to provide new or neglected explanatory insights (even if these aspects might not be the most important with respect to causal power).

These features place the second subtype of this explanatory approach closer to a constructivist or conventionalist epistemology, but the congruence analysis approach contains two methodological elements of control that work against any strong epistemological relativism.

A first – 'vertical' – element of control consists of an explicit separation of the two steps:

– deducing specific propositions and concrete predictions from abstract theories; and
– comparing these deduced expectation with empirical observations.

A second – 'horizontal' – element of control arises because a theory must show not only that its implications correspond to empirical observations but also that it has a higher level of empirical congruence than other theories, that it predicts crucial aspects of the empirical process more correctly than other theories, or that it leads to additional causal implications that are empirically corroborated and useful for theory development. In principle, a congruence analysis can also be conducted with only one theory, but such an approach loses the second element of control and is in many ways less compelling (see Section 4.3 for an extensive reflection on this point). In line with Peter Hall (2006), we stress that good theory-oriented social science is a 'three-cornered fight' involving empirical information and (at least) two different theories!

Overview

We proceed as follows: The first section of this chapter lays out the research goals and questions that are typically addressed by this approach to case study research (Section 4.1). We will then illustrate the epistemological foundation of congruence analysis, and we will provide a brief overview of diverse facets of the organization of knowledge that form crucial background assumptions for this approach: the vertical organization of knowledge with different levels of abstraction; the horizontal organization of knowledge and the differentiation of core concepts and peripheral concepts as the basic elements of theories; and a reflection on the centralization of the system of knowledge. We arrive at the definition of major terms within a CON approach and highlight the fact that, within a CON approach, we formulate specific and concrete expectations prior to the empirical investigation but that interpretation is of primary importance for connecting abstract propositions and concrete observations (Section 4.2). Because these foundations of the

CON approach have not been spelled out before in the literature on case study methodology, we provide a rather extensive discussion. Nevertheless, those who only want hands-on advice regarding a CON approach can simply scan this section, extract the definitions of major terms, and proceed with the following sections. Section 4.3 encompasses theory selection and the selection of cases. In fact, theory selection and specification comes first and case selection comes second; for the latter, it is important to reflect *a priori* on the relationship between cases and theories. We will formulate what it means to select 'crucial cases' within a CON approach with reference to the notions of 'most-likely cases' and 'least-likely cases'. The collection of information for conducting congruence analysis is briefly addressed in Section 4.4. In comparison to the other two approaches, the search for relevant observations is much more 'theory-driven', which means that the researcher must develop a thorough understanding of a set of theories before searching for confirming and disconfirming empirical evidence with respect to these theories and does the necessary 'soaking and poking' with a keen eye toward evidence that has the power to discriminate between the theories. In Section 4.5, we describe in more detail the techniques applied to make inferential leaps from empirical observations to the adequacy of explanatory theories. At the heart of this chapter is a template that shows the formal logic of this inferential leap from concrete observations to theoretical conclusions for the studied cases. Furthermore, we illustrate how this 'congruence analysis proper' is practiced with a broad spectrum of examples. Section 4.6 is devoted to the question of which kind of generalizing conclusions we can draw beyond the case(s) under investigation. The results of the congruence analysis are used to boost or undermine the aspirations of theories and paradigms to play an important role in scientific (and practical) discourses. Finally, we will lay out how the research typically unfolds and how to present the results (Section 4.7).

Examples

Throughout the chapter, we will illustrate the various steps within this explanatory approach with three pairs of examples. A first pair of examples has been chosen to represent our major subtypes within this explanatory approach: whereas Scott Sagan's study (1993) on risk-management concerning the safety of nuclear weapons represents the 'competing theories' approach, Graham T. Allison and Philip Zelikow's (1999) best-selling study on the Cuban Missile Crisis[3] is an example of the 'complementary theories' approach. Sagan's work has also been chosen because – in stark contrast to the COV approach – it shows that within a congruence analysis approach, a theory can receive more validation even though the 'final outcome' seems to point to the appropriateness of the rival theory. Allison and Zelikow's study most clearly shows the two-faced goals that can be attained with a CON approach: arriving at a more comprehensive understanding of a very important incident and providing strong evidence for the explanatory power of new theoretical approaches. Furthermore, the structure of their book is a perfect model for presenting the findings of congruence analysis – at least for the 'complementary theories' subtype. Andrew Moravcsik's (1998) contribution to the debate on how to explain European integration is a example of using congruence analysis for the struggle for paradigmatic dominance in an important subfield of political science. In contrast, Frank Schimmelfennig's research on the Eastern enlargement of the European Union (EU) and North Atlantic Treaty Organization (NATO) (2003) shows how an empirical congruence analysis can be used for developing and bolstering a new synthesis of major paradigmatic approaches in international relations (IR). The final two examples have been chosen to illustrate the fact that congruence analysis can be based on very different methods of data collection and data analysis. Whereas Elizabeth J. Wilson and David T. Wilson (1988)[4] generate the data in their study on organizational decision-making through in-depth interviews and apply statistical tools for the congruence test, John Owen (1997) draws primarily on the works of other scholars and historical sources in his study on the liberal basis of democratic peace. Some aspects will be further illustrated with reference to a case study on international water regulation conducted by Joachim Blatter (2009), although this study will be fully laid out only in Chapter 5.3 because we want to use it as a showcase for the sequential combination of CON and CPT approaches.

4.1   Research goals and research questions

Theories play many important roles in the social sciences. They not only provide meanings to empirical observations, but also structure the scientific discourse and influence the social and political praxis. Most consistent with the congruence analysis approach is the assumption that theories shape our knowledge about the social and political reality mainly by their focusing and framing effects. Established theories influence the perception of social scientists and practitioners alike by focusing their attention on some aspects of the social reality and – in consequence – by making them neglect other aspects of social reality. Furthermore, theoretical frameworks influence the perception of empirical realities by providing a consistent framework for interpreting this reality. As Allison and Zelikow argue for the area of foreign policy making:

> Professional analysts of foreign affairs and policymakers (as well as ordinary citizens) think about problems of foreign and military policy in terms of largely implicit conceptual models that have significant consequences for the content of their thought.
>
> (Allison and Zelikow 1999: 3)

In consequence, the struggle between paradigms and theories for recognition and for dominance cannot be discredited as *l'art pour l'art* but is one of the most important aspects of social science research. Nevertheless, congruence analysis is based on the premises that theories do not fully determine our knowledge about the social reality and empirical observations can be used to control whether theories provide correct and consistent predictions about social reality. The goal of empirical research is to provide evidence that indicates that an explanatory theory focuses on those aspects of reality that are most consequential for other aspects of social reality and/or that reveals those aspects of causal processes that are most meaningful and useful for social actors. Congruence analysis realizes that empirical research is embedded in a theoretical discourse, but it rejects theoretical determinism and epistemological relativism. Furthermore, acknowledging the relevance of paradigm and theories does not mean that we have to stick to theories and research programs that are connected to a specific paradigm – on the contrary – we strongly believe that case studies can cross the cleavages between divergent research paradigms – which allows not only for the creation of 'usable theory' (Rueschemeyer 2009) but also for theoretical innovation.

4.1.1 Research goals

In most important fields of the social sciences, we find a plurality of more or less specified theoretical approaches used to understand and explain the social and political processes and outcomes. These theories are usually aligned to overarching paradigms that reach beyond fields and sub-disciplines. We will provide a brief schematic overview of the relationship among theories and paradigms in the next section. For now, it is important to stress that the pro-typical goal of small-N studies applying congruence analysis is to make a contribution to the scholarly discourse on the relevance and relative importance of specific theories (= explanatory frameworks) and general paradigms (= meta-theories). In principle, such a contribution can take four forms:

- refining specific theories within a paradigmatic research program;
- developing a new theoretical synthesis within or across paradigms;
- strengthening the position of a theory in comparison to other theories in a theoretical discourse; and
- bolstering the aspiration of new theories to be recognized in a field of research.

As we will outline in detail later on, striving for these goals means that the researcher must first select the relevant theories, and then he can select the case(s) that are most appropriate for his specific goal.

Alternatively or additionally, the congruence analysis approach can also be used to explain specific socially important cases. In this case, the empirical case study is not instrumental for theoretical development and paradigmatic competition, but the theoretical approaches are used to explain the concrete empirical case(s). In consequence, case selection comes first and theory selection comes second. The following list of exemplary questions that lead to a congruence analysis indicates that skillful scholars are able to do both at the same time: use socially important cases to bolster a specific or new theory within a scholarly discourse and use important theories to provide explanatory insights into socially important cases.

4.1.2 Research questions

Typical research questions for a congruence analysis are the following:

- Does the 'high reliability organization theory' or the 'normal accident theory' provide the better framework for understanding and explaining risk management in complex organizations (Sagan 1993)?
- How can we explain governmental decision-making during the Cuban Missile Crisis? Which additional insights into governmental/organizational decision-making do we obtain by applying the organizational behavior model and the government politics model in addition to the dominant rational actor model (Allison and Zelikow 1999)?
- Is Liberal Intergovernmentalism (a general rationalist framework of international cooperation that includes the following elements: national preference formation, interstate bargaining and institutional

choice) the best explanation for European integration (Moravcsik 1998)?

- How can we explain the Eastern enlargement of NATO and of the EU? What can we learn from these enlargements regarding the role of institutions in IR and the debate between Rationalism and Constructivism as the main paradigms in IR in recent times (Schimmelfennig 2003)?
- Which theory of organizational decision-making is most consistent with the real decision-making processes in business organizations (Wilson and Wilson 1988; Wilson and Woodside 1999)?
- Are liberal identities, ideologies, and institutions the most important factors for explaining the war and peace making of democracies (Owen 1997)?
- Which theory of the policy process is best to explain long-term policy changes (Sabatier 1993)?
- Are the explanatory approaches within (the research program of) international Regime Theory (RT) sufficient for explaining trans-border water regulation, or do we need further explanatory approaches (Blatter 2009)?

Allison and Zelikow's book titles nicely illustrate their double ambitions: *Explaining the Cuban Missile Crisis* is the subtitle of the book. This indicates the goal is to explain the event that brought the world closest to a nuclear war. At the same time, the title reads *Essence of Decision*. This title shows the conviction of the authors that explaining the Cuban Missile Crisis more generally sheds light on organizational decision-making. The three explanatory approaches that they introduce are formulated at a rather abstract level. The authors write that these approaches can be applied to governments at different levels, other private organizations and 'other aggregate actors who one encounters in normal, everyday life' (Allison and Zelikow 1999: 7). In fact, that was exactly what occurred in the aftermath of the study.

In a similar way, the two goals show up in Schimmelfennig's (2001, 2003) study on the Eastern enlargement of NATO and the EU. In the book, he states that the 'basic goal is to explain the principal enlargement decisions of the EU and NATO in 1997' (Schimmelfennig 2003: 3). Nevertheless, he adds:

I show that the analysis of enlargement not only benefits from theoretical input from the general literature on international institutions and regional integration but also makes a valuable contribution to it. Eastern enlargement constitutes a puzzle for both rationalist and sociological theories of international institutions and lends itself to exploring novel ways of conceptualizing institutional effects and actor behavior in international politics.

(Schimmelfennig 2003: 3)

These examples show that an ideal congruence analysis focuses on the analysis of socially important cases, but even more importantly, it includes the most important theories in the field of research and promotes theoretical innovation. We want to emphasize, however, that not all social scientists or students in the social sciences can investigate events with a worldwide impact, but all should take into account the major theories in their field of interest – not only as a basis for a better explanation of their cases but also as a precondition for making a contribution to the theoretical discourse.

4.2   Ontological and epistemological foundations and affinities

In this section, we first illuminate the epistemological foundation of the CON approach. Next, we provide a brief systematic account of the basic aspects of the organization of knowledge, which lays the foundation for theory selection and specification (Section 4.3), for the congruence analysis proper (Section 4.5), and for the ways in which we draw generalizing conclusions beyond the cases of investigation (Section 4.6).

4.2.1   Illustrating the epistemological foundation of the CON approach

One of the typical metaphors used to illustrate that knowledge is relative and dependent on the specific approach to knowledge generation is the parable of the elephant and the blind men. According to the parable, a group of blind men encounters an elephant for the first time. They want to know what an elephant looks like, and each of them begins to investigate the elephant by touching the animal. Afterwards, they discuss their findings, and it becomes obvious that they ended up with very different ideas of what an elephant looks like, depending on whether they touched the foot, the ear, the tail or something else. For example, the man who touched one of the feet argued that an elephant looks like a tree.

The parable is usually invoked to argue that empirical studies with limited resources are always able to capture only a part of the reality. Nevertheless, we think that the parable is rather misleading not only because of the overly strong relativistic conclusion that is usually drawn from the story but also because it sidelines some other major challenges that we face in generating useful and meaningful insights into social reality. First, it is usually not emphasized that the descriptions that the blind men produce are not only influenced by the parts of the elephant that they investigated but also by their prior knowledge (for example, what a tree looks like). Second, the parable assumes that we can be so close to the empirical phenomenon that our senses are able to be in direct contact with 'reality'.

We think it is more illuminating to conceive the following situation as an illustration of the challenges we face in conducting theory-oriented empirical research in the social sciences.[5] Please assume that you are in charge of the security of villages in a wildlife reserve, and a technology company offers cameras as helpful tools (you are dependent on this help because your position comes with no additional funding). Therefore, the only technical means at your disposal are cameras that can be distributed across the habitat. First, you have to decide where to install the cameras, in other words, in which areas you want to focus your observations. You might base your decision on prior knowledge about the major causes of destruction of villages in similar environments. Nevertheless, the available data are so general that you hesitate to base the decision for your specific habitat on these data. Even more important for this decision is the fact that your decision is embedded in institutional and discursive contexts. For example, the fact that you are employed by the administration of the wildlife reserve provides strong incentives to investigate external causes and not causes of destruction within the villages. Furthermore, there is a public discourse proceeding (or a professional discourse within the administration of wildlife reserves) on the question of whether human villages can be tolerated in reserves with potentially dangerous animals such as elephants and another discourse on whether tourists should be permitted to camp within the wildlife habitat, as careless use of fire pits might cause firestorms. These discourses provide an initial orientation on which kind of causal factors to focus your observational investments.

The other major decision that you must make is which kind of cameras to use. There are two types of cameras available: infrared cameras that measure the temperature of the area and cameras that produce 'normal' images that can easily be deciphered by human eyes. Both types of cameras have disadvantages: the first type of camera can only capture strong differences in temperature, and the second type of camera is blind at night. Because all cameras have blind spots, it is certainly advisable to use both kinds of cameras, although this means that the number of areas that can be observed is limited, and a careful selection of these areas is in order.

This setup illustrates the following:

- The explanatory theories that researchers apply in their empirical investigations are embedded in broader practical and theoretical discourses. It is certainly a sign of progress that empirical social science is not fully determined anymore by external interests but rather is often driven by scholarly discourses, as this is the basis for intellectual autonomy. Nevertheless, a reflective scholar should be aware not only of the major scholarly debates and all relevant theoretical positions within these debates but also of the practical implications of these theories.
- The explanatory theories that researchers apply strongly influence the process and results of the empirical study: first, they guide the decisions about the 'technology' that scholars apply in collecting observations, and this technology strongly delimits (but not fully determines) what researchers are able to observe; second, based on these theories, scholars form expectations about the content and *gestalt* that emerges when the multiple observations are combined into full-fledged pictures and movies/storylines.
- Furthermore, the setting points to the fact that the inferences one draws from the observations are not dependent on the final outcome of process under investigation. If a village is not destroyed by a firestorm because of a last-second change in the wind direction, but the observations provide clear evidence that a tourist fireplace caused a firestorm channeled toward the village by natural context factors, the case study certainly creates a lot of leverage for the 'fire theory'.

4.2.2 Relationships between theories

Empirical research in the social sciences is embedded in practical and theoretical discourses. The main goal of a congruence analysis is to make a contribution to a scientific discourse, which is characterized by the implicit or explicit rivalry of divergent paradigms and theories. In consequence, the scholar must reflect much more intensively on the discursive context in which her research occurs than in other approaches. Today, most scientific discourses are only loosely coupled with practical discourses, and they are usually differentiated and structured through (sub-)disciplinary boundaries and by divergent fields of research. For scholars who want to be influential beyond a specific field of research or theoretically innovative, it is very helpful to have a broad theoretical horizon, which means that they should be able to apply general and abstract theories, and/or a broad range of specified theories. Nevertheless, for a sound congruence analysis, it seems even more important that the researcher know the most influential theories in his field of interest, that he reflects on the relationship between the selected theories, and that he explicitly justifies his selection of theories. Until now, there has not been much advice on how to select theories. In the following, we will provide some logical foundations for this task; applications and concrete examples will follow in Section 4.3.1. The following reflections are based on the premise that we can transfer insights from the literature on concept formation (especially Goertz 2006 but also Sartori 1984; Collier and Mahon 1993; Adcock and Collier 2001) to the task of causal theory selection, specification, and concretization.

If we want to describe the relationships between the theories we apply in an empirical study, we first have to reflect on how scientific knowledge is organized (or how scientific discourses are structured, to frame it in discourse-theoretical terms). Three aspects are especially important:

- the vertical differentiation of the system of knowledge;
- the horizontal differentiation of the systems of knowledge; and
- the centralization of the system of knowledge.

We will address these aspects sequentially. Ultimately, the reflections on the organization of knowledge will lead to a better understanding of the core features of the CON approach, and to a comprehensive and consistent terminology. We want to stress the instrumental aspect of this endeavor. We cannot take up the major debates in the philosophy of science; we only want to lay same logical and terminological foundations for empirical studies following a CON approach.

The vertical differentiation of knowledge

Vertically, knowledge systems are differentiated according to the level of abstraction. There are three basic levels of abstraction; each level is characterized by its content and its connections. We will briefly point to the content and the connections of each level for the process of causal theory formulation, which is presented in the right column of Table 4.1. The middle column on concept formation is added to illustrate the fact that we are transferring insights from methodological reflections from descriptive-comparative analysis to causal analysis.

Table 4.1   Three levels of abstraction in concept formation and in causal theory formulation

	Concept formation	Causal theory formulation
Most abstract level	Concepts	Paradigmatic perspectives: Ontological and epistemological assumptions
Intermediate level	Properties/attributes/ dimensions	Theoretical propositions: Constitutive concepts and causal connections
Most concrete level	Indicators	Empirical predictions: Concrete potential observations

Theories form the middle level of abstraction, and they contain specific propositions about constitutive concepts (elements of the theories) and causal connections between these concepts (the relational structure of the theories). On a higher, more abstract level, there are meta-theories (paradigms); they contain cognitive signifiers, which function as anchor points for the organization of knowledge (in other words, as focal points for the scientific discourse or as 'hard-core' scientific research programs in the sense of Imre Lakatos 1970). Paradigms provide the connections between theories in specific fields of research and more generic onto-logical and epistemological perspectives. On the lowest, most concrete level, there are the observable implications that we deduce from theories (predictions); they form the connecting points between abstract systems of knowledge and the empirical world.

The horizontal differentiation of knowledge

Horizontally, scientific knowledge is organized (scientific discourses are structured) as systems of centers and peripheries. This can be observed on two levels.

At the first level, scientific discourses consist of a multiplicity of paradigms, and these paradigms occupy more or less central places within the scientific discourse, depending on whether they are estab-lished/dominant or new/subordinate. We will take up this aspect below, where we reflect on the centralization of systems of knowledge.

Second, theories contain specific configurations of constitutive con-cepts. Each of these constitutive concepts occupies a more or less central place within the theories, which means that each theory has 'core concepts' and 'peripheral concepts'. The 'core concepts' represent the anchor point for paradigms, but paradigms comprehend not only the core concepts but also the full set of peripheral concepts that can complement the core concepts to formulate specific theories. In other words, a theory is a specified configuration of core and peripheral concepts and a subset of a paradigm that represents all possible configurations between the core concept and various peripheral concepts. Those who are interested in the logical structure of the relationship between theories and paradigms will get a more formalized characterization below, but let us first illustrate the meaning of core and peripheral concepts.

Core concepts can be filled in various ways – for those theories that are usually used in case study research, it is very common that they comprise a behavioral theory as a micro-foundation (for example, Rational Choice or Communicative Action). Some paradigmatic core concepts include 'social mechanisms' that connect structures and actions (see Section 3.2), but very often it is disputed how exactly the structural contexts feed into individual action and how the actions and interactions (re-)create structures (such disputes are a good justification and starting point for a doing a congruence analysis).

Specific theories do not only contain a core concept but also add further conceptual elements to provide full-fledged explanatory frameworks. For example, Schimmelfennig (2003) specifies three different rationalist explanations to explain the Eastern enlargement of NATO and the EU by complementing the core concept (rational decision-making of state actors) with three different peripheral concepts that contain the goals that the actors strive for: (a) security, (b) power, and (c) welfare (see Section 4.4. for a more detailed presentation).

Excursus: The relationship between paradigms and theories
in set-theoretical terms

It makes sense to understand the relationship between paradigms and theories as one that is based on a system of 'radial categories'. As David Collier and James E. Mahon (1993: 848–9) have laid out, in classic systems of categorization, there exist superordinate and subordinate categories, whereas in a system of 'radial categories', there are central and non-central categories. If we go down the ladder of abstraction within a system of knowledge that is organized according to classic categories, we add further properties (in concept formation) or further concepts (in causal theory formulation). If we go down the ladder of abstraction within a system of knowledge that is based on radial categories, we select a specific configuration of properties/concepts out of the full set of potential configurations of core concepts (CC) and peripheral concepts (PC). The crucial difference is that in a system of radial concepts, going down the ladder of abstraction does not imply increasing the 'intension' by adding further attributes/concepts. Instead, we increase the intension by reducing the number of attributes/concepts (by selecting some out of the full set of possible attributes/concepts) and by tightening the connection among the selected attributes/concepts. In both cases, though, going down the ladder of abstraction results in a decreasing 'extention' (range of cases).

In a paradigm, the relations among the concepts are as follows:

$$\text{Paradigm (P)} = CC * [PC_1 + PC_2 + PC_3 + PC_4 + PC_5];$$

whereby '*' means 'and' and '+' means 'or'.

In words: a paradigm is characterized by the core concept and the full set of potential peripheral concepts. Whereas the core concept is a necessary condition for characterizing a specific paradigm, individual peripheral concepts are not.

For a theory, in contrast, the relation among the concepts is the following:

$$\text{Theory (T)} = CC * PC_1 * PC_2.$$

In words: a theory is characterized by the core concept and a selected set of peripheral concepts. In a fully specified theory, all selected concepts have the status of necessary conditions. Furthermore, a fully specified theory contains propositions that define the relationships between the selected concepts.

These definitions help us to determine whether researchers are really comparing theories in the congruence analysis or comparing paradigms. If they treat all abstract concepts and propositions as necessary conditions, they test and compare theories; if the concepts and propositions are not considered necessary conditions, the congruence analysis is based on paradigms. These differences will appear when we observe our examples (see Section 4.4). Whereas Schimmelfennig (2003) is conducting his congruence analysis based on clearly specified theories, the study of Allison and Zelikow (1999) applies paradigms.

Mono-centric versus poly-centric systems of knowledge

Systems of knowledge can be organized as hierarchies with a single center or as polyarchies with multiple centers. Today, there are still some social theorists who aim for a fully integrated and consistent theoretical approach to understanding and to explaining the entire social world. Hartmut Esser, for example, has laid out such a full-fledged theoretical approach in seven volumes (Esser 1993, 1999–2001). At the heart of his endeavor is the expected utility theory, the behavioral model of the 'homo oeconomicus', which is also the basis for Rational Choice and Game Theories. Esser is able to integrate a large range of social theories into one consistent theoretical approach by adding material, institutional, ideational, and cultural structures as complementary concepts to his behavioral core concept. In consequence, his approach to the organization of knowledge in the social sciences is monocentric. Although many social scientists implicitly follow such a monocentric understanding of knowledge accumulation (by designing their empirical research on the basis of a single theoretical approach), the reality in most fields of research is characterized by a plurality of paradigms and theories, which partly compete with and partly complement each other. Acknowledging this reality leads to the conclusion that a congruence analysis should include a plurality of theories and not just one theory – a stance that will be further justified in Section 4.3.1.

Even if we recognize the fact that most fields of research are not characterized by the existence of a monopolistic paradigm with a single core concept, there is still room for diverse epistemological positions with respect to the question of how centralized a system of knowledge *should* be with respect to the horizontal organization of knowledge. Some would argue that it is a sign of maturity for a field of research if a clearly hegemonic paradigm or theory emerges because this development is interpreted as a movement toward a correct representation of a (single) objective reality, which in turn is the basis for rational decisions of social and political actors (arguably, we observe this state of the art in some fields of economics). Others would argue that a plurality of paradigms and theories is not only the basis for scientific creativity and progress but also a logical precondition for social and political choices.

Independent of one's own stance in this debate, a scholar who applies a congruence analysis approach with the aim to contribute to the scientific discourse should reflect on the existing horizontal organization of the system of knowledge. Ideally, a system can be either centralized (if there exists a clearly dominant paradigm or theory) or polycentric, whereby two or more theories occupy a similarly powerful position in the scientific discourse.

These reflections on the constellations among theories have implications for how we specify theories (Section 4.3.1), how we conduct the congruence analysis proper (Section 4.4), and how we draw conclusions beyond the cases under study (Section 4.6). Before we proceed with detailed descriptions and illustrations of these steps, it seems adequate to sum up the major implications of these reflections on the organization of knowledge for conducting good congruence analyses.

4.2.3   Implications for the congruence analysis approach

The presented reflections on the organization of knowledge help us to define a comprehensive and consistent set of terms for a CON approach. Next, we present arguments why a congruence analysis should include a plurality of theories and not only one; and finally, we point to features of the CON approach that might help to bridge the cleavages between divergent epistemological camps.

The terminology of congruence analysis

A congruence analysis begins with paradigms and theories that are located at a high level of abstraction. To test and compare these paradigms and theories empirically, we have to deduce implications on lower levels of abstraction. In the literature, we find a bewildering terminology used to denote the result of this step: many use the classic term 'hypotheses' when they lay out what they expect to observe if a theory has explanatory power (for example, Owen 1997: 58–61; Moravcsik 1998: 28; Schimmelfennig 2003: 226), others have used other terms: 'expectations' (Sagan 1993; Owen 1997), 'propositions' (Allison and Zelikow 1999), 'predictions' (van Evera 1997: 9; Wilson and Woodside 1999), and 'anticipations' (Owen 1997).

We think that it makes most sense to use the following terms for the following purposes:

- 'Propositions' specify the constitutive concepts and formulate the causal connections to define and characterize a paradigm or theory. Paradigms are usually characterized by a broad set of constitutive propositions and without a clear specification of causal connections. Theories, in contrast, are usually specified with the help of a small set of constitutive propositions including causal propositions.
- 'Hypotheses' are those propositions that specify the expected causal connections between the constitutive concepts of a theory. In consequence, hypotheses are a subset of propositions. The causal connections are usually formulated as configurations of necessary and – together – sufficient causal conditions that lead to specific outcomes.
- 'Predictions' formulate the concrete observations that we can expect in the empirical world. The term predictions should be reserved for those expectations that are on the same level of abstraction as the empirical observations.
- 'Expectations' include all propositions and predictions that we can derive from paradigms and theories. It is an umbrella term that helps

us to efficiently refer to all elements in the process of specification and concretization, which are necessary for making abstract explanatory approaches applicable for empirical analysis.

These definitions provide us with a comprehensive and consistent set of terms for the description of a congruence analysis. Furthermore, they allow us to bridge the cleavages between constitutive/interpretative and causal theorizing, and the corresponding epistemological camps. We will return to this below, wherein we provide examples showing that scholars do indeed formulate constitutive and causal propositions when they specify the expectations derived from different theories.

The advantages of a pluralist theoretical framework

In principle, a congruence analysis can be conducted based on one single theory. One can formulate the propositions that constitute a theory, deduce concrete predictions, and compare the propositions and predictions with the empirical observations. Nevertheless, such a limited form of congruence analysis has many disadvantages in comparison to a congruence analysis that applies a plurality of theories and derives its conclusions by comparing the level of congruence of these theories:

- In the stage of theory specification, the application of only one theory makes it impossible to use the most appropriate means of theory specification for a theory-oriented small-N study that clarifies the meaning of conceptual properties and propositions in one theory by contrasting them with conceptual properties and propositions from other theories (we will elaborate on this aspect in Section 4.4).
- In the stage of data collection, researchers who have introduced only one theory are very much tempted to search only for empirical information that confirms this theory. This includes not only the danger that disconfirming observations are sidelined but also the fact that empirical information that does not play a role with respect to this theory is neglected. This forecloses the opportunity that this information adds up to another – perhaps similar or even more consistent and relevant – explanation of the case(s) in comparison to the one that the researcher is focusing on. Whereas this danger always exists for deductive approaches to empirical analysis, it is clearly reduced if we apply a plurality of theoretical lenses.
- A further disadvantage arises during the stage when we analyze the data and draw inferences from concrete observations to abstract

theories. Often, we have a plurality of observations that we can relate to a specific expectation. It is very difficult to determine a certain number of congruent observations as a convincing threshold for deciding whether an expectation is confirmed or disconfirmed. This problem is multiplied when we take into account that we have formulated more than one proposition. In consequence, it makes much more sense not to apply the positivist logic of verification and falsification but to compare the number and relevance of observations that are congruent with Theory A and the number and relevance of observations that are congruent with Theory B to draw reflective and differentiated conclusions for the relative adequacy and relevance of the theories.

- Furthermore, only when we take into account divergent theories do we know which observations are 'crucial' – those wherein the two theories lead to contradictory expectations. In other words, comparing theoretical expectations upfront helps us to focus our empirical investigation on those aspects that are most relevant for drawing discriminatory conclusions for the theories.
- Finally, also for the last stage of drawing generalizing conclusions beyond the cases under investigation, it is advantageous to have applied a plurality of theories. A small-N study that draws only on one theory can logically never have a similarly strong impact on the theoretical discourse as would be the case if the congruence analysis included two or more theories. If the empirical result is strongly confirmatory for the single applied theory, the contribution to the theoretical discourse is very limited because the finding is neither innovative nor very convincing, as it has not been shown that the theory is better than alternatives. If the empirical result is mixed, the empirical study will not have an impact on the theoretical discourse at all. Moreover, if the congruence analysis strongly disconfirms the theory, the contribution to the theoretical discourse is much stronger if an alternative theory is presented. The alternative theoretical explanation can be developed in a purely inductive way and presented as a 'novel' theory. Nevertheless, for the accumulation of knowledge and for making progress in the social sciences, it is much better that the researcher connects the revealed empirical pattern with explanatory frameworks (theories or paradigms) within a specific field of research and – if necessary – also beyond the field of research or (sub)discipline. Ultimately, this inductive approach leads also to the situation that more than one theory is involved, albeit the temporal order of introduction of the two theories is different from the ideal way of doing a congruence analysis.

Constitutive and causal propositions

Within the CON approach, the specification of theories occurs through the formulation of constitutive and causal propositions, and usually, the causal propositions are formulated in the configurational terminology of causal conditions and causal mechanisms (see Chapter 3). We can illustrate these characteristics of the CON approach with a famous example: Andrew Moravcsik's (1998) study on European integration. In line with the dominant positivist tradition of Anglo-American political science, he uses the term 'hypotheses' to refer to the propositions he formulates for the three steps of European integration (national preference formation, interstate bargaining, and institutional choice). For the phase of interstate bargaining, Moravcsik (Moravcsik 1998: 55) deduces 'hypotheses' (his terminology; in our terminology: propositions) from two competing theories with respect to three elements: (a) underlying distribution of information and ideas, (b) negotiating process, and (c) outcomes – efficiency and distribution. In the following, we present some examples of his large set of propositions:

H1S (Supranational Bargaining Theory): Scarcity and asymmetry of technical, political, and legal information and ideas, relative to stakes, leave states less informed than EC officials. EC officials benefit from greater neutrality, political skill, technical expertise, administrative coherence or centrality in transnational networks. National positions should be unstable, due to changes in available information during negotiations.

H1I (Intergovernmental Bargaining Theory): Low cost relative to stakes means that information and ideas are widely and evenly distributed among national governments and members of domestic coalitions, with no supranational advantage. Residual asymmetries reflect the relative intensity of preferences concerning the issue in question. National positions are thus stable.

H2S (Supranational Bargaining Theory): Scarcity of information and ideas means that national governments cannot provide optimal levels of policy entrepreneurship. [...]

H2I (Intergovernmental Bargaining Theory): The most interested national governments and societal groups can act as effective policy entrepreneurs. [...]

H3S (Supranational Bargaining Theory): [...] Agreements are systematically biased towards outcomes preferred by supranational actors. [...]

H3I (Intergovernmental Bargaining Theory): [...] Governments that gain the most offer the most significant compromises or side-payments. Concessions on the margin are systematically biased towards outcomes preferred by governments least likely to support the 'core' agreement. Where credible for threatening countries and costly to the target governments, threats of exit and exclusion shift the outcome toward the state making the threat.

(Moravcsik 1998: 55)

The 'hypotheses' deduced from the two theories for the interstate bargaining process do not follow the classic co-variational form (for example, the more information is scarce and asymmetric, the more the agreements are systematically biased toward the outcomes preferred by supranational actors). Instead, H1S and H1I postulate assumptions about what constitutes the reality (scarce and asymmetric information relative to stakes or low costs of information relative to stakes) and the logical consequences for the distribution of information among the actors and stability of national positions. The propositions with respect to the negotiating process and negotiating outcomes contain further logical consequences of the constitutive assumptions in H1S and H1I. Nevertheless, they also contain further expectations that provide a richer picture of what we can expect if the Supranational Bargaining Theory is correct as well as what to expect if the Intergovernmental Bargaining Theory is the adequate analytic framework for explaining this step of European integration. Furthermore, although Moravcsik makes a considerable attempt to formulate the hypotheses he derives from the two theories as competing, an examination of H3S and H3I reveals that they are not always mutually exclusive. It might well be that the outcomes show both types of biases at the same time; hence, a bias toward supra-national actors and the least forthcoming countries.

Overall, the formulated 'hypotheses' contain constitutive and causal propositions, and the empirical implications of each proposition can be observed separately in the empirical part of the study.

The prior deduction of a plurality of expectations

Every theory-oriented empirical study relies on making inferential leaps between various levels of abstraction:

– Inferences from abstract paradigms and theories to specific and/or concrete expectations of what we will discover within the case(s) under study (in the form of propositions and/or predictions).

- Inferences from the set of empirical observations and from the comparison of these observations with the deduced expectations to the relative strength of the selected paradigms and theories to explain the cases under study and the role and relevance of these paradigms and theories in the broader theoretical discourse.

A good congruence analysis is based on explicit differentiation and a specific temporal order with respect to the two inferential leaps. The deduction of specific and concrete expectations from abstract theories is achieved in a first and separate step, followed by a second step wherein the expectations are compared with the empirical observations. A third step is to draw conclusions on the explanatory power of theories for the cases under investigation by comparing the levels of congruence between deduced expectations and empirical observations. Finally, further conclusions are drawn on the role and relevance of the theories in the wider theoretical discourse. It must be acknowledged, however, that both aspects – explicit differentiation and temporal ordering – are much more clear-cut in the final presentation of the research than in the actual research process (see Section 4.7). Nevertheless, the need to explicitly formulate and justify specific and/or concrete expectations prior to the presentation of the empirical information has many advantages with respect to the validity, reliability, and replicability of the final conclusions.

The primer importance of theory-led interpretation

Based on this emphasis on the prior formulation of expectations, it would be consistent to argue that a good congruence analysis demands not only the specification of theories through propositions but also the concretization through the formulation of observable predictions. Nevertheless, the examples that we use for illustrating the CON approach show a different picture. Only Wilson and Wilson (1988) actually concretize the expectations deduced from different theories so much that the ex-ante formulated statements come close to the low level of abstraction on which the empirical information is located (see Section 4.4). Much more common is to specify the theories by formulating precise propositions without the formulation of concrete predictions. In other words, scholars applying a congruence analysis most often do not 'operationalize' the theoretical concepts in the same strict sense as those who apply statistical techniques of analysis in large-N studies do by determining observable indicators for their variables prior to the collection of data. There are good reasons for this difference:

- In comparison to large-N studies, small-N studies use a much broader and more diverse set of indicators/observations for testing the congruence between theoretical expectations and empirical reality. Similar to those who use a CPT approach, scholars who apply a CON approach should think more like a detective and less like a statistician when they approach the empirical data. Nevertheless, within a CON approach (and in contrast to a CPT approach), they begin their search for evidence with clearly specified and theoretically characterized 'suspects'! The process of linking concrete observations to abstract concepts within a CON approach resembles less the process of operationalization as we know it from large-N studies but much more the process of writing a code-book when we do a content analysis. We begin with some basic anchor points derived deductively, but we proceed into the empirical field with an open mind and decide step-by-step whether or not we classify an empirical observation as congruent with a theoretical proposition.
- Because causal inference within a CON approach is usually not based on co-variation or correlation among variables and not on the comparison between cases, predictions and observations do not have to be transferred into metric measurement tools (as indicators do within a COV approach). The 'only' relevant criterion for judging the quality of predictions and empirical evidence within the CON approach is their concept validity, the question of whether the (predicted) observations express the meaning of the abstract conceptualization in an accurate manner.
- Within the CON approach the researcher does not reduce the meaning of an abstract concept to one or a few observable indicators (or of a theory to one causal hypothesis). Trying to secure the richness of concepts leads to concepts that often have fuzzy boundaries. This reduces the preciseness and transparency of the process to align empirical observations to abstract concepts. In consequence, scholars applying a CON approach must invest heavily in explicitly justifying their interpretation that a specific observation is, indeed, confirming or disconfirming a specific proposition and theory.
- Finally, because congruence analysis is a 'three-cornered fight', these justifications should always include the empirical observation and at least two theories. Therefore, it is more reasonable to begin by making inferential leaps between divergent levels of abstraction with concrete

observations and discuss their implications for the theories at a later stage of the research process. This last insight will become clear in Section 4.5, wherein we present all logical means to draw conclusions from empirical observation for a plurality of theories.

Overall, these reflections lead us to the conclusion that 'interpretation' plays a major role in conducting a congruence analysis. We are basically aware that this sentence leads us directly into the middle of major epistemological struggles. Therefore, we must add that we think 'interpretation' does not mean that the theories fully determine what we can observe in the empirical reality (as hard-core epistemological constructivists would argue). On the other hand, we want to stress the conviction that the leaps between concrete observations and abstract concepts is not such a technical and clear-cut matter, as the term 'operationalization' would suggest, and it is a major advantage of case studies to be able to reflect on these leaps not only in a general and ex-ante form but also rather extensively in respect to each major observation.

We have laid out the foundations of the congruence analysis approach much more extensively in comparison to the other approaches because this approach has not yet received much attention in the methodological debate on case studies and small-N research. In the following sections, we address the various steps of this approach and illustrate the best practices and available options with our set of examples.

4.3   Selecting theories and cases

Researchers who want to perform a congruence analysis face two important questions at an early stage of the research process:

- Which theories shall I select, specify, and apply?
- Which case(s) shall I select, specify, and investigate?

The formulations indicate that neither theories nor cases are 'natural givens' with clear-cut content and boundaries. Instead, theories and cases must be specified and delineated when answering these two questions. The fact that theories usually cannot be found 'out there' in the academic discourse or literature as clear-cut entities but have to be specified for each research project is most clearly formulated by Scott Sagan:

> The scholarly literature about complex organizations is large and diverse, but two general competing schools of thought on this specific issue exist. The first is the optimistic view of what I will call

'high reliability theory', whose proponents argue that extreme safe operations are possible, even with extremely hazardous technologies, if appropriate organizational design and management techniques are followed. The second school, what I will call 'normal accidents theory', presents much more pessimistic prediction: serious accidents with complex high technology systems are inevitable. The term school of thought was used deliberatively, since it is in many ways a better description of what exists in this literature on hazardous technologies than the term theories. The scholarship I will be analyzing is based on mixtures of abstract deductive logic and inductive empirical observations, and the authors within each school by no means agree on all details concerning organizational safety. Specific terms that appear often in this literature are not always used in a consistent manner. And perhaps most importantly the predictions of both schools are often imprecise. Nevertheless, proponents of each school do focus attention on a specific set of factors that they believe contributes to or decreases safety, and each school develops a set of general hypotheses that is meant to hold true in a variety of organizations across space and time. These ideas can therefore be viewed as nascent Social Science theories and can usefully be tested against one another.

(Sagan 1993: 13)

The order of the questions that we formulated at the beginning of this Section indicates that the selection and the specification of the case(s) are usually dependent on the selection of the theories. Overall, the selection process involves the following steps:

1. The researcher selects a field of interest, becomes acquainted with the state of the art, and identifies theoretical disputes and gaps.
2. The researcher decides what kind of contribution she wants to make to the scholarly discourse.
3. The researcher decides which theories will be applied to this task and justifies the selection and specification of theories with reference to the structure of the scientific discourse and the researcher's goals.
4. The researcher decides which cases will be investigated and justifies the selection and specification of cases with reference to the theories that she selected and specified.

The first two steps have been addressed in Section 4.1. We restate these steps here to show how the selection of theories and cases depends on prior decisions. Not all examples that we use for the congruence analysis follow these steps in the specified order; some begin with an interest in a specific political event (for example, the Cuban missile crises and Eastern enlargement). Nevertheless, all scholars face the challenge of selecting and specifying the theories they will apply in the empirical part of their study. As we will explain below, researchers whose main interest is to contribute to the theoretical debate should ideally choose their cases after selecting their theories and after reflecting on the relationship between the theories. Researchers who begin with an initial interest in a specific case also must reflect on the relationships between the theories they apply and the relationship between the theories and the case, if they want to draw theoretical generalizations beyond the specific case(s) under investigation in a reflective way.

4.3.1 Selection and specification of theories

All empirical studies aiming to contribute to a theoretical debate include a section that presents the 'state of the art'. This section fulfills (often only implicitly) the function of selecting the theories applied by the researcher for the empirical study. For a congruence analysis, the theories should be selected and specified in an explicit and reflective way. It should be standard practice to justify the selection of theories as explicitly as it has become standard for the selection of cases.

Three sets of questions are helpful for this task. The first set stimulates the researcher to reflect on the structure of the theoretical discourse; the second set animates him to clarify his theoretical aspirations; and the third set of questions makes the researcher aware of the trade-offs involved in the decision of how many theories should be specified and applied.

Analyzing and structuring the theoretical discourse

The first set of questions stimulates the researcher to reflect on the content and structure of the scientific discourse in the selected field of research:

– Which theories have been developed in the selected field of research?
– How is the scientific discourse structured? What are the major paradigms? What are the major theories aligned with these paradigms? Is there a dominant paradigm or theory? What are the major contenders for this dominant paradigm and theory?

To contribute to the body of knowledge, researchers should reflect on the state of the art in their field of research. For the theory-oriented congruence analysis, this means that researchers must provide an overview of the existing theoretical approaches and reflect on the structure of the scientific discourse. In Section 4.2.2, we presented some guideposts for these tasks. Until recently, most small-N studies have not provided a systematic discussion of the structure of the scientific discourse. Nevertheless, good case studies include explicit reflections on the structure of the scientific discourse that are used to justify not only the selection of the theoretical approaches but also the sequence in which they are applied. Schimmelfennig, for example, starts the first part of his book with the following statement:

> Rationalist theories of international institutions dominated the theoretical debate in International Relations throughout the 1980s. Moreover, club theory, the general rational theory of the size of organizations, is the best developed and most pertinent approach to explaining enlargement. For these reasons, I begin my analysis of Eastern enlargement with rationalist institutionalism.
>
> (Schimmelfennig 2003: 17)

Accordingly, Schimmelfennig begins the second part of the book as follows:

> In the course of the 1990s, sociological approaches to the study of international relations have increasingly challenged the dominance of rationalist theories. [...] Since the rationalist theories failed to explain why the EU and NATO should expand to include the CEECs [Central and Eastern European Countries], I turn therefore to sociological institutionalism in an attempt to solve the puzzle of Eastern enlargement.
>
> (Schimmelfennig 2003: 67)

Theoretical aspiration

A second set of questions forces the researcher to be clear and explicit about her goals and her contribution to the scientific discourse:

– Is the study meant to contribute to the scholarly struggle between scientific paradigms, or is the refinement of theories within a paradigm its major theoretical goal?
– If the study strives for theoretical innovation, are there sufficient theories within the field of research, or is it necessary to look for theories beyond this field of research?

Most small-N studies applying a congruence analysis approach focus on the major theoretical controversies in their field of investigation. Usually, this means that theories are selected based on different paradigms (for example, Sagan 1993: 13). Schimmelfennig, for example, justifies his choice of explanatory approaches accordingly:

> The debate between 'rationalism' and 'constructivism' – as the sociological approaches are now usually referred to – constitutes currently the focus of theoretical controversy in International Relations.
>
> (Schimmelfennig 2003: 67)

Nevertheless, it might be possible to compare theories within a specific paradigm. Wilson and Wilson (1988), for example, deduce predictions of decision-process activities from 'rational theory' and from 'bounded rationality theory', which can arguably be aligned to the same paradigm. Some scholars (for example, Sagan 1993; Moravcsik 1998) use their small-N studies to take sides in the struggle between dominant theories or paradigms within a specific field of research. To substantiate to their findings, authors must focus on important social and political events (for example, major decisions in the European integration process (near) accidents with nuclear weapons).

Other scholars primarily focus on theoretical innovation. To be successful, they not only have to show that established or dominant theories cannot explain the processes and results of their case studies (in a satisfactory way), but they must also show that newer or less prominent theories are more effective in explaining the cases or that they are able to fill important gaps. This means that in those cases where the established theories cannot provide an adequate explanation, an ad-hoc explanation is not sufficient. Instead, the empirical findings must be connected to theories and theoretical concepts outside the field of research. Allison and Zelikow (1999) identified 'organizational behavior theory' and 'governmental politics theory' as the paradigmatic approaches at the beginning of the 1970s that challenged the established unitary rational actor model in the study of foreign policy decision-making. Scholars sometimes go beyond the theories formulated in the case(s) field of research and base their alternative explanations on external or more abstract theoretical foundations. Schimmelfennig (2003) introduced 'rhetorical action' as the appropriate micro-foundation to explain the Eastern enlargement decisions of NATO and the EU after showing that Rational Institutionalism cannot explain the results and Sociological Institutionalism cannot explain the processes of Eastern enlargement. Because 'rhetorical action' has not been an established theoretical approach in IR, Schimmelfennig (2003 194–228) draws on Erving Goffman's social theory to lay out the theoretical foundations of this approach. He compares 'rhetorical action' to 'communicative action', a similar approach that had previously been introduced in the field of research.

Joachim Blatter (2009) proceeds quite similarly in his explanation of the strict water regulations at Lake Constance. First, he shows that all established explanatory approaches within the field of international environmental regulation cannot fully capture the cross-border decision-making process at Lake Constance. Next, Blatter departs from the theoretical repertoire of RT by applying the Advocacy Coalition Framework developed by Paul Sabatier for environmental policy analysis within domestic political arenas. This theoretical approach clearly shows more congruence with the empirical evidence than the 'epistemic community' approach or other cognitive approaches within RT. Nevertheless, some important inconsistencies and gaps remain. Consequently, Blatter turns to basic social science theory and introduces 'performance' as the theoretical concept most consistent with empirical information on the motives of actors and the structural context for breakthroughs in international regulations. The concept of 'performance' is also rooted in the tradition of Symbolic Interactionism and has developed in sociology and cultural studies as an alternative to the classic conceptualization of the *homo sociologicus*. 'Social interaction as performance does not follow the logic of appropriateness, but the logic of gaining attention' (Blatter 2009: 101).

For the systematic accumulation of knowledge, it seems important for a congruence analysis to begin with the most important theories within a field of research. If it can be shown that these theories cannot explain the results and processes sufficiently, further theories should be introduced. The researcher must first look for new or marginalized theories within the field of research. Next, he can incorporate theories from similar fields of research or more generic theories.

Number and relationship of selected theories

The third set of questions stimulates the researcher to think about how to present the theoretical setting for the empirical study:

– How many theories should be selected and specified?
– How do the theories relate to each other? Are they mutually exclusive or overlapping? Are they competing or complementary?

First, as we have argued above, a convincing congruence analysis involves more than one theory. The same arguments can be made against a quite common way of setting up the explanatory framework for small-N studies. Very often researchers set up a single explanatory framework by combining elements of divergent theories, then analyzing or interpreting the case(s) on the basis of this single theoretical framework. From a methodological point of view, such an *ex ante* integration is clearly inferior to combining the confirmed insights from different theories into a comprehensive explanatory approach after the empirical study (*ex post* integration). We will show how the latter can be accomplished convincingly in Section 4.6.2, where we illustrate the ways to generalize conclusions beyond the cases under study within a complementary theories approach.

A convincing congruence analysis requires more than one theory; but how many? We have stressed that theories are not 'natural givens', and there is a constant debate among scholars about the most adequate specification of theories. Consequently, the number of theories that a researcher applies for a specific empirical study is not fully determined by the scientific discourse; rather, it is up to each researcher to decide how differentiated the theoretical discourse should be and how many distinct theoretical approaches should be specified and tested separately. Sagan (1993) presented the theoretical field as two 'schools of thought' and integrated three different approaches into one of those school of thoughts labeled 'high reliability theory'. Allison (1971) scrutinized three different theories, and together with Zelikow (1999), he reformulated and updated each theory in the second edition of the book, and Wilson and Wilson (1988) derived their predictions from four theories of organizational decision-making.

Schimmelfennig presents his study in the context of the rationalist-constructivist debate in IR and structures his overall approach according to this paradigmatic struggle. Nevertheless, he convincingly argues

> that it makes [no] sense to test 'rationalism' against 'constructivism' in the study of enlargement. Both rationalism and constructivism are social metatheories defined by a set of assumptions about the world and about theory-building rather than by specific hypotheses. [...] There is a variety of substantial theories and hypotheses based on each metatheory.
>
> (Schimmelfennig 2003: 11)

Consequently, Schimmelfennig specifies three rationalist explanatory approaches (differentiated by the question of whether the state actors primarily strive for security, power, or welfare) and introduces four modes of action (habitual, normative, communicative, and rational) to trace the causal mechanism that leads from community norms and values to the outcomes of enlargement processes (Schimmelfennig 2003: 27–34, 157–63). Blatter (2009) goes even further in his analysis of transboundary water regulation and discusses three rationalist and three constructivist approaches developed within RT. He adds two further explanatory frameworks after showing that the various RT approaches are not sufficient to provide an adequate picture of the structural conditions and the causal mechanisms that lead to the strict regulations at Lake Constance.

When deciding how many theories to introduce and how to distinguish among the specifications within a paradigmatic approach, the researcher must consider the following consequences:

– A larger and more differentiated set of theories is likely to lead to more differentiated results. For example, if the researcher applies three different rationalist approaches rather than only one (see Schimmelfennig 2003), he is more likely to find confirmation for the rationalist paradigm. The same results if he does the same for the other, competing paradigm. In consequence, the study will probably not end up with a clear-cut result in favor of one paradigm, reducing the likelihood that it will be recognized and receive attention. However, differentiated results allow for fruitful combinations and innovations within and across paradigms, and convincing innovations have a good chance of receiving attention.
– A larger and more differentiated set of theories can lead to bolder theoretical conclusions. Researchers who show that they have considered all existing variants of the dominant paradigms without reaching a convincing explanation for the case(s) under investigation can more convincingly claim that a new theoretical approach is necessary. In contrast, researchers who fuse the approaches from different authors into one approach are more likely to be criticized for misrepresenting theoretical approaches.

The decision about the number of specified theories has consequences not only for the theoretical conclusions of the empirical study but also for the process of conducting a congruence analysis:

– A larger and more differentiated set of theories leads to more overlaps in the set of expectations. In other words, the final outcome and many other aspects of the process that lead to this outcome might

be 'overdetermined' in the sense of being in line with more than one
theory.
- A larger and more differentiated set of theories reduces the number
  of expectations and observations one can consider per theory (*ceteris
  paribus*, given a fixed amount of research resources).

Consequently, an approach with a larger number of theories will
focus on the (few) expectations and observations that have discriminatory power for the theories, whereas an approach with fewer theories
attempts to analyze the congruence between expectations and observations for as many aspects as possible to determine whether a particular
theoretical lens produces a consistent picture of the case. In other
words, the approaches differ with respect to the weight they give to
'external(horizontal)' and 'internal(vertical)' forms of control.

The selection and specification of theories is a crucial element of the
congruence analysis approach. Our lengthy treatment of this subject
should make it clear not only that theoretical and methodological questions are strongly connected but also that theory-oriented researchers
should be as explicit and reflective in their selection of theories as they
are in their selection of cases.

4.3.2 Selection and specification of cases

In a congruence analysis approach, which we present here as an ideal
type, the selection and specification of cases occurs after the selection of theories. We mentioned previously that in real-world empirical
research, the order can be reversed. In either method, the researcher is
faced with the following question:

- How is the case related to the theories?

In the following section, we present advice for selecting cases within a
CON approach, which is especially relevant for researchers who want to
contribute to the scientific discourse. Of course, it is possible to perform
a congruence analysis with the more modest goal of explaining a single
event that is of special interest for the investigator. In this case, the following reflections are not relevant for the researcher, but they become
relevant when others attempt to draw conclusions from the studied case
to the broader scientific discourse.

Case study methodology has a long tradition arguing that cases
should be selected with reference to theory, not according to systematic
(dis-)similarities among the cases or the imperative of variance in the
independent variable, as is the case in the co-variational approach (see
Chapter 2). The classical statement on this subject is by Harry

Eckstein (1975), who introduced the concepts of 'crucial cases', 'most-likely cases', and 'least-likely cases'. For an adequate understanding of 'crucial cases' within a CON approach, one must go beyond the focus on variables and the corresponding variable-scoring observations that are usually aligned to the notions of 'most likely' and 'least likely'.[6] Furthermore, one must consider not only the relationships between theories and cases but also the constellation of theories within the scientific discourse.

4.3.3 Crucial cases

'Crucial cases' within a CON approach can be defined in a first simplified approximation as cases that are 'most-likely cases' – or better: very likely cases (see footnote 6 and preface) – with respect to a dominant or established theory in scientific discourse and, at the same time, 'least-likely cases' – better: very unlikely cases – with respect to a peripheral or new theory. This definition is very much in line with Eckstein, who states: 'Crucial case study obviously proceeds best when a case is treated in both senses [as a most-likely case and as a least-likely case] and confronted with both theory and countertheory' (Eckstein 1975: 119). Nevertheless, for an adequate definition of 'very likely cases' and 'very unlikely cases' within a CON approach, these terms must be defined more precisely, resulting in a more nuanced perspective on the 'theoretical crucialness' of cases. The full implications will become obvious in Section 4.6, where we show how theoretical conclusions can be drawn beyond the investigated cases.

An adequate understanding of these case-selection strategies within a CON approach is facilitated by the use of Bayesian logic. Slightly modifying Gerring (we substitute 'hypothesis' for 'theory'), a Bayesian approach to empirically testing a theory is as follows:

> The degree to which t [a theory] is confirmed by e [a set of evidence] depends [...] on the extent to which P (e|t) exceeds P (e), that is, on how much more probable e is relative to the theory and background assumptions than it is relative just to background assumptions. [...] Thus, the stranger the prediction offered by a theory – relative to what we would normally expect – the greater the degree of confirmation that will be afforded by the evidence.
>
> (Gerring 2007b: 234, with reference to Howson
> and Urbach 1989: 86)

In other words, the riskier an explanatory proposition or a theory is, given what we know about the case and given what we would perceive as 'normal', the more potential leverage the corresponding evidence has for this theory in a theoretical discourse. The potential is realized if the risky proposition receives clear confirmation through the congruence analysis proper. The decisive step in applying these Bayesian insights to a CON approach is to realize that the 'background assumptions' and the 'normal expectations' are derived from two different sources:

1. from contextual factors within the cases and
2. from the constellation of theories within a scientific discourse.

Eckstein (1975) argues that two important studies have had a significant impact in the social sciences because the authors selected 'most-likely cases' and 'least-likely cases'. A brief recapitulation shows that Eckstein's description of these studies is in line with the understanding of 'most-likely cases' and 'least-likely cases' as defined for the CON approach. Eckstein points to Malinowski's influential study on obedience to norms, in which Malinowski chose a primitive, socially coherent society for empirical analysis. This was a 'most-likely case' for the assumption held by other anthropologists that obedience to norms is automatic and spontaneous in small and homogeneous societies because individuals are strongly embedded in the collective. When the findings conflicted with this assumption, the assumption was seriously undermined. The impact of Malinowski's study has been strong because he challenged an assumption that was widely held and because he showed that the assumption did not hold even under the most favorable circumstances.

According to Eckstein, Michels chose a 'least-likely case' to bolster the claim that oligarchy in organizations is a ubiquitous phenomenon because the distinction between delegates and ordinary members invariably leads to the former's power over the latter. To construct a particularly strict test for this theory, Michels chose the German Social Democratic Party during the Weimar Republic. As Eckstein explains, the antecedent conditions did not look promising for this theory: the party was dedicated to grassroots democracy and associated ideologies, represented classes whose interest was in such a democracy, had elaborate intra-party democratic procedures and the delegates had the same social background as the members. All of these characteristics made the equivalence between organization and oligarchy extremely unlikely in this case. Nevertheless, Michels demonstrated that even this organization had an oligarchic structure (Michels 1962, as discussed in Eckstein 1975: 118).

In consequence, Eckstein argues that Michels' study has been 'crucial' for the oligarchy in organization hypothesis because it holds even under the most unlikely circumstances.

Nevertheless, for a thorough reflection on how 'crucial' or important a case is for a theoretical discourse, the researcher must go one step further and consider a plurality of theories and their position in the theoretical discourse. This demand is partly met by Allison and Zelikow, who write about the virtue of focusing on the Cuban missile crisis:

> In the context of ultimate danger to the nation, a small group of men weighed their options and decided. Such central, high-level, crisis decisions would seem to be ideal grist for Model I [Rational Actor Model, JB and MH] analysis. Model II and Model III are forced to compete on Model I's homeground. Dimensions and factors uncovered by Model II and Model III in this case should be particularly instructive.
>
> (Allison and Zelikow 1999: 7)

A closer look at this statement and the overall setup of the study reveals that the argument is not completely formulated in the cited statement. In this statement, Allison and Zelikow compare the context of the Cuban missile crisis to only one theory (Model I). No explicit reflection occurs on how 'strange' the contexts were for the organizational behavior model or for the governmental politics model. Implicitly, the proposition that the Cuban missile crisis is a strict test for Models II and III relies on Allison and Zelikow's overall setup of the analytic framework. They present Model I as the dominant perspective and the other models as complementary alternatives (Allison and Zelikow 1999: 4–5). Ultimately, the answer to the question of whether a case has a 'crucial' impact on a theoretical discourse depends not only on ex-ante reflections on its likeliness in respect to theories but also on the results of the congruence analysis proper. Only if the major conceptual aspects of a dominant theory are empirically disconfirmed and the major conceptual aspects of a non-dominant theory are empirically confirmed a case study will have a substantial impact on the theoretical discourse. We will return to this point in Section 4.6, where we suggest how to draw systematic conclusions beyond the investigated cases within a CON approach.

4.4 Formulating expectations and collecting data

A thorough knowledge of theories is crucial for selecting cases and lays the groundwork for the next steps in the congruence analysis approach. For each theory selected by the researcher, she must specify the implications for the cases under study. Furthermore, the theoretical frameworks and the corresponding expectations guide the collection of empirical information. For these stages, the researcher is confronted with the following questions:

– How shall I specify the expectations?
– How shall I concretize the expectations?
– How shall I collect the data?

For each of these questions, there is a variety of possible answers within the CON approach. In the following subsections, we will identify the alternatives in principle and provide examples.

4.4.1 The specification of propositions

Explanatory propositions can be specified in three principal ways (see Section 4.2):

– We can formulate the constitutive and causal propositions of an explanatory framework as comprehensively as possible. The set is usually large and emphasizes constitutive over causal propositions. Consequently, the explanatory framework comes closer to a paradigm than to a specific theory.
– We can focus on the causal relationship between two conceptual elements of an explanatory approach and formulate the causal propositions as precisely and clearly as possible. This is usually done by proposing that specific empirical expressions of abstract concepts are necessary and/or sufficient conditions for a specific expression of another abstract concept (a step in a causal chain or final outcome). Thus, the set of propositions is smaller than within the first type of theory specification.
– We can focus on comparing the expectations derived from divergent theories when we formulate constitutive and causal propositions. The propositions and predictions derived from different theories can be convergent, contradictory, or complementary. The set of propositions includes constitutive and causal propositions for which the divergent theories lead to contradictory expectations.

Our set of examples shows that some authors closely follow one of these ideal types, whereas others combine the divergent ways of theory specification.

Schimmelfennig's *The EU, NATO, and the Integration of Europe*

We begin with an example of the second approach because it sets high standards to which we can refer when describing further examples. In the first part of the book, Schimmelfennig (2003) derives a differentiated and precisely specified set of propositions for Eastern enlargement from three different theories, which share the conceptual core of the rational institutionalist paradigm. For the first theory – the security approach – Schimmelfennig deduces the following propositions in the form of necessary preconditions:

> According to the security approach, enlargement will take place if it is necessary and efficient for both the non-member state (S) and the member states (M) of the organization (O) in order to balance the power or threat of another state or coalition of states (the rival R). The following specific conditions must be jointly present for a state to seek membership:
>
> (1) R is (becoming) more powerful than S or threatens S.
> (2) S is not capable of balancing the power or threat of R internally.
> (3) O is less powerful or threatening than R.
> (4) O is able to deter R from attacking S or to defend S effectively against an attack by R, or R is unalterably aggressive.
> (5) The security benefit for S of membership in O are higher than those S would reap from any other relationship with O.
>
> (Schimmelfennig 2003: 30)

For the organization (EU, NATO), Schimmelfennig specifies the following necessary preconditions:

> (1) R is (becoming) more powerful than O or threatens O.
> (2) O is not capable of balancing the power or threat of R on its own.
> (3) S is less powerful or threatening than R.
> (4) For each M, the accession of S enhances its net internal and external security, or those members that benefit from the membership of S possess the bargaining power or provide the compensation to make M agree to the accession of S.
> (5) For each M, the security benefits of the membership of S are higher than those of any other relationship with S, or those members that benefit from membership more than from any other relationship with S possess the bargaining power or provide compensation to make M agree to the accession of S.
>
> (Schimmelfennig 2003: 30)

Schimmelfennig formulates similar sets of necessary preconditions from the other two theories in the rationalist paradigm (the power and welfare approaches; Schimmelfennig 2003: 32–3). Furthermore, Schimmelfennig reflects explicitly on the relationship among the various preconditions. Each condition within an approach has the status of a necessary condition. In other words, each approach is disconfirmed as an explanation for Eastern enlargement if one of the preconditions is not fulfilled. Schimmelfennig applies the 'principle of charity' to the rationalist paradigm by specifying each of the three theories as sufficient for confirming the rationalist paradigm: 'If a single approach produces a successful explanation, I count this as a confirmation of rationalist institutionalism as a whole' (Schimmelfennig 2003: 35).

In the subsequent empirical chapters on NATO and the EU enlargement, Schimmelfennig evaluates the evidence for each formulated precondition and finds that the necessary preconditions for the nonmember states are fulfilled. Therefore, Rational Institutionalism can explain the bid for membership, but none of the three specified sets of preconditions for the organization (EU, NATO) existed, so Rational Institutionalism is not able to explain why the member states within NATO and the EU accepted the applications.

Overall, Schimmelfennig's first chapters concentrate only on causal factors (specified in the language of necessary and sufficient conditions) and on the outcome to disconfirm Rational Institutionalism. Next, he follows the same procedure for Sociological Institutionalism and confirms this approach as far as preconditions and outcomes are concerned. Later, Schimmelfennig went beyond input factors and outcome to derive empirical implications from Sociological Institutionalism for the process of enlargement. As with Rational Institutionalism, he considered two different theories within this paradigm (differentiated by their divergent micro-foundation/action-formation mechanisms, habitual action, and normative action). For the normative action approach, he formulates five hypotheses (we provide only a selection here):

(N1) The CEECs' desire to become NATO and EU members was a corollary of their identification with the Western international community and its constitutive values and norms.

(N2) [...].

(N3) The Western organizations offered membership to, or reacted favorably to the membership requests of, democratic CEECs.

(N4) [...].

(N5) ...

(Schimmelfennig 2003: 162)

For the 'habitual-action theory', Schimmelfennig formulates a similar list of hypotheses, but the combination of the two approaches is very different from the way he connected the different rationalist theories. Schimmelfennig argues:

> The main assumption the habitual and normative action hypotheses have in common – and that distinguishes them from the other process hypotheses [which he formulated in later chapters, JB/MH] – is that social values, norms and identities [...] shape the actors' identities, interests, and preferences. [...] Therefore, in order to test these process hypotheses, the most important facts are the enlargement preferences of the member and applicant states. If the preferences are, in general, uniform among the relevant actors, follow the community values, norms and identity and correspond to the enlargement rules of the organization, the analysis supports the sociological-institutionalist perspective.
>
> (Schimmelfennig 2003: 163)

Consequently, the two theories are not presented as two potentially different pathways to enlargement but as theories that share three necessary preconditions, which can be evaluated by examining the enlargement preferences of the member and applicant states. This approach is less 'charitable' in comparison to the treatment of the rationalist paradigm, and the specification of the empirically tested proposition follows a different approach. It corresponds to the third approach in our list, which focuses on contradictory expectations.

Allison and Zelikow's *Essence of Decision*

The primary example for the first approach, which specifies paradigms by formulating a broad set of propositions, is Allison and Zelikow's (1999) study on the Cuban missile crisis. The authors differentiate three decision-making paradigms in international politics (rational actor, organizational behavior, and governmental politics paradigm), discuss the history and the theoretical foundations of each paradigm, and specify the following aspects for each paradigm: (a) the basic unit of analysis, (b) 'organizing concepts' (including micro-foundations such as the Rational Choice Theory for the first model), (c) 'dominant inference patterns', (d) 'general propositions' (also, for the second and the third paradigms, 'specific propositions'), and (e) the typical evidence used within such a paradigm. Allison and Zelikow formulate many general and specific propositions as causal claims between explanatory factors and specific outcomes, such as the following: 'The existence of an organization with specific capacities for doing something increases the probability that its output/action/option will be chosen by the leadership of the organization and the government' (Allison and Zelikow 1999: 176–7).

In comparison to Schimmelfennig's approach, the causal claims are less clearly specified with respect to what we can expect for the cases under study. Furthermore, the specification of the paradigms not only includes a list of general and specific propositions but also goes beyond the formulation of these kinds of causal expectations to provide a complete picture of each paradigmatic approach for explaining decision-making in international politics (and beyond). Finally, the authors formulate some of their specific propositions in a competitive manner, not in the sense that they formulate mutually exclusive expectations, but in the sense that some explanatory factors are seen as more important than others (for example, 'The probability of nuclear attack is less sensitive to balance and imbalance or stability and instability (as these concepts are employed in Model I strategists) than it is to a number of organizational factors', Allison and Zelikow 1999: 182).

Nevertheless, their research design and their empirical sections do not allow for these claims to be tested systematically. Allison and Zelikow do not structure the empirical sections of their study according to their propositions (as Schimmelfennig does) but according to the three major puzzles that emerge in the Cuban missile crisis – the Soviet decision to place offensive missiles in Cuba, the United States (US) decision to react with a blockade, and the Soviet decision to withdraw the missiles. This means that their study includes not one but three cases. In the end, consistent evidence is found for each paradigm. Their major claim is that the second and third paradigms produced new insights and explanations that the first paradigm could not provide (Allison and Zelikow 1999: 379–89).

Sagan's *The Limits of Safety*

Scott Sagan and Andrew Moravcsik's way of formulating the theoretically derived propositions are fully in line with the third ideal type. Their reflections on what we can expect from different theories for the studied cases culminate in tables that juxtapose the different propositions (Moravcsik 1998: 28, 55, 69; see Section 4.2.2, where we restate some of Moravcsik's propositions).

Scott Sagan (1993) formulates seven competing propositions for the 'high reliability theory' (HRT) and for the 'normal accidents theory' (NAT), including the following:

> HRT 1: Accidents can be prevented through good organizational design and management.
>
> NAT 1: Accidents are inevitable in complex and tightly coupled systems.
>
> [...]
>
> HRT 3: Redundancy enhances safety; duplications and overlap can make a 'reliable system out of unreliable parts'.
>
> NAT 3: Redundancy often causes accidents; it increases interactive complexity and opaqueness and encourages risk taking.
>
> (Sagan 1993: 46)

Specification, in this approach, means focusing on those propositions where the divergent theories lead to contradictory expectations. A major difference from the second way of specifying propositions is that the propositions do not focus on the outcome of the process. Only two of the 10 aspects for which Moravcsik formulates hypotheses refer to outcomes (efficiency and distribution of interstate bargain, institutional form); the other eight concepts refer to aspects of the political process (for example, timing of shifts in preferences, the negotiation process). Sagan formulates competing propositions for the outcome (HRT 1 and NAT 1; see above) but argues that two competing theories cannot be evaluated by looking at the outcome.

> Because neither theory provides a precise estimate of the likelihood of serious accidents with hazardous technologies, it is impossible to determine the precise number of accidents, which, if discovered over time, would support or weaken the theories. [...] [I]mprecise language suggests that the two theoretical schools have a common estimate about the probability of dangerous accidents despite the strong difference in the tone of their conclusions: Perrow may look at a glass of safety and fit it 1 percent empty; high reliability theorists may see the same glass of safety as 99 percent full.
>
> (Sagan 1993: 48)

Consequently, Sagan focuses his empirical analysis on specific mechanisms. The two theories present very different assumptions about the relevance and causal roles of these mechanisms (for example, redundancy and organizational learning).

Owen's *Liberal Peace, Liberal War*

John Owen's (1997: 58–63) hypotheses represent a mix between the second and the third approaches to theory specification. Owen presented the following propositions following an extensive argument for explaining the war- and peace-making of liberal states by focusing on the perceptions of liberal elites. He sums up his reflections on idealist, realist, and materialist theories of democratic peace in the following competing hypotheses:

> 1.a. Liberals will perceive a foreign state as liberal if it matches their criteria for Liberalism within their own state; conversely, they will perceive a foreign state as illiberal if it violates those criteria.

> 1.b. Liberals will perceive a foreign state as liberal if that state poses no threat to them, may help or is helping them to oppose a state or states that threaten their own state. Liberals will perceive a foreign state as illiberal if it poses a threat to them. The more powerful, the closer, and the more hostile a foreign state is, the more threatening it is.

> 1.c. Liberals will perceive a foreign state as liberal if their immediate material well-being depends on good relations with that state and as illiberal if their immediate material well-being would be served by hostile relations with that state.
>
> (Owen 1997: 58–61)

The three hypotheses represent clearly competing causal propositions. Nevertheless, Owen's attempt to develop propositions with discriminatory power among the theories goes further. He argues that an important element in testing his 'liberal ideology theory' against contending realist theories is the assumption that liberal elites develop their perceptions and positions before a crisis emerges and do not change these positions during the crisis because they interpret the statements and actions of the other country through their ideological lenses. Consequently, Owen (1997: 57) states that he will treat an 'update' of perceptions based on the signals liberal actors receive from the other country and changes in the positions of liberal elites during a conflict as indicators of the rival 'realist theory'.[7]

4.4.2   Concrete expectations: Predictions

Most scholars who follow the congruence analysis approach do not formulate the expectations they deduce from theories as concrete predictions. This means that the ex-ante formulated expectations are not

Table 4.2 Predictions of four models of decision-process activities

Decision phase and operating mechanism	Rational model	Bounded rationality	Political model	Garbage can model
1. Problem definition				
Do the participants view the problem in the same way?	Y	P	N	P
Does the problem definition represent the goals of the organization?	Y	Y	N	Y
2. Search for alternative solutions				
Is search limited to a few familiar alternatives?	N	Y	P	P
Are potential solutions considered simultaneously and compared with one another?	Y	P	N	N
3. Data collection, analysis, and use				
Is information collected so that an optimal decision can be made?	Y	N	N	N
Is control over data collection and analysis used as a source of power?	N	N	Y	N
4. Information exchange				
Is information biased so as to conform to the preference (position) of the person transforming it?	N	Y	Y	N
Is information exchange negatively affected by people entering and leaving the decision process and changing their focus of attention?	N	P	N	Y
5. Individual preferences				
Do preferences change as problems become attached to or detached from the decision?	N	P	N	Y
Are individual preferences a function of personal goals and limited information about the alternative?	N	Y	P	P
6. Evaluation criteria trade-offs				
Are criteria for a solution agreed on *a priori*?	Y	P	P	N
Do trade-offs across solution criteria occur?	Y	N	P	N
7. Final choice				
Is the first alternative that exceeds the cut-off level(s) selected?	N	Y	P	N
Is the alternative chosen one that is expected to maximally benefit the organization, compared with other alternatives?	Y	P	N	P

Note: Y(es) = the theory predicts a positive answer to this question; N(o) = the theory predicts a negative answer to the question; P(artial) = the theory has no clear prediction for this answer.
Source: Wilson and Woodside (1999: 220),[8] based on Wilson and Wilson (1988).

on the same (low) level of abstraction as the empirical observations. The inferential leap between concrete observations and specific, but still abstract, propositions is completed later, when the empirical data are analyzed and interpreted. Nevertheless, there are studies that purport to formulate 'predictions' in the sense that we have defined them. Wilson and Wilson (1988), in their study on organizational decision-making, formulated 14 questions (two for each phase of a decision-making process) and deduced *a priori* the answers that they saw as most consistent with the four theories they selected (see Table 4.2).

They called this a 'prediction matrix'. We will discuss their way of comparing these predictions with empirical data in Section 4.5. We will discover that also in this study, the 'observations' are not on the same level of abstraction as the formulated 'predictions'. Three members of the research team must interpret the collected data to decide the extent to which the reality of decision-making is in line with the expectations deduced from the theories.

Sagan formulates the expectations he derives from 'high reliability theory' and 'normal accident theory' in two steps. In the theoretical chapter, he formulates contradicting propositions, and in the following chapters on specific cases, he applies the theories by formulating specific predictions for the cases. For the Cuban missile crisis, for example, he combines the propositions formulated for the 'high reliability theory' with empirical information about the state of affairs during the Cuban missile crisis:

> The five factors would lead a high reliability theorist to predict that a nuclear alert during the Cuban missile crisis would be an extremely safe military operation. [...] From this perspective, it would be surprising if a set of serious accidents occurred in October 1962.
>
> (Sagan 1993: 58)

The combination of the propositions derived from the 'normal accidents theory' and other empirical information about the situation leads to completely contradictory predictions. The contradictory predictions are formulated at the beginning of the empirical chapters. The rest of the chapter provides not only information about the (near-)accidents that occurred but also information on the role of specific mechanisms emphasized by the two theories (Sagan 1993: 62–116).

4.4.3   The collection of information and production of data

The kind of data that are used for a congruence analysis can be very diverse, as are the methods to collect and produce this information.

Our set of examples reveals a broad spectrum. Owen draws primarily on existing scholarly literature and newspaper articles to reveal the perceptions and preferences expressed by liberal elites in situations before and during political crises that (might) have led to war. Allison and Zelikow use a broad array of primary and secondary sources for their three detailed and distinct reconstructions of the decision-making process during the Cuban missile crisis. Especially helpful for their endeavor was their access to the tape recordings of White House deliberations during the crisis. Furthermore, the authors conducted numerous interviews with participants and observers (Allison and Zelikow 1999: 312–3).

Most analysts collect existing information, but sometimes the data are produced by the scholars. This is the case when scholars interview the actors and observers of the process they analyze. Wilson and Wilson (1988) draw primarily on this kind of self-generated data in their study on organizational decision-making. After producing their prediction matrix, the authors conducted in-depth interviews with several members of four different organizations (buying centers in a university). The interviews were guided by the questions formulated in the predictions matrix, but they were semi-structured and included open questions. In addition to the transcripts of these interviews, the researchers collected other documents with relevant information on the decision-making process (Wilson and Woodside 1999: 219). The interviewers did not ask the questions from the prediction matrix directly; rather, they attempted to stimulate narrative storytelling about the decision-making process: 'Please describe, in your own words, the decision-making process that you and your colleagues experienced in buying the copier' (Wilson and Wilson 1988: 590). Thus, the acquired data was qualitative in nature. Before the scholars could use statistical techniques to analyze the data, it had to be translated into quantitative data. In the process of interpreting the transcripts and documents, the researchers decided on the right 'answer' to their 14 questions for each case and compared these answers with their deductions from the four theories (see the next section, which describes in more detail how the authors analyzed the data they collected and produced).

4.5   Data analysis – The congruence analysis proper

At the heart of the congruence analysis approach is a systematic comparison of the collected empirical information with the expectations deduced by the researcher from divergent theories. First, we present the logical foundations of this task, and then we describe the various ways scholars pursue this form of data analysis.

4.5.1 The steps of the congruence analysis proper

The congruence analysis consists of the following steps:

1. The empirical information (the set of observations) is compared with the expectations deduced from one theory (A). The comparison, which most often involves inferential leaps between different levels of abstraction, is based on interpretation and requires explicit reflection and justification. The comparison can lead to the following results:

   (a) the observations are in line with the expectations;
   (b) the observations are contradictory to the expectations; or
   (c) the observations are not in line with the expectations, but they also do not directly contradict the expectations; instead, they lie outside the set of expectations that can be linked to theory A.

2. The same empirical information is compared with the expectations deduced from another theory (B). This comparison can lead to the same types of results.

3. The results of the two comparisons of empirical information and theoretical expectations are combined to evaluate the relative explanatory power of the two theories for the case(s) under investigation.

There are various ways to proceed in implementing these steps. Table 4.3 provides the logical foundations for conducting this form of data analysis in a way that is methodologically consistent with the CON approach. Furthermore, the table helps to identify the ways to proceed with the congruence analysis proper, which we will illustrate with some examples.

4.5.2 The full set of possible conclusions

A congruence analysis that is most consistent with the notion of a 'three-cornered fight' (Hall 2006) begins the analysis with the empirical observation and simultaneously reflects on its congruence with theory A and theory B. Given that both comparisons can lead to three possible results, the combination can produce nine potential conclusions for

Table 4.3 Ways of drawing conclusions in the congruence analysis proper

	Observation(s) in line with expectations deduced from theory B	Observation(s) in contradiction to expectations deduced from theory B	Observation(s) beyond the expectations deduced from theory B
Observation(s) in line with expectations deduced from theory A	Conclusion A: Connections to other observations	Conclusion B: Strong evidence for preferring A to B	Conclusion C: Evidence underscores explanatory power of A
Observation(s) in contradiction to expectations deduced from theory A	Conclusion D: Strong evidence for preferring B to A	Conclusion E: Strong evidence for the need for other theories	Conclusion F: Evidence undermines explanatory power of A
Observation(s) beyond the expectations deduced from theory A	Conclusion G: Evidence underscores explanatory power of B	Conclusion H: Evidence undermines explanatory power of B	Conclusion I: Evidence for the need of expanded or other theories

each observation (see Table 4.3). The nine possible types of conclusions can be clustered into the following groups:

– The most important empirical evidence with the strongest theoretical conclusion is provided by those observations that are simultaneously in line with one theory and in contradiction with the other theory (conclusions B and D). For a competing theories approach, these are clearly the most valuable observations.

– Observations that are confirming or disconfirming for a theory but cannot be connected to another theory represent clear but less important evidence and lead to weaker theoretical conclusions (conclusions C, F, G and H). These observations usually form the bulk of observations. For a competing theories approach, these observations must be aggregated in some form, and the aggregated results must be compared with the results of the other theory to draw strong theoretical conclusions. For a complementary theories approach, those observations that are in line with a non-dominant theory are the most valuable.

– Observations that are in line with the expectations of both theories provide less clear evidence. Especially for a competing theories approach, these might be seen as useless observations. Nevertheless, a CON approach is based on a holistic understanding of theories as a consistent set of concepts that are linked together in a coherent way. Consequently, a purely technocratic approach of comparing individual observations with single expectations is not adequate. For the interpretation of observations that fit both theories at first sight, it is helpful to examine the set of connected observations. The internal consistency of a cluster of observations serves as a second (horizontal) point of reference when deciding whether an empirical observation is evidence for one or another theory.

- Finally, Table 4.3 reveals that a sound congruence analysis also takes into account observations that are important for explaining the case but are in line with neither theory A nor theory B. The first possibility, that an observation contradicts the expectations of both theories, is an important piece of evidence that leads to strong theoretical conclusions (conclusion E). If an observation cannot be connected (positively or negatively) to both theories, we can conclude either that a theory has to be expanded or that another theory is needed (conclusion I). Note that such a conclusion is based on the assumption that these observations have been identified as 'important' for explaining the case(s) under investigation. Because they fall outside the expectations that we can identify from the theoretical starting points, this identification can only be based on the 'natural foundations' of causal-process observations (see Chapter 3). In Chapter 5, we provide an example (Blatter 2009) that shows how causal-process observations provide the empirical foundation for arguing that a new theory is necessary to explain the outcome of interest.

4.5.3 Examples: Applications of the congruence analysis proper

The following examples demonstrate that scholars proceed with the congruence analysis proper in different ways.

Owen's Liberal Peace, Liberal War

John Owen (1997) begins the congruence analysis proper with the presentation of empirical observations and performs a two-step comparison of these observations with the expectations that he deduced from theories. In his theoretical chapter, Owen deduces three hypotheses from three theories to consider what shapes liberals' perceptions of foreign states: (a) Idealism: liberal ideology, (b) Realism: balance of threat, and (c) Rationalism: parochial interest (Owen 1997: 58–61). Nevertheless, in the empirical section of his book, Owen begins by describing 10 political crises between the US and foreign states that (potentially could have) led to war in the nineteenth century. For each crisis, he draws on a large set of primary and secondary sources to detail how the liberal elites in the US (and their major factions, for example, Federalists versus Republicans) and in the other country perceived the adversary country. For each case, Owen structures the historical reconstruction by answering the following questions: (a) How liberal was the US, and how liberal was the other country? (b) How did the US perceive the other state, and how did the other state perceive the US? Furthermore, Owen describes the actions, interpretations, and reactions during each crisis and closes each case study chapter with a short summary, in which he draws initial conclusions from the crises regarding the adequacy of the hypotheses. In other words, Owen aggregates the plurality of observations in a non-formal way and provides an initial judgment with respect to the congruence of the observations with the theories. Often, he finds that the information provides evidence for more than one theory.

In the third part of his book, Owen 'engages in a structured, focused comparison of the cases to see if two crucial expectations of [his] argument are borne out' (Owen 1997: 185). By drawing on the findings of the case studies, he discusses for each case whether the perceptions and the causes of these perceptions are in line with the idealist, the realist, or the rationalist theory. Because he applies this kind of congruence analysis for both countries, each crisis actually consists of two cases. Owen (1997: 208) sums up the findings of the comparative congruence analysis in a table that reveals that there is evidence for the 'idealist theory' in 17 of the 19 cases, 6 cases contain evidence for the 'realist theory', and observations point to the 'rationalist theory' in ten cases.

It is important to note that, when Owen is formulating the overall findings of his small- to medium-N study, he does not simply draw on the larger number of cases in line with the 'idealist theory' in comparison with the cases that exhibit observations congruent with the other theories. He acknowledges that for two cases, Realism is indeed a better explanation than his idealist account, and for two other cases, Realism best explains the perceptions of many actors. Owen interprets all other cases as confirming the core of his 'idealist theory', that liberal ideology shapes the perception of the other country. He counts not only cases for which he has found evidence for the 'idealist theory' but also cases for which he has found evidence for the idealist and for alternative theories. He uses different kinds of evidence and logic to argue that ideology is the crucial factor shaping perceptions. For a first group of cases, Owen uses causal-process observations and shows that changes in perceptions closely follow institutional changes. For other cases, Owen convincingly shows that ideology clearly shapes self-interest. Actors perceive their interests in a way that other actors and external observers would find irrational, and they do this in line with their ideology.[9]

Owen primarily uses evidence that confirms one of the three theories, and he draws the corresponding types of conclusions (types C and G in Table 4.3). His analysis is not geared toward detecting disconfirming evidence. Accordingly, the summary table in his study contains no negative scores for the theories. Because he is aggregating the individual observations and conclusions on the level of cases, he ends up with many cases that show some congruence with multiple theories. He uses discriminatory observations (close temporal connections between institutional and preference change, interests that are more consistent with ideology than with rational calculation) and the corresponding kinds of conclusions (types B and D in Table 4.3) only at a late stage in the data analysis.

Wilson and Wilson's *'Degrees of Freedom' in Case Research of Behavioral Theories of Group Buying*

Wilson and Wilson's approach (1988) to data analysis proceeds differently. For each concept (an element of the organizational decision-making process), the empirical data are compared to the predictions derived from all four theories, and confirming or disconfirming conclusions are drawn for all applied theories (see Table 4.2). In other words, these authors draw conclusions according to types A, B, and D in our typology. Wilson and Wilson take a more quantitative approach to the aggregation of individual results from the congruence analysis, and they apply statistical techniques when comparing the congruence between empirical data and expectations derived from different theories. As we have explained (Section 4.4.2), these authors developed a 'prediction matrix' by deducing the expected answers to 14 questions from four theories of organizational decision-making. They collected data on decision-process activities in four buying centers in different departments of their university. The major source of information was semi-structured interviews, and this information was complemented by documents from the buying centers (purchase order requests). The transcripts of these interviews formed the major source of empirical information. The research team compared the statements of the interviewees with the deduced expectations from the theories. Three 'judges' (members of the research team) independently searched for answers to the formulated questions in the empirical material and decided whether the empirical evidence was fully, partly or not at all in line with the predictions of the theories. Each judge made 56 evaluations (seven phases x two statements each x four cases), and the team tested the inter-judge reliability of the evaluations. Next, for each case, the number of 'hits' (congruence between reality and prediction) for each theory was counted. In three of the four cases, the bounded rationality model clearly received the most hits. The authors conducted a chi-square test to determine whether the number of hits was significantly higher than the number that could be expected by chance, and they applied a z-test to determine whether the number of matches for 'bounded rationality theory' was significantly greater than the hits for the other three theories. These statistical techniques were applied for each individual case and for the results of all cases (Wilson and Woodside 1999: 222).

In the original study, Wilson and Wilson not only compared the level of correct predictions between the four theories, but also formulated hypotheses concerning the level of congruence they expected for each theory given the characteristics of the decision-making process under investigation (buying decisions for copier machines). Consequently, the conclusions drawn by Wilson and Wilson (1988) were quite different from those in the revised study presented by Elizabeth J. Wilson and Arch G. Woodside (1999). The high level of congruence for 'bounded rationality theory' was in line with their theoretical expectations. However, they were surprised by the lower, but still significant congruence between the empirical results and the expectations derived from the political model and the garbage can model. These findings were not what they expected given the context conditions (Wilson and Wilson 1988: 592–3). The difference between the original study (Wilson and Wilson 1988) and the reconstruction of the study (Wilson and Woodside 1999) nicely illustrates the difference that a Bayesian approach to case study research makes. Formulating specific expectations based on the context conditions of the investigated cases leads to quite different interpretations of the same results of the congruence analysis proper than a simple comparison of the level of congruence between the theories. Nevertheless, Wilson and Wilson did not reflect on the position of the four theories they applied in the theoretical discourse. This reduced their ability to draw conclusions from their findings for the broader theoretical discourse beyond the cases under investigation (see Section 4.6).

Another way to proceed with the congruence analysis proper can be found in the studies of Schimmelfennig (2003) and Blatter (2009).[10] In contrast to Wilson and Wilson, these authors do not simultaneously compare the empirical data with expectations from different theories.

However, evidence that is not in line with theoretical expectations plays a much more important role in their analytical proceedings.

Schimmelfennig's *The EU, NATO, and the Integration of Europe*

Schimmelfennig (2003) takes up the propositions that he formulated in his theoretical sections and painstakingly explains the extent to which they are in line with the empirical data in his two case studies. For NATO enlargement, Schimmelfennig (2003: 37–44) shows that all of the conditions deduced from the security approach in the rationalist paradigm (see Section 4.4.1) were fulfilled for the Central and Eastern European Countries (CEEC), but this was not the case for the formulated conditions for the NATO member states. After demonstrating that the empirical reality is not in line with the security approach with respect to member states, he compares the congruence between the propositions of the power approach and the empirical evidence and comes to the same conclusion: none of the rationalist approaches can explain why member states accepted the NATO enlargement (2003: 43–51). He proceeds in the same way for his second case – EU enlargement – and produces the following finding: Rationalist Institutionalism can explain the interest of the CEEC in joining NATO and the EU, but it cannot explain the willingness of the member states of these two organizations to accept their bid because the preconditions deduced from rationalist approaches are not in line with the empirical findings. After showing that the empirical findings are not sufficiently in line with rationalist expectations, Schimmelfennig turns to an evaluation of the propositions that he deduced from Sociological Institutionalism. This chapter is structured according to the theoretical propositions. First, Schimmelfennig refers to primary and secondary sources to show that NATO and the EU are international communities with a liberal political culture. Second, with reference to databases like POLITY and Freedom House, he tests the sociological institutionalist hypothesis that only states that exhibit a certain level of liberal culture are accepted as new members. Overall, this kind of data shows a high level of congruence with the formulated propositions on the relationship between causal conditions and outcomes.

Nevertheless, in the second part of the book, Schimmelfennig shows that the empirical information does not correspond to the expectations derived from Sociological Institutionalism with respect to the process of enlargement. For this argument, Schimmelfennig presents data that indicate that the preferences of many member states and the initial steps in the enlargement process do not confirm Sociological Institutionalism.

At the beginning of the final part of the book, Schimmelfennig develops two alternative theoretical mechanisms that link individual state preferences and community norms (rhetorical action and communicative action), and he deduces partly competing observable implications (2003: 193–226). He tests the partly congruent and partly competing implications by interpreting the authoritative speech acts of representatives of the major actors in the process of NATO expansion. Schimmelfennig presents many examples of statements by CEEC countries as confirming evidence for the rhetorical action hypothesis. He explicitly states why these statements are more in line with the theoretical concept of rhetorical action than with communicative action (2003: 235). The most convincing evidence for the rhetorical action proposition is presented when Schimmelfennig shows that most skeptics of Eastern enlargement did not change their preferences; they were silenced because they could not argue against the liberal community values they had previously upheld. Schimmelfennig then discusses alternative explanations. He stresses that rhetorical action is confirmed by empirical evidence, but he acknowledges that there are other plausible explanations based on materialist theories. Consequently, rhetorical action loses the status of a necessary condition to explain NATO enlargement. Thus, he embarks on another case study (sequential selection of cases!) and selects a case in which this alternative explanation is less likely – the EU enlargement process. In this case study, he focuses on the intergovernmental decision-making process and attempts to disentangle the potentially confounding effects of bargaining and shaming (Schimmelfennig 2003: 264–5). In fact, he provides considerable empirical evidence in line with Rhetorical Action Theory and uses the case study to further elaborate on the various elements of this theory: 'rhetorical commitment', 'rhetorical argumentation', and 'rhetorical entrapment'.

Overall, Schimmelfennig mainly compares empirical information with the expectations from only one theory. He shows the extent to which the data are in line with the first established theory and what gaps remain, and then he does the same with the next established theory. In his final attempt to make a case for Rhetorical Action Theory, he uses confirmatory evidence and the corresponding types of conclusions (C, G in Table 4.3).

These examples show that there are different ways to proceed with the congruence analysis proper and that, after comparing the congruence of the empirical information with the expectations deduced from theories, scholars use different ways of reaching conclusions for the theories' adequacy to explain the investigated cases. We will show in the next chapter how further conclusions can be drawn beyond the studied cases.

4.6 Direction of generalization

A congruence analysis can be used to shed light on important social or political events, and it is a strong approach for generating systematic evidence if the explanation of these events is disputed. Nevertheless, most scholars applying a CON approach want to use the findings of their case study to contribute to the broader theoretical discourse. In contrast to statistical generalization (see Chapter 2), no claim is made that findings can be generalized to a population of similar cases. Instead, generalizing conclusions are drawn for the theoretical discourse. To highlight the fact that the theoretical discourse represents the functional equivalent of the population of similar cases in the COV approach and the set of causal configurations that enable specific kinds of outcomes in the CPT approach, we could call the entity for which we draw conclusions the 'population/set of theories' that is recognized as relevant in this discourse. The existing population/set of relevant theories and the position that specific paradigms and theories inhabit in the scientific discourse significantly shape the way scholars and practitioners perceive and approach the world. Furthermore, these theories form the primary structure of university curriculums and play a pivotal role in socializing elites. Consequently, the struggle for recognition and relevance among paradigms and theories is of crucial importance for the social sciences. The CON approach not only provides the methodological foundation to make this struggle more reflective but also for allowing a productive encounter of theories from different paradigms.

In principle, there are two major ways to use the findings of the congruence analysis for the broader theoretical discourse. The results of the empirical study can be used as munitions in the struggle for hegemony between competing theories. Alternately, the findings can be used as arguments for the adequacy and fruitfulness of new or marginalized theories or new combinations of theories. We will first provide the logical foundations for theoretical generalizations within a competing theories approach. Then, we provide some examples that show how theoretical generalization takes place within the second subtype of the CON approach, the complementing theories approach.

4.6.1 Theoretical generalization within a competing theories approach

We have emphasized our conviction that there are very good reasons to conduct empirical research with the goal of contributing to the scientific struggle for theoretical recognition and dominance. The conclusions that we can draw from small-N studies for the broader theoretical discourse depend on four aspects:

- the positions of the applied theories in the scientific discourse;
- the likeliness of theories to explain the case(s), which can be estimated upfront on the basis of context conditions or general characteristics of the case(s);
- the empirical support that the theories receive in the empirical study; and
- the real-world relevance of the studied case(s).

We have discussed in detail in earlier chapters the first three aspects of the CON approach, but we have addressed the latter aspect only within the CPT approach. Nevertheless, it seems obvious that a study on the major integration steps of the EU or a study on the Eastern enlargements of NATO and the EU has a stronger impact on the theoretical discourse in the field of IR than a study on a policy-field-specific agreement between Spain and Portugal, for example.

We assume that a small-N study (like any other study) has the strongest impact if it modifies the positions of theories within the scientific discourse by undermining dominant theories and by strengthening new theories. Consequently, a case has the highest level of relevance for the theoretical discourse if it is a 'very likely case' with respect to the dominant theory and a 'very unlikely case' with respect to an alternative theory and if the congruence analysis leads to clearly better results for the alternative theory than the dominant theory. This is how we defined 'crucial cases' in Section 4.3.1 with reference to the literature. Table 4.4 goes a step further and shows that cases can have various degrees of 'crucialness'. Scholars should reflect on the position of the applied theories in the theoretical discourse and on the 'likelihood' of the cases they select for all relevant theories. Scholars can use these reflections to select cases that have a good chance of being theoretically relevant. Nevertheless, the relevance of the small-N study for the theoretical discourse ultimately depends on the empirical findings.

Table 4.4 The relevance and crucialness of cases for the theoretical discourse

Number of case-type	Dominant theory		Alternative theory		Theoretical relevance ('crucialness')
	Context conditions	Empirical result	Context conditions	Empirical result	
1	Very likely	Disconfirmation	Very unlikely	Confirmation	Very strong
2	Very likely	Disconfirmation	Likeliness unclear	Confirmation	Very strong/strong
3	Likeliness unclear	Disconfirmation	Very unlikely	Confirmation	Strong
4	Very unlikely	Disconfirmation	Very unlikely	Confirmation	Strong
5	Very likely	Disconfirmation	Very likely	Disconfirmation	Strong
6	Very unlikely	Confirmation	Very likely	Disconfirmation	Strong
7	Very unlikely	Confirmation	Likeliness unclear	Disconfirmation	Strong/medium
8	Likeliness unclear	Disconfirmation	Very likely	Confirmation	Medium/strong
9	Very likely	Disconfirmation	Likeliness unclear	Confirmation	Medium
10	Very unlikely	Confirmation	Very unlikely	Disconfirmation	Medium
11	Likeliness unclear	Confirmation	Very likely	Disconfirmation	Medium/weak
12	Very likely	Confirmation	Very likely	Disconfirmation	Weak/medium
13	Very likely	Confirmation	Likeliness unclear	Disconfirmation	Weak
14	Very unlikely	Disconfirmation	Very likely	Confirmation	Weak
15	Likeliness unclear	Confirmation	Very unlikely	Disconfirmation	Weak/very weak
16	Very likely	Confirmation	Very unlikely	Disconfirmation	Very weak

Notes: This table refers to theoretical generalization within a competing theories approach; therefore, it is assumed that if one theory is confirmed, the other is disconfirmed.
Furthermore, this table has been changed in comparison to the hard-cover edition; we have exchanged the more common terms "most-likely" and "least-likely" with the more adequate terms "very likely" and "very unlikely". For an explanation see endnote 6 of this chapter (which is new in comparison to the hardcover edition) and the preface of this paperback edition.

We have not included the fourth factor that influences the theoretical 'crucialness' of a small-N study – the real-world relevance of the case(s) under investigation – in the table for two reasons. First, including this factor would have made the table overly complex and would have distracted from the main message of the table: the 'crucialness' of a case depends on the *a priori* expectations and the empirical findings with respect to two theories, not just one theory. Once again, it is obvious that it is important to conceive of the CON approach as a 'three-cornered fight' involving empirical evidence and at least two theories.

The other reason is that the fourth factor is located outside the scientific system and serves as a reminder that the struggle for recognition and dominance in the theoretical discourse take place not only on the bases of methodological rigor and formal logic, as the table seems to suggest. The impact of small-N research on the theoretical discourse depends on the real-world relevance of the selected cases and on the reputation of the scholars and their institutional affiliations.

This point leads us to one of the major problems and dangers of the CON approach, which is especially virulent within a competing theories approach: the goal of contributing convincingly to scientific discourse demands a significant investment in theoretical knowledge and specification, which might come at a price. It is no accident that two of our examples of the competing theories approach have drawn strong criticism. Scott Sagan has been criticized for misrepresenting the literature he used to develop the 'high reliability organization model', and it has been shown that Andrew Moravcsik made grave mistakes in the interpretation of the empirical material that he used for his theoretical stance in favor of Liberal Intergovernmentalism (Lieshout, Segers, and van der Vleuten 2004).

4.6.2 Theoretical generalization within a complementary theories approach

There are ways to draw generalizing conclusions for the theoretical discourse beyond the claim that one theory is better, more valid, or more relevant for a field of research than another theory. These ways strive primarily for theoretical innovation and not for theoretical dominance.

A first example is Frank Schimmelfennig's study, which used empirical findings from the study on the eastern enlargement of NATO and the EU to draw conclusions for the broader theoretical discourse between rationalists and constructivists within the field of IR. Schimmelfennig

(2003: 283–5) sums up the results of the various steps of his congruence analysis by scrutinizing a sequential causal framework for IR in which the first step – preference formation – takes place according to rationalist theories, whereas the second step – international interaction – is structured according to the norms and values of Sociological Institutionalism. Schimmelfennig argues that this sequential explanatory framework represents a new theoretical synthesis in IR, whereas other sequential combinations of the two paradigmatic approaches have been previously formulated. Schimmelfennig (2003: 284) mentions Legro's (1996) suggestion of combining the two paradigms in the opposite way and explaining preference formation by domestic organizational culture and international interaction on the basis of strategic rational action. Schimmelfennig's contribution to the theoretical debate is not limited to a new configurational synthesis of the two major paradigms within IR; it includes another innovation. He uses the two case studies to convincingly show how community values influence rationalist state actors. In other words, he shows how the two paradigmatic approaches in IR can be linked by a specific causal mechanism: rhetorical action. This action-formation mechanism was not previously introduced in IR theory, at least not in such a convincing way. To make this theoretical innovation compelling, it is necessary to develop this causal mechanism on the basis of fundamental social science theory and to bolster its empirical adequacy and relevance through a methodologically sophisticated small-N study.

Joachim Blatter's study on international environmental regulations at Lake Constance illustrates another way to use the empirical findings of a case study to bolster the claim that theoretical innovation is necessary in a field of research. In his concluding chapter, Blatter (2009: 106–7) reflects on the consequences of his empirical findings for the theoretical discourse. An initial and theoretically less far-reaching conclusion would be to recognize 'performance' as another behavioral mechanism that complements the existing population of action-formation causal mechanisms within RT. Nevertheless, Blatter argues that his findings represent a more fundamental challenge for RT because the functionalist assumptions at the heart of RT are not sufficient to explain international environmental regulations. The regulation is not functionally necessary, and the major stimulus for the transboundary regulations did not come from within the policy-field of regulation. Consequently, his findings provide further support for those who argue that the (often implicit) fundamental assumptions of RT must be overcome and that international regulations are embedded in the broader process more than has been assumed by the policy-field-focused theories in this field of research. Like Schimmelfennig, Blatter shows that he is not alone in this kind of theoretical reasoning; in recent years, international water regulations have increasingly been examined in terms of the 'securitization' of environmental politics. Nevertheless, again like Schimmelfennig, Blatter proposes a different role of transnational water policy for international security. His empirical study and further examples described briefly in the concluding chapter show that water can serve as a stimulus for international cooperation and environmental innovation and is not necessarily a source of conflict and war.

Neither Schimmelfennig nor Blatter claims that their theories or theoretical syntheses represent the most important explanatory approaches in their fields of research. Nevertheless, their studies and theoretical conclusions challenge fundamental assumptions of hegemonic paradigms in these fields and provide evidence that other causal processes and results are possible. In other words, they complement the established repertoire of theories and causal mechanisms. The final test for whether these case studies are 'crucial', in the sense of theoretically relevant, is left for the scholarly community, which can adopt these theoretical innovations or ignore them.

4.7 Presenting findings and conclusions

The documentation of a congruence analysis follows a clear deductive template. First, the scholar introduces and justifies the selection of theories to be applied in the empirical study into the theoretical discourse. Next, the theories are specified and expectations are deduced. In comparison to the other explanatory approaches in small-N research, the description of the discursive context in which the study takes place and the justification and specification of theories plays a more important role and demands more attention. In the following chapters, the empirical information is presented and the congruence analysis proper is performed. At the end of the congruence analysis, the researcher sums up the results for the cases under study. Finally, the researcher reflects on the broader implications for the theoretical discourse.

All CON approaches share this deductive way of presenting the small-N research project. Nevertheless, we can further differentiate two major ways to proceed:

– A first way is to introduce and specify all of the theories in a theoretical chapter, which focuses on the divergent propositions and expectations that can be deduced from these theories. The empirical material in the next chapters is presented and discussed with an eye toward all of the introduced theories, and initial conclusions are drawn at the end of each empirical chapter. The researcher systematically presents the results of the empirical investigations in a separate chapter and compares the level of congruence for the various theories. Finally, the researcher draws further conclusions beyond the investigated cases. For us, Owen's study represents the best example of this way of structuring the documentation.

– A second way to proceed is to work with different 'cuts'. The overall line of argumentation is scrutinized only briefly in an introductory chapter. Next, an initial theory and its empirical implications are described and compared with the empirical evidence. This leads to an initial result, which usually highlights what the theory can explain and what gaps remain. Then, the next theory is introduced, specified, and tested. Once again, the results are discussed, and remaining gaps are highlighted. This procedure is reiterated until no major gaps remain in explaining the studied cases. Finally, the scholar reflects on the implications of the results for the theoretical discourse. Frank Schimmelfennig's book serves as a perfect model for this way of presenting the findings of a congruence analysis.

As in all empirical studies, the reality of the research process is much less linear than its presentation in the documentation. A parallel selection and specification of theories and cases often takes place because the researcher must determine whether his first information and intuition holds. Furthermore, the process of linking empirical information to theories takes place much more iteratively in comparison to the way it is presented in the final documentation. It must be stressed, however, that a good congruence analysis depends on a thorough knowledge and understanding of a plurality of theories. Only if you have a solid idea about what you are looking for can you recognize compelling evidence when you see it.

4.8 Summary

The congruence analysis approach is the most appropriate method for researchers who want to contribute to the theoretical discourse within a field of research. Scholars who apply a CON approach are convinced that paradigms and theories are important in the academic world and beyond because they focus attention on specific aspects of social events, and they provide the basic frameworks for understanding the world. A congruence analysis is based on fundamental paradigms and 'thick' theories and not only on plausible reasoning which is sufficient to formulate a hypothesis in the COV approach. Paradigms are consistent worldviews, and theories are configurations of abstract concepts that can be specified through a set of constitutive and causal propositions.

A core feature of the CON approach is that it is a 'three-cornered fight' in which the empirical evidence is compared with expectations deduced from at least two different theories. Researchers who apply a CON approach should reflect explicitly on the structure of the theoretical discourse to which they hope to contribute and on the status of the theories they select within this discourse. Together with *a priori* information and the findings of the case study, these reflections form the basis for the broader conclusions that can be drawn from the small-N study. The researcher tries to select cases that are potentially crucial for the theoretical discourse. Cases that are 'very likely cases' for the dominant theory and 'very unlikely cases' for the alternative theory have a greater potential of being 'crucial cases'.

With respect to empirical evidence, a congruence analysis can take into account variable-scoring observations and causal-process tracing observations. Usually, the latter takes precedence. The search for information is 'theory driven', and the selection and presentation of the empirical information are organized in ways that facilitate the drawing of conclusions for the comparative validity and relevance of theories. The data analysis – the congruence analysis proper – involves three steps: (a) the comparison of the empirical information with one theory, (b) the comparison of the empirical information with another theory, and (c) the comparison of the results of (a) and (b) to draw conclusions about the comparative merits of the theories. The results of the congruence analysis can be used to argue that a specific theory is 'better' than other theories, which represents the competing theories approach. Within a complementary theories approach, the results can be used to introduce further theories in a field of research or to develop new theoretical syntheses.

5
Combining Diverse Research Approaches

The previous chapters outlined three approaches to case study research. In this chapter, we will discuss fruitful combinations of the different case study approaches. Furthermore, we show how case studies (that is, small-N studies) can be connected to large-N studies that use statistical methods to perform data analysis and medium-N studies that apply Qualitative Comparative Analysis (QCA) for this task.

We combine divergent research approaches and designs because they have strengths that complement one another. Therefore, combining the various approaches and designs increases the leverage of the research. Nevertheless, combining the different approaches might not always be as easy and fruitful as it seems. We are aware that a lively methodological debate is currently occurring about the extent to which combining small-N studies (that is, qualitative research) with medium-N or large-N studies (that is, quantitative research) makes sense (for example, Lieberman 2005; Haverland 2007; Fearon and Laitin 2008; Rohlfing 2008; Seawright and Gerring 2008; Kuehn and Rohlfing 2010; Wolf 2010). In general, we do not share the skepticism that has been raised against the idea of combining qualitative and quantitative research because we have found fruitful combinations of the two types of research. Nevertheless, we believe that usually a separate and sequential application of different research approaches and designs is more appropriate than the mixing of various approaches and techniques within the same study.

In the first paragraph of Section 5.1, we provide an overview of the major reasons for combining approaches and designs. In Sections 5.2 and 5.3, we present examples that exhibit the two most important combinations of divergent case study approaches:

1. complementing the co-variational approach (COV) with causal-process tracing (CPT) and
2. using causal-process tracing (CPT) as an integral element of or as a complement to a congruence analysis (CON).

At this point, it will become clear again why the chapter on causal-process tracing has a central place in our book. Although we identified specific research goals and questions in which CPT serves as an adequate standalone research approach, one can also usefully apply causal-process tracing as a technique for drawing causal inferences to answer research questions for which the COV and CON approaches represent the optimal choices as overall research designs.

In Sections 5.4 and 5.5, we examine the most important ways through which case studies can be connected to large-N and medium-N studies. Because we aim to take terms seriously, we do not call these combinations 'mixed-methods' or 'mixed-method strategies' (as, for example, Lieberman 2005). Although we realize that – unfortunately – these terms have become widespread, we hold this stance for various reasons.

First, the word 'mixed' might wrongly imply that different approaches or methods are mixed together within a single study. As will be shown in Section 5.2, case study researchers actually mix different techniques to draw causal inferences within the same study. Nevertheless, we propose that applying one case study approach after the other is the better way to go since then it is possible to tailor each study coherently for specific purposes. Furthermore, when we combine small-N studies with large-N or medium-N studies, this always takes place sequentially. That is, one type of study, which has its own goals and methods for performing data generation and data analysis, is followed by the other type of study, which has other goals and other methods for performing data generation and data analysis. The two studies are not mixed but clearly separated and utilize a sequential application. The second study draws upon the findings of the first study while constructing the analytic framework and/or selecting the cases to be studied.

Second, the term 'method' is too general since it is used for both, for the techniques to generate data and for the techniques to analyze data. In the following we are not concerned with combining different methods of data generation (for example, surveys and narrative interviews). Instead, we want to show how various techniques of data analysis can be applied independently and in a sequential manner. As a result, we use the terms 'combined case study approaches' and 'combined research designs' instead of the term 'mixed methods'.[1]

In Section 5.4, we present research designs that combine case studies with large-N studies. We show how a large-N study can be augmented through case study analyses by focusing on causal-process observations. Usually, the goal of the case study is to find empirical evidence for the theorized pathway or for the conceptualized causal mechanisms that lead from a cause to an effect after the effect of a cause has been estimated by a statistical analysis. We also discuss how new hypotheses can be generated by performing an intensive case study of cases that have been identified as 'deviant' in a prior large-N study. Additionally, we examine how a case study can serve as a plausibility probe for a hypothesis that is then put to a comprehensive test in a large-N multivariate study using statistical analysis.

In Section 5.5, we scrutinize a combination of case studies and medium-N studies whereby the latter apply QCA. Because causal-process tracing and QCA are both based on configurational thinking, it seems very adequate to use CPT in order to bolster or to test the internal validity of the findings of a prior QCA study. Nevertheless, we could not find any study that applies a sequential combination of QCA and CPT for these goals. What we found is an instance, in which a scholar selected a contradictory case from a prior QCA study and showed – by comparing it to a consistent case – that it was timing that made all the difference. Furthermore, we present a study that applies at first various case study techniques and later on QCA for analyzing the same (nine) cases.

We end up with some reflections on the practical preconditions to combining different case study approaches and connecting small-N to medium-N or large-N studies (Section 5.6). Individual researchers are able to combine different study approaches, but the growing demand for combinations of small- and medium- or large-N studies will require more collaboration among scholars with different methodological skills. A necessary condition for such collaborative work is a non-fundamentalist and non-hegemonic attitude toward epistemology and methodology. Case study research that recognizes methodological plurality and that is located within the 'epistemological middle-ground' can pave the way toward more collaborative research projects in the social sciences.

5.1 Combining approaches and designs: Purposes and possibilities

In the literature, we find that scholars combine qualitative and quantitative research methods or divergent research designs for many reasons (for example, Greene, Caracelli, and Graham 1989; Bryman 2006). We distinguish four main reasons for connecting small-N studies to large-N or medium-N studies. These reasons are essentially identical to the reasons for combining divergent case study approaches. Table 5.1 displays the four purposes and the resulting sequences of the divergent approaches and studies.

5.1.1   Strengthening concept validity of descriptive inference

The first reason for combining different approaches is to strengthen the validity of the descriptive inferences that we draw from empirical observations for the cases under investigation. In this book, we are primarily concerned with causal inferences, not descriptive inferences. Nevertheless, one of the strong assets of case study research is that we can draw a detailed picture of the outcome or the cause(s) of interest. These detailed descriptions are much more useful for the theoretical discourse and for practitioners outside of the investigated cases if we connect these descriptions to abstract concepts in a reflective and systematic manner. In other words, the quality of our descriptions depends on a reflective specification of concepts that we use to interpret and to classify the factors and results of a causal process. The CON approach contains the most sophisticated advice for connecting abstract concepts and concrete observations. It makes us especially aware of the fact that divergent theories might look differently at a certain concept or that an abstract concept like 'stable democracy' can be specified quite differently depending on the theory of democracy.

In consequence, it makes sense to conduct a congruence analysis of a single case first and to use the gained insights for a sophisticated conceptualizing of the variables in a second case study that looks at a plurality of cases and applies co-variational analysis. In a similar way, we can connect a congruence analysis to large-N or medium-N studies. A co-variational case study as a prelude for large-N studies might also enhance the descriptive validity of the latter. By conducting a case study based on a COV approach before performing a large-N study, we obtain many insights into the adequacy of the indicators and measurement scales as well as a better understanding of how to integrate the different types of data (see Section 2.6). These insights will increase the conceptual validity of the large-N study, which, in turn, is a precondition for making accurate descriptive and causal inferences.

Table 5.1   Reasons for combining different case study approaches and for connecting small-N with large-N and medium-N studies and the resulting sequences

Purpose	Sequence of case studies	Sequence of small-N (case studies) and large-N or medium-N studies
Strengthen the concept validity of descriptive inferences (theory/concept formation and measurement)	1. CON 2. COV	1. Small-N study (COV, CON) 2. Large-N/Medium-N study -> Variables/conditions are conceptualized and measured on the basis of the findings of the small-N study
Strengthen or test the internal validity of causal inferences (effect/outcome and mechanism/process)	1. COV 2. CPT	1. Large-N/Medium-N study 2. Small-N study (CPT) -> Select 'onliers' (based on statistical analysis applied in the large-N studies) or causal configurations with high leverage and consistency (based on the techniques of fsQCA applied in the medium-N studies)
Complement the range of relevant variables, conditions/mechanisms, or theories	1. COV or CON 2. CPT	1. Large-N/Medium-N study 2. Small-N study (CPT) -> Select 'outliers' (from the statistical analysis of the large-N study) or 'contradictory cases' (from the truth-table of the medium-N study)
Increase the external validity (generalization to larger populations of cases)	1. CPT or CON 2. COV	1. Small-N study (COV, CPT) 2. Large-N/Medium-N study -> Select more cases that are less similar with respect to the independent and control variables (for the large-N studies) or less similar with respect to the outcome (for the medium-N studies)

We will not go further into the details here or provide examples in the following section because this book focuses on those methodological aspects that are primarily concerned with making causal inferences. Just one last remark: Whereas the purpose of strengthening internal descriptive validity is fulfilled by the first study for the second study, for all following purposes it is the study that is conducted in the second step that fulfills the stated goal.

5.1.2   Strengthening or testing the internal validity of causal inference

A second and often-mentioned reason for adding another, different type of study is to test the internal validity of the causal claim that has been made based on the evidence and methods applied within the first study. Nevertheless, in real social science research, scholars do so for a slightly different reason. The term 'testing' implies that the result of the second study can either bolster or undermine the findings of the first study. However, most scholars who combine co-variational analysis and causal-process tracing present only those findings of the causal-process tracing that strengthen the results of the co-variational analysis. Furthermore, scholars often apply the two methods of drawing causal inferences not sequentially but together. Both features represent common practice as we will see in Section 5.2. A radical adherent of 'Critical Rationalism' would be skeptical of this practice. Our 'epistemological middle ground' allows for a milder verdict because a coherent set of variable-scoring observations and causal-process observations increases our confidence in the causal claim. Nevertheless, we prefer to apply CPT in a distinct second study because a clear-cut sequential combination allows for much more openness with respect to the result of the second study. Using CPT to test the results of the co-variational analysis is not yet common in case study research. The same is true for using CPT as a testing device for the internal validity of the findings derived from a correlation-based statistical analysis in large-N studies. However, an increasing number of methodologists are proposing this combination and provide advice on how scholars should select the cases for the CPT-focused case study based on the findings of the large-N study (for example, Gerring 2007a; Rohlfing and Schneider 2011). In order to test the internal validity of the finding of the large-N study, scholars should choose cases that are well predicted by the multivariate model. In other words, they should select cases that are 'on the regression line' (see Section 5.3). To test the causal inferences of a QCA-based medium-N study with CPT, we should select cases that show a causal configuration with high levels of 'consistency' and 'coverage'. These measures indicate the correctness and the empirical relevance of the causal configuration within the population of investigated cases.

5.1.3   Complementing the range of variables, conditions, mechanisms, and theories

If we add causal-process tracing to COV- or CON-based case studies or to large-N/medium-N studies, we might identify further relevant variables, conditions, mechanisms, or theories. Although these insights might emerge as a side effect of our attempt to test the findings of the first study, one can also view the identification of these causal factors and their theoretical reflection as a distinct objective.

First, innovation and not testing is the main purpose for conducting the second study. This will be shown in Section 5.3, where we will present a study that complements a congruence analysis with causal-process tracing in order to bolster the claim that further theoretical perspectives are necessary in a specific field of research.

Second, when we complement large-N or medium-N studies with causal-process tracing in order to identify additional causal factors, we select different cases in comparison to the cases that we select when we want to use CPT to test the internal causal validity. If the first study is a large-N statistical analysis, then we select 'outliers'. Conversely, if the first study is a medium-N QCA study, then we select 'contradictory cases', which are cases that show the same causal conditions but different outcomes (for a sophisticated discussion of the case selection strategies after regression analysis and QCA, see Rohlfing and Schneider 2011).

5.1.4   Increasing the external validity of causal inferences

The final major reason for combining different approaches and studies is to determine whether the findings of the first study can be generalized toward a wider population of cases. Within small-N studies, one can best accomplish this task by utilizing the COV approach, though in a limited fashion. Therefore, this goal represents the main rationale for complementing a small-N study with a medium-N or large-N study. First, a scholar can complement a small-N study based on the COV approach with a large-N study that applies statistical techniques to reveal correlations and, thus, determine whether 'x makes a difference' in a wider population of cases. Secondly, a scholar can complement a small-N study based on the CPT approach with a medium-N study that applies

QCA and, thus, determine whether the causal conditions and configurations revealed in the small-N study are necessary and sufficient for producing a specific type of outcome in a wider population of cases. Note, that this combination presupposes an understanding of generalization that is closer to 'statistical generalization' (as defined in Section 2.7) than to 'possibilistic generalization' (as defined in Section 4.6).

Thirdly, complementing a congruence analysis with a large-N study based on statistical techniques is very uncommon but possible as has been shown by Schimmelfennig (2003). He tested the first finding of his congruence analysis, which states that Sociological Institutionalism can explain the decisions to enlarge the EU and the North Atlantic Treaty Organization (NATO), with a large-N study taking into account earlier enlargement decisions and enlargement decisions of other organizations (Chapter 6 of his book). However, Schimmelfennig significantly reduced the complexity of the 'cause' when he conducted the large-N study after the case study (that is, from a large set of causal conditions to three indicators of one variable; see Schimmelfennig 2003: 126).

5.2 Combining co-variational analysis and causal-process tracing

The combination of COV and CPT is probably the most practiced combination in case study research. We will discuss two variants. In each variant, the causal-process tracing is preceded by a cross-case comparison. The first variant is useful for X-centered research, which aims to establish the effect of a specific factor. Accordingly, COV dominates in this case. The second variant resonates well with studies that attempt to explain a specific outcome: Y-centered research. In this case, the researcher focuses on CPT.

5.2.1 X-centered combination of COV and CPT

In a case study based on the COV approach, a researcher aims to establish the causal effect of a specific independent variable. We called this approach 'X-centered research'. To isolate the causal effect, one selects cases that vary with regard to this independent variable but show similar values for the other potentially influential variables. As we discussed in Chapter 2, scholars do not regard a mere observation of a co-variation between the independent variable as sufficient proof of a *causal* relationship. Even if the investigator successfully controls for all of the other relevant variables and even if the researcher can show that the cause precedes the effect if he or she chooses an intertemporal comparison, the resulting co-variation does not constitute proof. To provide a compelling explanation, the researcher also needs to establish a plausible connection between the cause and the effect (that is, an explanation for why the independent variable affects the dependent variable). In accordance with the COV approach, one only needs to make 'a plausible argument' for this connection. However, to further increase the confidence that the relation between the independent and the dependent variable is a causal one, the scholar can augment the COV approach with causal-process tracing. Hence, after the cross-case comparison has established that the independent variable of interest co-varies with the dependent variable, the researcher can delve into one or more cases to establish whether the causal process has actually unfolded as assumed. Through an in-depth study, the researcher seeks to develop a comprehensive storyline and identify the 'smoking guns' and 'confessions' that will increase the plausibility of the argument that the hypothesized causal process has been at work.

Note that causal-process tracing might also be useful even if the dependent variable does not co-vary with the independent variable, or in other words, when the dependent variable has a similar value across cases despite different values of the independent variable. In this case, the researcher cannot establish a causal effect. Yet, the investigator can engage in causal-process tracing to determine why the independent variable had no effect. In other words, the researcher can determine at which point in the assumed process the results failed to follow the predictions. Doing so may lead to a refined hypothesis that includes further necessary conditions or the researcher might formulate more clearly the scope conditions under which the hypothesis holds.

An example of an X-centered study that combines COV and CPT is Alon Peled's study on two public management reform initiatives in Israel (Peled 2002). Peled aims to determine not only the impact of the initiatives on the fate of public management reform in Israel but also whether the process by which administrative reforms are implemented affect the bureaucrats' willingness to cooperate in future reforms. The goal of this study is to broaden the debate on public management reform. Many studies have focused on the ideas that underlie new public management reforms. For example, Peled wants to draw attention to the implementation stage of the reform process (2002: 219). New public management ideas can be implemented through an 'open book' or a 'top-down' style of reform. An 'open book' style is characterized by an incremental, participatory, and consensus-oriented process, whereas a 'top-down' process is secretive, top-down, and centralized (2002: 217–22). Peled hypothesizes that an 'open book' reform style facilitates future reform attempts. This argument is based on the assumption that such reforms create 'trust among organizational members' and that this trust is 'the engine that produces commitment, loyalty and productivity', which, in turn, facilitates future reform attempts (2002: 220). Peled's case selection is in accordance with the COV approach. He selects the cases based on where the independent variable 'reform style' varies. He then chooses a reform launched by the Israeli Civil Service Commission (1994–96), which aimed to make the public sector more entrepreneurial and self-empowered, and a reform initiated by the Israeli Ministry of Finance (1989–98), which aimed to reduce the costs of public management information systems. At the same time, Peled holds a number of factors constant. Both reforms unfolded in the same country and in the same period of time. Moreover, both reforms were informed by new public management ideas. Having controlled for these factors, he can concentrate on the legacy of the reform. However, rather than only scoring the variables to make a 'static' comparison, he actually traces the dynamics of the reform process. For instance, for the open book reform, he analyzes the origin of the reform by focusing on the Civil Service Commission's vision and establishes the open book character of the reform process. Additionally, Peled traces the early reform movements, its initial success, the growing opposition against the reform, the end of the reform, and how the reform, even though it was abolished, created a favorable environment that inspired future reform attempts (Peled 2002: 222–9). He studies the top-down reform undertaken by the Ministry of Finance in a similar manner, again tracing the origin of the reform and the reform process, and he shows how the top-down style led to frustration and opposition, which eventually hampered the Ministry's future reform efforts (Peled 2002: 229–37). Peled conducted this analysis in an intensive manner, especially with regard to the Ministry of Finance's relatively less researched reforms. He not only conducted 80 interviews with the advocates and opponents of the reform but also consulted parliamentary records, the ministry's internal documents and specialized newsletters (Peled 2002: 218). His causal-process observations are crucial to his argument because they provide evidence suggesting that the style of the reform process affected the civil servants' motivation. The author emphasizes what we termed 'confessions' by referring very often to the explicit statements in which actors explain their behavior. The study includes occasionally lengthy quotes from interviews with the key actors in the reform process. For instance, the minister of Environmental

Affairs stated that the Civil Service Commission reform has 'helped us to create opportunities to promote issues that were on the agenda for a long time' (quoted in Peled 2002: 228), whereas other 'confessions' provide evidence that the Ministry of Finance's reform left behind 'scorched earth' (Peled 2002: 236). A senior civil servant at the Education Ministry stated the following:

> I believe that the real motive [of a new reform attempt of the Ministry of Finance, JB and MH], is their desire to control everything that happens in every ministry. In this sense they are still living according to Bolshevik standards.
>
> (quoted in Peled 2002: 236)

By constructing a comprehensive storyline, Peled was able to reconstruct the sequence of events. His evidence suggests that the 'open book' style of reform created a climate conducive to future reform not only after the initial stage of the reform process (that is, the successful completion of the pilot program) had succeeded but also after the reform suffered a 'premature death' (Peled 2002: 227) a few years later. This finding provides powerful evidence for the argument that the civil servants' commitment to reforms is not related to the content of the reforms but the manner in which they are implemented.

As the example demonstrates, augmenting the cross-case comparison by employing COV while using within-case evidence generated by CPT helps not only to establish the effect of the independent variable but also to determine whether the causal process connecting the cause and the effect has worked as assumed. Combining variable-scoring observations with causal-process observations increases the leverage of the causal inferences. That is, combining both approaches generates support for the argument that a specific factor impacts the findings of the study.

However, we offer a cautionary note. If scholars use CPT to complement COV, then they will be strongly tempted to search and/or present only those causal-process observations that fit the findings of the co-variational analysis. To cast off all such doubts, the investigator should specify ex ante and as precisely as possible what the causal path that connects the independent variable with the dependent variable looks like. Moreover, the investigator should anticipate any arguments claiming that other causal processes might have been at work here and should try to make observations related to those arguments.

5.2.2   Y-centered combination of cross-case comparisons and CPT

The aforementioned variant can be applied to studies examining the effect of a specific factor: X-centered research. COV is especially applicable in these studies. Can scholars who are interested in the causes of a specific outcome, Y-centered research, where CPT is especially applicable, also use the elements of the COV approach? They cannot if they follow the ideal-typical approach, because COV requires them to select cases that show *variation* on the *independent* variable. However, in the chapter on the co-variational design, we also briefly reviewed the method of agreement, where scholars select cases that have *similar* values for the *dependent* variable (that is, a common outcome). Because of this case selection criteria, the method of agreement falls outside of COV as defined in our book (see Chapter 2). However, the method of agreement can be useful for making causal inferences because it allows one to eliminate rival explanations (that is, those conditions that are not shared by cases with a common outcome). Applying the method of agreement can be a first step to reducing the number of possible explanations for the outcome of interest. Therefore, the method of agreement provides the preconditions for a more focused causal-process tracing.

To provide an example of this type of combination, we revisit Skocpol's (1979) study on social revolutions, which was presented in Chapter 3. Skocpol's study begins by comparing three cases with a common outcome: social revolutions. These cases are China (1911), France (1789), and Russia (1917). She selects the 'positive cases' (that is, cases in which the outcome is present) by examining their scores on the dependent variable. Then she applies Mill's logic regarding the method of agreement. That is, she identifies the conditions that these three cases have in common. She also eliminates the conditions that these cases do not share because these conditions have no explanatory power. Then she selects the 'negative cases'. She investigates the cases in which social unrest but no social revolutions occurred. These cases are quite similar in all other aspects as well. Specifically, she examines pre-revolutionary Russia (1905) as well as episodes of English, German, Japanese, and Prussian history (Skocpol 1979: 37). She shows that these cases in which revolution failed to occur have a number of conditions in common with the cases in which social revolutions occurred. By comparing the similarities, she proves that these conditions could not have caused the revolutions. She explains this argument in the following way:

> France, Russia and China will serve as three positive cases of success-ful social revolutions, and I shall argue that these cases reveal similar causal patterns despite their many other differences. In addition, I shall invoke negative cases for the purpose of validating various particular parts of the causal argument. In doing so, I shall always construct contrasts that maximize the similarities of the negative case(s) to the positive case(s) in every apparently relevant respect except the causal sequence that the contrast is supposed to validate.
>
> (Skocpol 1979: 37)

Through case comparisons based on the logic of agreement, Skocpol shows that a number of factors, such as relative deprivation and urban worker revolts, could not have caused the social revolutions (see also Mahoney 1999: 1160; Moses and Knutsen 2007: 103–6). In the rest of her study, she focuses on the factors that 'survived' the cross-case com-parison. These factors include the combination of 'conditions for state break down' and 'conditions for peasant revolt' (see also Mahoney 1999: 1158). She argues that social revolutions occur only if *both* conditions are present. Hence, she argues that a causal configuration serves as a necessary and sufficient condition for social revolutions.

As presented extensively in Chapter 3, Skocpol also shows *how* and *why* these conditions produce social revolutions. Hence, she engages in causal-process tracing. Skocpol herself argues that the cross-national comparison serves as a cornerstone of her research design. However, for many observers, her narrative analysis (that is, the reconstruction of the causal processes) renders her book a compelling treatment of revolutionary processes (Mahoney 1999: 1157; Sewell 2005: 97).

Skocpol's study shows that cross-case comparisons that involve the method of agreement can serve as the first step within a Y-oriented research project. The method of agreement allows one to eliminate a number of explanations. Additionally, within-case analysis based on causal-process observations strengthens the internal validity of the causal inference. This analysis provides a comprehensive storyline that includes both causal chains and causal conjunctions, which describe the exact process by which specific initial conditions lead to peasant revolts and state breakdowns. Together, these factors constitute the necessary and sufficient conditions that have enabled social revolutions to occur.

5.3   Combining congruence analysis and causal-process tracing

Another potentially fruitful combination of different approaches to case study research is the combination of congruence analysis and causal-process tracing. This combination can manifest itself in two different forms: (1) when CPT is embedded into the congruence analysis or (2) when CPT is added to the congruence analysis in a second distinct step.

5.3.1   Causal-process tracing as part of a congruence analysis

In the first variant, CPT is embedded into the congruence analysis. Many scholars who are applying a CON approach explicitly specify the causal propositions in the configurative and temporal language of causal chains and causal conjunctions. For these scholars, causal-process observations are necessary for determining the congruence between theoretical expectations and empirical reality. As a result, these scholars combine CPT and CON in their small-N studies.

Consider, for example, Moravcsik's study on EU integration, which we discussed in our chapter on congruence analysis. Moravcsik formulates the following hypotheses, which focus on the temporal order of events based on two competing theories (that is, the geopolitical and economic theories of national interest formation):

> Geopolitical theory: Shifts in preferences and policies follow the onset and precede the resolution of major geopolitical events that reveal new information. Generally we expect over time that concern about the USSR or colonies declines; concern about federalism may deepen.

> Political economic theory: Shifts in preferences and policies follow the onset and precede the resolution of major economic problems. Preferences for integration slowly intensify over time with rising trade flows, capital mobility, and policy convergence.

> (Moravcsik 1998: 28)

Moravcsik tests these competing predictions by using causal-process observations for all of the major countries and for all of the major steps of the European Integration process in the empirical chapters of his book. He summarizes his findings as follows:

> The timing of shifts in preferences and positions offers further support for the political economic theory. Important changes in the

priorities, policies, and preferences of national governments appear to have reflected shifts in the domestic and international economic environment. Examples include the clear impact of French devaluation in 1958 on business demands, the rapid British response to economic exclusion from the EC, and the response to global trends towards liberalization of service provision in the 1980s. [...] By contrast, important geopolitical events – the Suez Crisis of 1956, the founding of the French Fifth Republic in 1958, the collapse of the Fouchet Plan negotiations in 1962, the Anglo-American agreement at Nassau in 1963, [...] – do not seem to have led to expected shifts in national preferences concerning the EU.

(Moravcsik 1998: 475)

This summary shows that not only the timing of economic and geopolitical events but also the timing of changes in preferences and positions are critical to his argument. Accordingly, the kind of causal-process observations that we call 'confessions' play an important role in generating the necessary data for testing the competing propositions.

5.3.2 Causal-process tracing as an inductive addition to the deductive congruence analysis

Joachim Blatter (2009) applies congruence analysis and causal-process tracing in his study on international regulations designed to protect Lake Constance. His study shows that the CON approach follows the deductive logic involved in evaluating existing theories, whereas the CPT approach fits the inductive logic of theoretical innovation.

Lake Constance (Bodensee) is the third largest lake in Western Europe and lies on the borders of Germany, Switzerland, and Austria. The cooperation of these riparian states has led to an impressive record of environmental achievements in respect to the lake. Blatter's study focuses on the regulation of motorboats, which is a policy field that the overseers of Lake Constance pioneered. Blatter primarily aims to show that to understand the breakthrough in international environmental regulations at Lake Constance, scholars must move beyond the 'theories of international regimes' (RT). RT is a research program that dominated the study of international environmental regulation in North America and Europe from the 1980s to the beginning of the new century. This research program has developed a sophisticated and differentiated set of theoretical approaches to explain the emergence of international regulations in specific policy fields, where the field of water politics has played a major role (for example, Haggard and Simmons 1987; Hasenclever,

Mayer, and Rittberger 1996). Furthermore, RT researchers have accumulated an impressive amount of empirical knowledge (for example, Breitmeier, Young, and Zürn 2006).

In the first part of his study, Blatter applies the entire set of explanatory approaches established within the RT literature. Based on each theoretical approach, he deduces the specific necessary and sufficient conditions required to produce an international regulatory agreement and compares his predictions with the empirical realities of the case.

First, he examines the rationalist approaches. All rationalist or interest-based approaches are based on a functionalist background. In contrast to simple Functionalism in which international cooperation is explained by 'problem pressure' (that is, the functional need for regulation), rationalists believe that the need for regulation is a necessary but insufficient precondition to the rise of an international regime. Rationalists assume that joint regulations occur only in 'problematic situations', where various interdependencies induce all of the actors involved to cooperate to maximize their own interests. In these situations, the rational pursuit of individual interests can lead not only to collectively irrational results but also to suboptimal results from the viewpoint of the individual actors. Conversely, cooperation can produce superior results. In the international field, a 'problematic situation' (that is, strong transboundary interdependencies) must exist before international regulations can emerge. Nevertheless, to constitute sufficient conditions, 'problem pressure' and 'problematic situations' must be combined with additional structural conditions that facilitate the creation of international law. Based on the literature on RT, Blatter constructs three specifications of rationalist theories by complementing the two core conditions with different structural conditions: a 'situation structuralist' perspective, a 'multi-level game' approach and a 'realist' conceptualization. For example, within the situation structuralist approach, 'problem pressure' and a 'problematic situation' must be complemented by an interest constellation among the riparian states that facilitates cooperation. An upstream–downstream situation that results in an asymmetric interest constellation hinders the creation of joint regulations. In contrast, a situation in which all sides profit from regulation and all sides must pay a similar price renders joint regulations feasible.

In his empirical chapters, Blatter (2009: 85–91) addresses the two core conditions that constitute the necessary elements in all rationalist explanations. First, he argues that the two major environmental problems

associated with motorboats (that is, the destruction of valuable ecosys-
tems and the pollution of the water with toxic substances) lacked either
the 'problem pressure' or the 'problematic situation' element. Next, he
addresses the complementary conditions and shows that there were no
interest constellations, multilevel structures with environmentally oriented gatekeepers or hegemonic actors. As a result, Blatter dismisses the
rationalist explanations.

Next, Blatter (2009: 91–6) analyzes social constructivist approaches.
Initially, he examines the established approaches (that is, informational, cognitive, and normative approaches) within RT. He discovers
that the predictions drawn from these approaches are more congruent
with empirical observations. For example, the cognitive approach draws
on the existence of transnational and transgovernmental 'epistemic
communities' strongly oriented toward the environment. Blatter finds
that this approach explains to a considerable degree why policymakers
placed and kept the motorboat issue on the cross-border political
agenda. However, in comparison with the 'Advocacy Coalition Framework' (ACF; Sabatier and Jenkins-Smith 1993) (that is, an approach
from outside the domain of RT), the 'epistemic community' approach
provided a far less complete picture of the reality at Lake Constance.
The congruence between the expectations deduced from the ACF and
the group and belief formation processes observed at Lake Constance
was quite high. Nevertheless, this approach failed to explain when
and why riparian states actually agreed on binding and demanding
standards.

Overall, the results of the congruence analysis revealed that the
ACF, which was developed to explain policy changes in the domestic
realm, showed a higher level of congruence than all of the explanatory approaches within RT. For the theoretical discourse, this finding
is important because it indicates that the differences between domestic policy making and international policy making might no longer
be strong enough to justify the existence of distinct theories and
explanatory approaches in international relations (IR).

Nevertheless, a gap in the explanation of the regulations at Lake
Constance still existed. To address this point, Blatter pursued other
theoretical explanations. After using a deductive CON approach to show
that all of the existing explanatory approaches could not explain the
cross-border motorboat regulations, Blatter (2009: 96–100) developed
an alternative inductive explanation of cross-border regulations drawing on causal-process observations. First, he recounts the history of
the joint regulations while emphasizing the temporal orders of the

potential causal conditions and regulatory outcomes. By doing so, he shows that the two breakthroughs in the joint regulations did not occur when the environmental debate on motorboats peaked. Instead, they occurred when the idea of Euroregion-building reached the shorelines of Lake Constance, and various cross-border networks competed to represent the *Euregio Bodensee*. The temporal contiguity between Euregion-building and the regulatory breakthroughs and the non-contiguity between the environmental discourse and the regulations provide the first empirical evidence for the alternative explanation.

Because Blatter provides additional causal-process observations to bolster his claim that we must examine the general (that is, not specific to any policy) relationship among the riparian political entities in order to understand why international environmental regulations were created. First, he shows in detail how the Internationale Bodenseekonferenz (IBK), a network of government leaders from the German and Austrian Länder and the Swiss Cantons around the lake, helped pave the way toward a joint agreement. Blatter finds that the regional IBK presented the second breakthrough in the negotiations to the public instead of the International Commission of Navigation for Lake Constance, which was formally in charge of regulating the motorboats on the lake. We can interpret this observation as a 'smoking-gun observation'. It clearly depicts the dense link between Euregion-building and motorboat regulation. Second, Blatter presents evidence that resembles 'confessions'. He finds that the IBK announcement calls the regulations 'pioneering work' and indicates that these 'regions are of special importance in Europe, they give important impulses and offer solutions' (Blatter 2009: 100). Blatter uses this quote to support his claim that the IBK was motivated to address the highly symbolic issue of motorboat regulation primarily because the IBK wished to gain attention and recognition as an emerging political entity.

Next, Blatter connects his empirical findings to abstract theoretical concepts. He argues that the IBK's motivation is best captured by the theoretical concept of 'performance'. Drawn from cultural sociology, this concept claims that (political) actors perform symbolic actions to receive attention and recognition. Performative actions are especially warranted in transformational situations in which the existing political entities (for example, nation states) are challenged by new entities (for example, cross-border regions) and in which a new entity aims to obtain recognition and legitimacy by presenting itself as a problem solver. The action-formation mechanism of performance will only lead to cross-border regulation during the periods in which cross-border cooperation is perceived to be positive in the public discourse. In our methodological terminology, Blatter theorized his explanation by introducing a situational mechanism (that is, discourses that emphasize polity transformations), an action-formation mechanism (that is, entities perform symbolic actions to receive attention and recognition), and a transformational mechanism (that is, because cross-border regional identities trump national identities, no actor can continue to block the regulations).

In the last sections of his study, Blatter reflects on the wider empirical and the broader theoretical relevance of his findings. He shows that his causal mechanism likely played a helpful role in other fields of environmental cooperation at Lake Constance. Furthermore, he points to a diverse set of international water regulations in which the causal mechanism appears to have worked as well (that is, the River Rhine and Elbe water regimes). He does not claim that performance is a necessary or a sufficient condition for all international water regulations. His reflections on the broader theoretical relevance of his findings correspond to the manner through which we generalize within the CON approach. One conclusion indicates that his findings point to additional social and causal mechanisms complementing the other approaches within Regime Theory (RT). Another conclusion suggests that the findings undermine the adequacy of the functionalist, policy-oriented, paradigmatic framework that underlies RT. In the context of this methodological reflection, it is important to note that the second conclusion draws generalizations based on a higher level of abstraction than the first conclusion because the second conclusion not only contributes to the established approaches within a research program but also questions the core concepts of this research program. Additionally, this conclusion points to other promising theoretical frameworks and paradigmatic anchor points that exist beyond this program.

In sum, the COV and CON approaches profit significantly by adding causal-process tracing. From a methodological point of view, pursuing the different approaches sequentially would be optimal. Unfortunately, the current publication context hinders attempts to combine divergent case study approaches in this manner because one requires extensive space to present the empirical findings of case study research, especially within the CPT approach. Most journals that apply strict word limits are no longer willing to provide the space needed for this task. The current trend toward electronic journals might help overcome this structural impediment for case study research.

5.4 Connecting case studies to large-N studies

The previous sections showed how different case study approaches can be combined. However, combining case studies with large-N or medium-N studies may also be useful. In this section, we focus on the combination of small-N and large-N studies. In the next section (5.5), we will examine combinations of small-N and medium-N studies. Case study approaches can be combined with large-N designs in two ways. The case study must either augment the large-N study or precede the large-N study.

5.4.1 Case studies augmenting large-N studies

To combine case studies with large-N studies, an investigator can perform a multivariate regression analysis or a similar analysis and then conduct a case study. The case selection in the small-N study is based on the results of the large-N study. The first reason for this combined design is to increase the internal validity of the research. Through the multivariate regression, the scholar can establish the causal effect of a series of independent variables. The case study provides evidence concerning the causal pathway. As we discussed in the context of the COV approach, the concept of causality typically involves three elements: co-variation between variables, temporal ordering (that is, the cause needs to precede the effect), and control for alternative explanations. We also added the causal pathway to this list of elements. Given that all other variables are held constant, one can interpret the difference in the dependent variable observed in a co-variational design (that is, most similar systems design) as the causal effect of the independent variable. This effect is similar to the causal effect estimated in a large-N study based on multivariate regressions or related techniques. Through a multivariate regression, one can establish the average change in the value of the dependent variable associated with the change in one unit of the independent variable while controlling for other variables (see also Seawright and Collier 2004: 275–6). The regression coefficient of the respective variable (β) provides the size of the causal effect. Unlike case studies based on COV, large-N research can measure the effect of a series of independent variables rather than one independent variable because it is built on a larger number of cases and does not depend on control through case selection.

However, identifying statistically significant effects provides no guarantee that the theoretical explanation given for the effect is valid or that the hypothesized causal pathway is correct. The causal effect might have worked by using a different pathway than the one considered by the investigator. In this sense, no difference exists between COV and large-N research (see Section 5.2). Gerring (2007a: 45–8) presents a number of examples in which case studies have cast doubt on the connection between the independent variable and the dependent variable assumed in large-N research. One of these examples concerns research into democratization. The existence of a robust, statistically significant relationship shows that former British colonies are, on average, more democratic than countries colonized by another country. Scholars have argued that this relationship is due to a diffusion effect – that is, the transfer of British governmental and representative institutions and the tutoring of the colonial people in the ways of British government (Rueschemeyer and Stephens 1997: 62). However, intensive case studies conducted by Dietrich Rueschemeyer and John Stephens revealed that the association between British colonialism and democracy is only partially due to diffusion effects. On this point, the researchers wrote, '[t]he interaction of class forces, state power and colonial policy must be brought in to fully account for the statistical results' (Rueschemeyer and Stephens 1997: 62).

As stated previously, one of the major strengths of case study research is that it can reveal the traces of causal mechanisms and causal pathways. Thus, after establishing the causal effects, a researcher can conduct case studies to find direct empirical evidence showing that the causal mechanisms or the hypothesized causal pathway has worked as assumed (see also George and Bennett 2005: 35; Fearon and Laitin 2008: 756–9). In other words, the research nests the case study research into the large-N research.

Evan S. Lieberman (2005) was one of the first researchers to explicitly show what a nested design should look like. We mostly follow his template. First, a scholar conducts a large-N study. If the multivariate model yields a robust and statistically significant relationship between the independent variables and the dependent variable results, then the researcher can conduct a case study. Note that if the multivariate model has weak predictive power, then the researcher should not nest a case study in it. If there is no causal effect, then there is no causal pathway. In that case, the researcher would be better off conducting an explorative case study before testing a (new) multivariate model (see below).

Second, the researcher needs to select a case (or cases) that is (are) accurately predicted by that model. Even if the model achieves robust results, it may not accurately predict all of the possible cases. However, because the researcher aims to determine whether the causal pathways have unfolded as expected, the researcher does not need to focus on the cases that the model has failed to explain (see the reasons for focusing on weakly predicted cases below).

To identify the accurately predicted cases, the researcher can plot the scores of the dependent variable against the scores predicted by the model. The resulting graph is the so-called 'regression-line'. Then the researcher needs to select cases whose actual values are close to the predicted values (that is, 'on-the-line' cases, 'small residuals', or 'typical cases') (Lieberman 2005: 444; Seawright and Gerring 2008: 229–30; Rohlfing and Schneider 2011: 14).

Ingo Rohlfing and Carsten Q. Schneider argue that researchers should apply a clear-cut criterion as to whether a case is a typical case or a deviant case. This is because once the working of the hypothesized causal pathway can be confirmed for one or two cases, the result can be generalized to all other typical cases, but not to the deviant cases (Rohlfing and Schneider 2011: 14). While Lieberman proposes to work with standard deviations for the distance of a case to the predicted value, Rohlfing and Schneider propose to use prediction interval for classifying cases into typical and deviant cases.

Regarding the number of cases selected, Lieberman suggests that scholars should choose more than one case and that these cases should vary on the values of the independent variables that are central to the model. On this point, he states the following:

> By selecting cases with varied scores on the explanatory variables, the scholar can use SNA [Small-N Analysis, JB and MH] to demonstrate the nature of the predicted causal effects associated with the model on contrasting contexts.
>
> (Lieberman 2005: 444)

Take Fearon and Laitin's argument concerning the causes of civil war. We briefly reviewed this study in Chapter 2. Fearon and Laitin (2008) argue that per capita income can be seen as a proxy for a state's capacity. The researchers delineate the expected causal pathway for both rich states and weak states.

> Thus we would expect to find that in rich states nascent insurgent groups are detected and easily crushed by the police [...], while in poor states we should find would-be insurgent groups surviving and

growing due to the states' incompetence [...] and virtually absence from parts of their territory.

(Fearon and Laitin 2008: 763)[2]

In other words, the researchers argue that the existence of insurgent groups is a necessary condition for civil war. However, this condition is not a sufficient one. Only if the state lacks the capabilities needed to establish a counterinsurgency can these groups develop into a powerful enemy of the state and engage in a civil war. Otherwise, the state contains or even destroys these groups. By showing that insurgent groups are successfully controlled by the police in rich states but not in poor states, the researchers can make their claims more compelling.

Fearon and Laitin leave open the question whether these well-predicted cases vary on other explanatory variables as well. We would caution against the advice to choose well-predicted cases that vary on many different explanatory variables. We would rather side with Rohlfing and Schneider who argue that cases should be selected that vary on the independent variable of interest and – by implication – the dependent variable, but not on other independent variables (Rohlfing and Schneider 2011: 20). Following the logic of our COV approach, this mode of case selection allows to isolate the causal pathway of the independent variable of interest, as the other independent variables could not have caused the different values of the dependent variable. Which independent variable is of interest is up to the researcher, but it should be a variable that is statistically significant; hence a variable that according to statistical conventions has been shown to have an independent effect on the dependent variable.

In short, an intensive study of one or a few well-predicted cases can help scholars enter the 'black box' between the independent variables and the dependent variable. Scholars can employ a detailed analysis of accurately predicted cases to reveal whether the hypothesized causal mechanisms actually work in these cases.

In addition, researchers might be interested in the cases that are located off the regression line, hence 'large residuals' or 'deviant cases' (Seawright and Gerring 2008: 302–3; Rohlfing and Schneider 2011: 22). These poorly predicted cases are also called 'outliers'. Many large-N studies treat outliers as a nuisance or as non-relevant anomalies that may have been produced by measurement errors. Under certain circumstances, scholars drop these cases from the sample and re-run their analysis. However, as Lijphart has argued in his 1971 methodological article on case studies, scholars may consider studying deviant cases if their goal is to identify hitherto omitted explanatory variables that may help expand the population of well-explained cases.

As in the previous design, a scholar nests a case study into a large-N study. The investigator conducts a comprehensive large-N research to test for the causal effect of a series of potentially relevant variables based on the existing theories in his or her field of study. After performing the analysis, the researcher plots the actual values of the dependent variable against the line capturing the predicted values.

In contrast to the previous design, the researcher selects a case (or cases) that is (are) not explained by the model. In other words, the researcher conducts a case study of the deviant cases. How can the scholar explain these outcomes? The research goal becomes Y-oriented. The researcher investigates the details of the case in an inductive manner to uncover variables that have been disregarded or to follow hunches that have not yet resulted in well-specified and measurable variables (Lijphart 1971: 692; George and Bennett 2005: 34; Lieberman 2005: 445–6; Gerring 2007a: 105–15; Rohlfing and Schneider 2011: 16).

Although Lijphart defined the deviant case study as a single case study, it can also be conducted as a comparative case study. For instance, two or more deviant cases may cluster together in the scatterplot. By comparing these cases with cases that are well explained (that is, cases that are close to the 'line'), one might inductively determine the theoretically meaningful differences between the two groups of cases. Suppose that an investigator is interested in determining the causes of economic wealth in a country. His model relies heavily on regime type. He finds a positive relationship between democracies and wealth. However, there are also a number of countries clustered together that are wealthy without being democratic. By comparing this group of countries with the well-explained countries, he discovers that the former consists of oil-producing countries. Hence, his deviant case analysis has enabled him to identify a new wealth-creating factor: the provision of oil. The researcher can include this factor in a new multivariate model that likely better fits the cases.[3]

Note that some authors, including Fearon and Laitin (2008), argue that scholars should not deliberately select the cases that are 'on' or 'off' the regression line. Instead, the scholars should randomly select their cases because deliberate selection may lead to selection bias. The researcher may select cases that he or she knows relatively well, and these cases may have been on the researcher's mind when he or she developed his or her causal model in the first place (Fearon and Laitin

2008: 764–6). We sympathize with this view, but we also note that the suggested alternative may pose many practical difficulties. Following the alternative method, the researcher may select cases in which the investigator has difficulty accessing sufficient high-quality data to convincingly classify the cases (necessary for a co-variational analysis) or to generate a 'comprehensive storyline' that includes 'smoking guns' and 'confessions' (necessary for causal-process tracing).

5.4.2 Case studies preceding large-N studies

In some instances, a researcher may prefer to conduct the case study before conducting the large-N study. For example, consider a case study based on COV. In this case, the investigator aims to establish the causal effect of a specific factor. The investigator must control for the rival explanations by holding the factors suggested by these explanations constant. To do so, he selects cases in which these variables have similar scores. Careful case selection increases the internal validity of the research. At the same time, the researcher only establishes the causal effect of the variable in these most similar systems. As discussed in Chapter 2, Haverland showed that the number of veto points affects the degree to which countries adapt to the environmental obligations set by the European Union (EU). However, he has only established this effect for the rich, technologically advanced and environmentally conscious EU member states. As a result, the findings may only be generalizable to a relatively small population. In other words, the external validity of the results is limited.

A researcher may choose to prioritize internal validity over external validity if he or she is interested in a specific case. For instance, if the researcher is evaluating the effect of a specific policy change or an innovation in a specific organization and if he or she only uses the other case (or cases) as a control case, then the researcher may choose to focus on the internal validity of his or her study.

The researcher may also choose to focus on internal validity if his or her study is a plausibility probe. Eckstein provides the following definition of a plausibility probe:

> In essence, plausibility probes involve attempts to determine whether potential validity may reasonably be considered great enough to warrant the pain and costs of testing, which are almost always considerable, but especially so if broad, painstaking comparative studies are undertaken.
>
> (Eckstein 1975: 108)

Eckstein discusses Almond and Verba's five-country comparison *The Civic Culture* as an example of a plausibility probe. He describes their study as 'hardly large and dubiously representative' (Eckstein 1975: 110). This study probes the researchers' argument concerning the relationship between a country's political culture and its degree of political stability. However, the study is neither large enough nor sufficiently representative to serve as a definitive test of their argument.

Hence, comparing a few cases may well serve their goal of probing the validity of their argument about the effect of a certain factor. Because the results show that the factor affects the cases being compared, the investigator may have sufficient reason to engage in a large-N study. Researchers may utilize random selection to show that they can discern the causal effect while examining a sample that is representative of a larger population. By doing so, the researchers increase the external validity of their study (see also George and Bennett 2005: 35).

For example, consider how Haverland's study on the impact of institutional veto points fits within the development of studies on the EU. In the 1990s, a few researchers interested in the EU decided to stop analyzing European integration (that is, the scope and degree of the delegation of authority from member states to the EU) in favor of studying the effect of the EU on its member states. Scholars have labeled this research perspective 'Europeanization research'. This research raised several questions. To what extent and in which direction does the EU shape its member states' policies, structures and processes? Which factors determine the degree to which the member states adapt to the EU directives? Which factors can explain the cross-national differences that soon became recognized? To be sure, prominent theories in Comparative Public Policy and Public Administration may have been usable. However, rather than engaging in large-N studies, the researchers adapted the existing theories to the new phenomenon and probed these explanations by conducting comparative case studies. Christoph Knill and Andrea Lenschow were some of the first scholars who conducted a systematic comparative case study. They examined the fate of a number of environmental directives in Germany and the United Kingdom (UK) and found that the degree of fit between the national status quo and the European requirements affected the degree to which the member states adapted to the EU directives (for example, Knill and Lenschow 1998). Haverland's study examined another environmental directive and compared Germany, the Netherlands, and the UK. He found that rather than the degree of fit, the existence of veto points impacted the countries' degree of adaptation. One can view both studies as plausibility probes for their respective arguments. Once the researchers were able to demonstrate that these variables have effects in the small-N setting, they became promising candidates for large-N testing. Accordingly, scholars have used both factors in large-N studies focusing on a much broader and diverse sample of cases and, hence, have increased the generalizability of the results (see, for instance, Linos 2007).

5.5 Connecting case studies to medium-N studies

Since Charles Ragin published *The Comparative Method: Moving beyond Qualitative and Quantitative Strategies* (1987), Qualitative Comparative Analysis (QCA), which was later renamed as Crisp Set QCA (csQCA), and further refined as fuzzy set QCA (fsQCA), has become known as a 'third way' or 'middle ground' between case studies (small-N) and large-N studies (see, for example, Rihoux and Ragin 2009). Charles Ragin introduced QCA to fill the gap between case studies that include fewer than 6 cases and statistical analysis that contains more than 80 cases (Ragin 2000: 21–30).[4]

The approach is based on the same type of configurational thinking introduced in Chapter 3, where we discussed causal-process tracing. To recap, configurational thinking assumes that almost all social outcomes are caused by a combination of causal factors, that divergent pathways to similar social outcomes exist (equifinality), and that the effects of the same causal factor may differ depending on the context and combination (causal heterogeneity) (Ragin 2008: 109–46). Whereas CPT applies configurational thinking within cases, QCA performs cross-case analysis. Accordingly, we expected to find empirical studies combining QCA and CPT. As we show in Table 5.1, one can use CPT in a second study to test the internal causal validity of the findings from a QCA study. In order to do so, one has to select a typical case for those causal configurations which have high levels of coverage and consistency (for a more detailed elaboration on how to select cases after a QCA, see Rohlfing and Schneider 2011). However, we could not find any sound study that uses CPT for this purpose (Rohlfing and Schneider cannot point to existing case studies that follow their methodological advices). What we found is a study (Emmenegger 2011a) that applies CPT for the investigation of a 'contradictory case' (that is, cases that exhibit the same causal configuration but different outcomes) to identify additional conditions that must be fulfilled to produce certain outcomes (Rihoux and de Meur 2009: 48–56).

Much more common is a combination in which case studies are conducted prior to a QCA analysis. In this combination, a scholar first conducts the case study with a few cases as a plausibility probe. Next, the scholar determines whether the causal configuration(s) revealed in the small-N study is(are) necessary and sufficient for producing a specific type of outcome by employing QCA and a larger, more diverse set of cases. Another common combination (for example, Johnson 2005) uses case studies to generate data within a study that applies QCA to perform data analysis.[5] However, this kind of combination misses the opportunities for revealing causal insights that case study approaches exhibit in addition to QCA. Since it is much more common we start with an example in which the case study precedes QCA.

5.5.1 Qualitative Comparative Analysis as a follow-up to case studies

Fritz Sager (2002, 2005, 2006) applied case studies and QCA to determine which institutional settings provide fruitful conditions for generating and implementing integrated land use and transport policies in metropolitan areas. Based on two competing paradigms within the metropolitan governance literature (that is, the progressive model and the public choice model), Sager identifies four major institutional factors of influence (that is, organizational centralization, territorial consolidation, professionalization, and autonomy of the bureaucracy) and deduces four sets of competing hypotheses. Furthermore, he develops a differentiated set of dependent variables (that is, formal rationality, substantial rationality, and implementation). In his first step, he tests the hypotheses by using a case study design. While referring to Lijphart's comparable cases strategy (that is, the most similar systems design; see Chapter 2) Sager selects four Swiss metropolitan areas that are similar in many respects but different in their institutional features (Sager 2002: 84). Furthermore, within these four metropolitan areas, he first investigates six political decision-making processes, which constitute the 'most similar cases', and later analyzes three more cases such that he has a total of nine cases (Sager 2002: 107, 165). In the empirical chapters, he proceeds as follows. First, Sager describes in detail the outcome of each case and aggregates the scores for the divergent dependent variables into one aggregate outcome. Second, he conducts a limited type of congruence analysis for each case to determine to what degree the four causal conditions and the outcome correspond with the progressive model or with the public choice model. Third, he evaluates the causal hypotheses based on a cross-case analysis that uses dyadic scores and cross-tabulation. For most of his hypotheses, he finds a strong co-variation among the cases, but the co-variation is almost never fully deterministic. For example, with respect to the influence of the bureaucracy's autonomy on the implementation process, three cases show that the administration is autonomous and that the implementation is successful. Conversely, in four cases, the bureaucracy is not autonomous, and the implementation was not successful. Based on these seven cases, Sager concludes that the progressive hypothesis is confirmed, though two examples do not follow this hypothesis. Finally, Sager conducts additional analysis to determine how the different dependent variables relate to each other. His most important finding is that organizations only implement substantially rational solutions if these solutions have been developed in formally rational processes, if the organizational structure is centralized and if the bureaucracy has a high level of autonomy (Sager 2002: 246).

In a later publication, Sager (2005) used QCA to analyze the same cases. The QCA technique allows him to more precisely present the results. For example, he shows that organizational centralization is a necessary condition to implementing substantially rational solutions but that an autonomous bureaucracy is not. Specifically, he found successful cases in which an organization lacks an autonomous bureaucracy but compensates for its absence through strong territorial consolidation (Sager 2002: 245). However, for another important finding, Sager (2002: 244–5, 2005: 246–7) needs the insights gained through the case study analysis in order to show that an additional explanatory factor conditionalizes the positive effect of professionalization on the implementation of substantially rational solutions. An organization will implement a solution only if the professional experts who formulated the solution are located within a public administration (that is, the experts are not private consultants).

In a second QCA study that analyzed 17 cases from 9 different West European countries, Sager applied his theory to a large and more diverse population to determine its generalizability (Sager 2006). By doing so, he confirmed the results from the first study. Emboldened by his conclusions, Sager argues that 'the results [...] show that well coordinated policy decisions are only implemented in institutional settings that correspond to the progressive model, thus promoting this model rather than the public choice model' (Sager 2006: 433).

Overall, this example indicates that a QCA can complement a case study analysis in two different respects. First, it can be applied as a different technique for analyzing the same cases. Doing so reveals the comparative strengths and weaknesses of the divergent methods of data analysis. That is, whereas QCA generates more logical stringency, case studies allow for more comprehensive explanations and reveal new factors of influence, which are highly relevant for practitioners. Second, scholars can use QCA studies to test whether the given explanation also applies to further cases. Note that QCA can cope with more cases than a case study and these cases can be less similar in comparison to the cases needed to apply a co-variational analysis.

5.5.2   Case studies as a follow-up to a Qualitative Comparative Analysis

Patrick Emmenegger's (2010, 2011a) work on job security regulations in Western democracies represents a combination of medium-N and small-N studies that is still rare: He conducts case studies as a follow-up to a QCA analysis and uses the results of the QCA analysis in order to select useful cases for a focused causal-process tracing. The goal of the case study is to explain the liberal regulations in Denmark, which represents a contradictory or non-consistent case in respect to the findings of the QCA analysis (Emmenegger 2011a). According to the QCA analysis which included 19 Western democracies, the existence of high levels of non-market coordination, strong labor movements, moderately strong religious parties, and few institutional veto points represents one of three identified causal configurations that lead to a high level of job security regulations.[6] Denmark displays all these conditions but did not follow the other Nordic countries toward a high level of job security regulation. Instead Denmark exhibits what has become famous as 'flexicurity': the combination of liberal job regulations (which makes hiring and firing easy) and generous unemployment insurance benefits. First, by applying within-case and cross-case analysis Emmenegger shows that 'flexicurity' cannot be explained by functionalist arguments and has not been the result of a 'grand strategy'. Rather, it is the result of a 'non-event' (Emmenegger 2011a): in contrast to other Scandinavian countries Denmark did not turn toward higher job security regulations at the end of the 1960s and the beginning of the 1970s. Using Sweden as a comparative case that exhibits the same causal configuration as Denmark and high levels of job security regulations (hence, a consistent case for the Nordic path) helps in various ways to focus the tracing of the causal process in Denmark. First, the comparison makes it possible to identify the time when the regulatory paths of the two countries diverged, and second, the Swedish case provides a template of necessary and jointly sufficient factors for a successful turn toward higher regulations (Emmenegger 2011a: 19 contains a figure that nicely visualizes the causal chain of necessary and sufficient conditions in the Swedish case). With the help of this template, Emmenegger is able to identify the small but crucial differences between the two countries in respect to the strength of leftist parties and in respect to time when the unions changed their strategy. Crucially important for the failure to turn toward higher job security regulations in Denmark was the fact that the unions changed their strategy (from attempts to achieve stronger regulations through collective bargaining with the employers to reach their goals by demanding public legislation) some years later than the Swedish unions and at that time the window of opportunity had been closed because the leftist coalition government in Denmark (which has always been weaker than the corresponding leftist government in Sweden) lost its majority in the 1973 election (Emmenegger 2010: 283–8).

Two insights should be stressed when we reflect on how causal inferences are drawn in Emmenegger's case study:

– The cross-case comparison helps not only to exclude many theoretically possible explanations for the outcome in Denmark (in contrast to Emmenegger we would not call it a most similar systems design because the analysis is not X-centered but Y-centered), but is also very helpful in identifying causal chains and causal conjunctions, which represent temporal configurations of necessary and jointly sufficient causal conditions. Emmenegger's case selection corresponds to the advice that Rohlfing and Schneider (2011) provide.
– Nevertheless, the main epistemological fundament for drawing causal inferences remains in the within-case analysis and the cogency of Emmenegger's conclusion is based to a large part on a dense description of the temporal unfolding of events (including reflections on the perceptions and anticipations of actors).

Overall, currently we are witnessing an explosion of methodological reflections on how small-N, and large-N, or medium-N studies can and should be combined. Combinations that exhibit explicit methodological reflections are still rare, though. Hopefully, the forgoing sections help to overcome this situation.

5.6   Preconditions for combining different explanatory approaches

The discussion above implicitly assumes that a single researcher executes the combined research design. However, combining a case study and a large-N study is demanding if one wants to perform both tasks well. On this point, Frieder Wolf argued the following:

> Keeping track of the latest refinements of quantitative modeling and multiple regression estimation technique – requiring a non-trivial level of econometric understanding as well as the maintenance of large databases – at the same time as immersing oneself into the intricacies of several cases – usually requiring language skills as well as securing and digesting vast amounts of primary sources and cultivating contacts with expert interview partners – places a considerable burden on the shoulders of researchers.
>
> (Wolf 2010: 147)

Therefore, we emphasize that a combined research design does not need to be conducted by a single researcher. Several researchers who bring their own special skills and assets can collaborate to execute this design. Researchers can also conduct this type of study sequentially over a longer period of time, during which different researchers address the same research debate. George and Bennett (2005) illustrate this point by examining the history of research on the debate over inter-democratic peace. In the first phase of research (that is, from 1960 to 1985), scholars were involved in large-N studies. They examined the correlation between regime type and war and found that democracies engage in wars as often as other types of governments. However, democracies do not commit to war against each other. Hence, these scholars comprehensively showed that democracies do not fight each other. However, these analyses could not explain *why* democracies do not fight each other. Because of their advantages in the areas of measurement validity, the reconstruction of processes and causal heterogeneity, the case studies that were conducted in the 1980s and 1990s were able to shed light on the causal mechanism (George and Bennett 2005: 37–59). Nevertheless, if a division of labor exists, then George and Bennett are correct in arguing the following:

> Effective collaboration requires that even as researchers become expert in one methodological approach, they must also become conversant with alternative approaches, aware of the strengths and

limitation, and able to make informed reading of their substantive results.

(George and Bennett 2005: 35)

5.7   Final remarks

We have now arrived at the end of our book and feel that we have come full circle. We started by embedding case study research into the overall methodological debate over research designs. We then provided a definition of a case study and extensively laid out the foundations and elements of three approaches.

A core message of this book is that there exist not only one or two ways for conducting case study research but that it makes sense to distinguish three different approaches. Such a differentiated typology of case study approaches allows for consistent alignments of research goals/questions, epistemological fundaments, rules of selecting cases (and theories), ways to generate data and to draw causal inferences, and understandings and directions of drawing conclusions beyond the investigated cases (generalization). The various approaches have clear affinities to specific research fields and (sub-)disciplines; for example, those who do research in Comparative Politics will almost certainly feel an affinity to the COV approach, whereas IR scholars probably are more comfortable with the CON approach. If it is true, as we argued in the introduction, that the boundaries between (sub-)disciplines are getting perforated, then those scholars who have a broader spectrum of theories and methods at their disposal will certainly profit.

It has to be stressed though that the perforation of boundaries should not be accompanied by fuzziness and unreflected 'mixtures' of theories or methods. Our book makes clear why causal-process tracing has become such a hot issue among case study researchers: because it can play an important role in all case study approaches. In order to make causal-process tracing a helpful complement to other approaches, we not only need a clearly specified understanding of what causal-process tracing is but also an understanding of causal-process tracing that has the capacity to really complement the deductive COV and CON approaches. We think that pointing to the critical realist epistemological fundament and comparatively narrow definitions of causal-process tracing and causal mechanisms is more useful in this respect than the broad understandings of causal-process tracing and causal mechanisms that we find in other methodological treaties on case studies.

Nevertheless, we try to strike a careful balance between emphasizing the productivity of differentiation and distinction, and the pragmatic need for combinations. The last chapter pointed to fruitful ways to combine these approaches and to connect them with large-N studies and medium-N studies. Although we have emphasized the advantages and possibilities of case study research, we believe that a better understanding of the social world ultimately requires not only small-N, medium-N, and large-N research individually but also sensitive combinations of all three types of research.

Notes

1 Relevance and Refinements of Case Studies

1. In principle, this corresponds to the main message of Gary Goertz and James Mahoney (forthcoming), who show that in the social sciences there are 'quantitative' and 'qualitative' cultures or paradigms that have distinct epistemological roots and different practices of concept formation and of drawing inferences. Internally, these cultures or paradigms are coherent. For case study research, we think that it makes more sense to distinguish three and not only two approaches. Using the term 'approach' instead of 'paradigm' points to the fact that we see the three case study approaches not as distinct as the two cultures that Goertz and Mahoney scrutinize, but as partly overlapping and complementary.

2 Co-Variational Analysis

1. The contrast between X-centered and Y-centered research is also called 'factor-centric' versus 'outcome-centric' research designs (Gschwend and Schimmelfennig 2007: 7–8), the 'effect of a cause' approach to explanation versus the 'causes of an effect' approach (Mahoney and Goertz 2006: 230), and 'forward looking' versus 'backward looking' (Scharpf 1997: 22–7; see also Ganghof 2005).
2. In addition, studies that select on the dependent variable may end up with no variation in the independent variable or with more than one independent variable that varies. This would imply that the logic of our co-variational approach would not lead to identifying the cause of the difference in the dependent variable. Selection on the dependent variable is however in line with causal-process tracing that assumes causal configurations.
3. Strictly speaking, the term 'spatial' denotes a geographical situation: different regions, countries, or communities. Here, it is used more loosely. It can also denote entities such as different companies, organizations, or leaders, even though they are located in the same geographical area.
4. This book is about case studies, which imply an intensive form of research. This means that investigators can only focus on a few cases. Note that cross-sectional and intertemporal designs can also be used for a large number of cases. Such designs, however, can be more aptly labeled quasi-experiments. Hence, in line with the logic presented here, one can compare, for instance, many cases of government reform with many cases of non-reform to establish the effect of reforms (comparison group design; see, for example, Lyons and Lowery 1989 for an application); or one does not compare two cases over time, but takes each year as a 'case' (the interrupted time series design, see Cook and Campbell 1979); or one combines both into a

multiple interrupted time series design (see Meier 1980 for a helpful application). Such research is necessarily more superficial regarding individual cases. It is not possible, for instance, to know each case well enough to use context-sensitive indicators (see Section 5.2). Therefore, these are not case studies as understood in this book and fall outside of its scope.

5. This description of this hypothetical study is informed by Gerring's discussion of a real study by Abada and Gardeazabal (see Gerring 2007a: 159–60).

6. There are a number of comprehensive treatments of Mill's method of difference, his method of agreement, and ways to combine these (see, for instance, Frendreis 1983; Faure 1994).

7. See also Chapter 5, where we discuss the combination of case study approaches that Skocpol (1979) uses. She begins her analysis with cases selected on the scores of the dependent variable and in accordance with the method of agreement and then proceeds by using causal-process tracing.

8. Some readers might find the distinction between prior knowledge and theories artificial and redundant. We have chosen to make this distinction because we develop a precise definition of theory in Chapter 4. This definition distinguishes theory from paradigmatic perspectives (on a higher level of abstraction) and from empirical predictions (on a lower level of abstraction). These distinctions should also clarify that within a COV approach one does not need 'theories' to fulfill these functions, even though, for the coherence of the scientific debate, it should be the preferred source for these functions.

9. If theoretical reasoning does not lead to a conclusive answer, the investigator can seek to combine the co-variational approach with causal-process tracing or congruence analysis (see Chapter 5).

10. We would have to expand our understanding of statistical generalization to a more Bayesian understanding to accept this form of generalization as statistical generalization.

11. This section draws heavily on Haverland (2005).

12. Note, however, that the original research does not include a full-fledged counterfactual analysis.

3 Causal-Process Tracing

1. This is often overlooked by those who want to press all alternatives to the co-variational template under the heading of 'process-tracing'. The term 'process' refers to the object of the observation and not the process by which the scholar tries to reach valid conclusions (through some kind of Bayesian updating, for example). The examples from political science that Brady, Collier, and Seawright (2006: 365–7) introduce for illustrating their understanding of causal-process tracing are in line with our understanding because time plays a major role, which is not the case with their examples outside of political science (Brady, Collier, and Seawright 2006: 360–5). In not one of the latter examples is the temporal unfolding of a causal process crucially important for drawing causal inferences. Therefore, they are much better subsumed under the methodological approach that we call congruence analysis.

2. The implicit question is: 'Who is responsible?' Newspaper reports of investigations into the catastrophic accident stressed the fact that the explosion of the platform was the result of a 'series' or 'chain' of problems and mistakes. Whereas the investigations of the involved companies focused on specific conditions that led to the accident (proximate causes), reflective commentators reminded readers that the major structural causal factor was the dramatically growing demand for oil (for example, Neue Zürcher Zeitung 9.9. 2010: 3, 23).

3. The in-depth studies revealed that the contributions were also quite different, such that it becomes clear that the concept of 'equifinality' depends on how differentiated one conceptualizes the outcome.

4. This represents a very different approach in comparison to Gerring's (2001) attempt to extract a 'minimal core definition' of the term 'causal mechanism' through an inductive analysis of the usages of the terms within the literature. As a consequence, we arrive at a different definition.

5. The cross-case technique of analyzing causal configuration through QCA shows a clear affinity to the kinds of causal configuration in the left column. Most often, the causal factors are not grounded in basic social theories, the QCA is strongly connected to a static comparison that is logically affiliated to causal conjunctions, and although most applicants of QCA do not explicitly reflect on the difference between additive and interactive causality, it seems that most existing studies assume additive causality (conclusions based on the overview provided by Rihoux, Bol, and Rezsöhazy 2011).

6. This form of presentation is actually a mix between a COV approach and a CPT approach. The vertical dimension is more in line with co-variational thinking because it represents the causal factors as continuous variables; the horizontal dimension is more in line with the logic of causal-process tracing because it presents the development in a continuous time stream. Sybil Rhodes and Arus Harutyunyan (2010) – see following footnote – present the results of their cases studies in figures which represent a mix between 'variable-centred' graphics and 'event-centred' graphics even more clearly.

7. We made up our example for didactic purposes with 'findings' that allow rather clear-cut interpretations. In real social science research, findings are much more messy. This can be observed in a study that strongly resembles our hypothetical example in respect to the two different conceptualizations of the influence of democracy and in respect to presenting the findings (Rhodes and Harutyunyan 2010).

8. We deliberately use the term 'co-variational thinking' instead of co-variational approach (COV) because we specified the latter as an X-centered approach that attempts to select cases on the grounds that they do not differ, except with respect to the one independent variable of interest, and which draws causal inference based on the fact that X and Y co-vary across the (spatially or temporally differentiated) cases and all other independent variables have similar values. Co-variational thinking is not restricted to such a narrowly specified research design.

9. The entire cluster of observations that make the smoking gun a convincing piece of evidence for a specific causal claim can be seen as functionally equivalent to the data-set observations that reveal the co-variation among the scores of the dependent variable and the scores of the dependent variable within a COV approach (see Chapter 1).

10. Nevertheless, sometimes we are more interested in the question of whether it was a gun that was used for the killing (for example, in the context of political debates on gun restrictions).

11. According to Gerring (2007a: 177), 'Brady's conclusion did not rest on a formal research design but rather on isolated observations [...] combined with deductive inferences.' This characterization, in our view, devalues 'causal-process observations'.

12. Reprinted from *The American Journal of Sociology* 104(4), James Mahoney, 'Nominal, Ordinal, and Narrative Appraisal in Macrocausal Analysis', 1154–96, © 1999 by The University of Chicago, with permission from The University of Chicago Press.

13. There are studies that are more thoroughly reflective in this respect. For example, Larry J. Griffin (1993), who is applying an 'event-structure analysis', or Jack Levy's analysis (2007) of necessary conditions in the outbreak of World War I.

14. Tannenwald's usage of the terms 'pathway' and 'mechanism' is different in her book in comparison to the first presentation of her study in *International Organization* (IO). In her earlier IO publication (Tannenwald 1999: 462), she aligns the term 'causal mechanism' with what we would call specific context or configurational factors: domestic public opinion, world opinion, and personal conviction. The more theory-oriented terms force (Realism), self-interest (Rationalism), and legitimacy (Constructivism) are labeled 'pathways'. She partly corrects this unconvincing labeling in her later book, wherein she uses the words as synonyms (for example, Tannenwald 2007: 47–51, 64).

15. George and Bennett (2005) call this kind of generalization 'contingent generalization'. Nevertheless, this term, which was introduced first by George and Smoke (1974) in their attempt to specify the conditions under which deterrence fails, is still very much inclined toward an X- or variable-centered method of thinking. The terminology implies a reading such as 'X is only making a difference (for Y) under the context conditions Z and W'. This is fully in line with the COV approach. In contrast, the terms 'configurational' and 'possibilistic' imply a configurational and Y-centered method of thinking and, therefore, correspond much better to the CPT approach.

16. In this section, we use 'causal configurations' and 'causal combinations' interchangeably, although in Section 3.2, we have clarified that a causal combination is a subtype of a causal configuration. In contrast to a causal mechanism, it is unnecessary for a causal combination to include specifications of the three types of social mechanisms that make a full-fledged multilevel model of explanation complete. Nevertheless, as our example indicates, the boundary between causal combinations and causal mechanisms in real case study research is not as clear-cut as definitional terms imply, and the term 'configurations' is better suited to denote the meaning of this kind of generalization.

17. Tannenwald and Schimmelfennig are also addressing the question of whether their findings can be generalized toward similar cases, actors, and fields. Tannenwald (2007: 374–83) does this in a qualitative manner, whereas Schimmelfennig (2003: 112–51) adds a large-N event-history analysis to his small-N study. Both kinds of generalization rely on further empirical

information, whereas possibilistic generalization requires information about the state of the art in the field of research or in the theoretical and paradigmatic discourse.

4 Congruence Analysis

1. Note that as in the co-variational approach, congruence analysis engages in comparison. However, the comparison is twofold and concerns different aspects. First, it is a comparison between expectations deduced from theory and actual observations in the empirical world. Second, the analysis of congruence between theoretical implications and empirical observations is conducted in a comparative way, involving at least two theories. In contrast, the co-variational approach compares observations within one case with observations in another case.

2. Teaching the original hardcopy version of the book, we have realized that students tend to opt too hastily for the complementary theory type. Even if the final goal is to establish whether and how two or more theories are complementary, one should always start with a competing theory approach. Pitting theories against each other helps to elucidate more convincingly and more precisely which theory has more explanatory power with regard to what aspect of the empirical world. For the advantages of a pluralist theoretical framework see also pp. 161/167.

3. Allison published a first version of *Essence of Decision* in 1971. Allison and Zelikow published a thoroughly revised version in 1999. In the following, we refer to the newer book.

4. The original study published by Elizabeth J. Wilson and David T. Wilson in 1988 has been represented in a methodologically oriented article written by Elizabeth J. Wilson and Arch G. Woodside (1999). We will draw on both sources.

5. We deliberately use the same fictive example that we use for illustrating the added value of causal-process observations in Chapter 3 to make clear that the CON approach emphasizes very different aspects of small-N research in comparison to the CPT approach.

6. As we seek to be sensitive to language and terminology, we exchange Eckstein's terms "most-likely" and "least-likely" with "very likely" and "very unlikely." This is because the terms "most" and "least" suggest that we have collected information about an entire population of potential cases and that we were able to identify *the* "most" and *the* "least" likely case, or in other words the most extreme ones out of this population. But within a congruence analysis approach, having such knowledge for all potential cases is not a necessary condition for case selection. What is necessary, though, is an explicit and convincing justification of why there are strong or many reasons to expect that a selected case will very likely be explained by a specific theory or why there are strong or many reasons to expect that it is very unlikely to be explained by a specific theory. In the preface, we provide an extended explanation why we found it important to make this change when we had the opportunity to slightly modify the manuscript of the hardcopy edition for the paperback edition.

7. This example shows that causal processes and temporality play a role in congruence analysis. Nevertheless, in contrast to a CPT approach,

Owen does not try to identify 'smoking-gun observations' that show, in detail and with certitude, that peace and war decisions were made on the basis of liberal perceptions. He concentrates on those observations (persistence of perceptions) where the rival theories yield competing predictions.

8. Reprinted from *Industrial Marketing Management* 28(3), Elizabeth J. Wilson and Arch G. Woodside, 'Degrees-of-Freedom Analysis of Case Data in Business Marketing Research', 215–29, © 1999 Elsevier Science Inc., with permission from Elsevier.

9. For a third group of cases, Owen goes beyond the use of specific observations to bolster the claim that liberal ideology is the major factor shaping perceptions. Owen points to the fact that the overall congruence between the idealist hypothesis and the empirical evidence is strong (17 out of 19 cases). He argues that this congruence is especially important because the 'idealist theory' predicted novel findings in contrast to Realism and parochial interest. Whether this claim holds can be disputed; Idealism is certainly not a novel theory in the scholarly discourse on democratic peace. Nevertheless, scholars applying a CON approach refer to the position of theories in the scientific discourse when drawing conclusions from cases. These further conclusions should be separated from the congruence analysis proper.

10. The latter study will be reconstructed in Chapter 5 because Blatter complements the CON approach with a CPT approach. Nevertheless, the part of the study that follows the CON approach closely resembles Schimmelfennig's approach.

5 Combining Diverse Research Approaches

1. For an intriguing discussion of various ways to combine methods of data generation and data analysis, see Junk (2011). His differentiation of method parallelization and method triangulation is especially relevant for those who apply causal-process tracing.

2. If a scholar selects cases that vary on the independent variable(s) and that are accurately predicted by the model, then these cases also vary on the dependent variable. Hence, in the civil war example, the scholars select cases in which rich countries are free of civil war and in which poor countries experience civil wars.

3. Rohlfing and Schneider (2011: 22–5) provide detailed suggestions concerning the uncovering of omitted variables and causal mechanisms by comparing typical and deviant cases.

4. A detailed explanation of QCA and related approaches is beyond the scope of this book (for excellent textbooks, see Ragin 2000; Schneider and Wagemann 2007; Rihoux and Ragin 2009; for a recent overview of existing QCA studies, see Rihoux, Bol, and Rezsöhazy 2011).

5. Ironically, those who cannot read German may think that the example presented in the following also serves as an example of the type of combination in which case studies are only used to generate data. They may think this way because in his English journal article that uses QCA to analyze data, Sager

argues that 'the case studies [...] provide the primary data for the actual comparison [...] They identify the values the variables take on in each case' (Sager 2005: 240). However, we will show that in his German dissertation (Sager 2002), he first analyzed the Swiss cases by employing the analytic techniques of two case study approaches (that is, COV and CON).

6. Emmenegger calls the causal configurations 'paths' which is adequate since he presents the results of a static QCA analysis and also, for each path (state capitalist, Continental European managed capitalist, and Nordic managed capitalist pathways) illustrates the historical development within the countries that belong to a specific causal configuration. Nevertheless, only in the case study (Emmenegger 2010) he traces the historical developments in Denmark and Sweden in detail.

Bibliography

Adcock, R. and D. Collier (2001). 'Measurement Validity: A Shared Standard for Qualitative and Quantitative Research.' *American Political Science Review* 95(3): 529–46.

Allison, G. T. (1971). *Essence of Decision: Explaining the Cuban Missile Crisis.* New York: Longman.

Allison, G. T. (2011). [personal webpage], online: http://www.hks.harvard.edu/about/faculty-staff-directory/graham-allison [accessed 09 August 2011].

Allison, G. and P. Zelikow (1999). *Essence of Decision: Explaining the Cuban Missile Crisis.* New York: Longman.

Babbie, E. (2001). *The Practice of Social Research,* 9th edition. Belmont (CA): Thomson Wadsworth.

Bates, R., A. Greif, M. Levi, J.-L. Rosenthal, and B. Weingast, eds. (1998). *Analytic Narratives.* Princeton: Princeton University Press.

Bennett, A. and C. Elman (2006). 'Complex Causal Relations and Case Study Methods: The Example of Path Dependence.' *Political Analysis* 14(3): 250–67.

Bennett, A., J. Lepgold, and D. Unger (1994). 'Burden-Sharing in the Persian Gulf War.' *International Organization* 48(1): 39–75.

Bevir, M. and R. A. W. Rhodes (2002 [1995]). 'Interpretive Theory.' In *Theory and Methods in Political Science,* ed. D. Marsh and G. Stoker. Basingstoke: Palgrave Macmillan, 131–52.

Bhaskar, R. (1979). *The Possibility of Naturalism: A Philosophical Critique of the Contemporary Human Sciences.* Brighton: Harvester.

Bhaskar, R. (1989) *Reclaiming Reality: A Critical Introduction to Contemporary Philosophy.* London and New York: Verso.

Blatter, J. (2009). 'Performing Symbolic Politics and International Environmental Regulation: Tracing and Theorizing a Causal Mechanism beyond Regime Theory.' *Global Environmental Politics* 9(4): 81–110.

Blatter, J. and T. Blume (2008). 'In Search of Co-Variance, Causal Mechanisms or Congruence? Towards a Plural Understanding of Case Studies.' *Swiss Political Science Review* 14(2): 115–56.

Blatter, J., F. Janning, and C. Wagemann (2007). *Qualitative Politikanalyse: Eine Einführung in Forschungsansätze und Methoden.* Wiesbaden: Verlag für Sozialwissenschaften.

Brady, H. E. (2004). 'Data-Set Observations Versus Causal-Process Observations: The 2000 U.S. Presidential Election.' In *Rethinking Social Inquiry: Diverse Tools, Shared Standards,* ed. H. E. Brady and D. Collier. Lanham: Rowman & Littlefield, 267–72.

Brady, H. E. and D. Collier, eds. (2004). *Rethinking Social Inquiry: Diverse Tools, Shared Standards.* Lanham: Rowman & Littlefield.

Brady, H. E., D. Collier, and J. Seawright (2006). 'Towards a Pluralistic Vision of Methodology.' *Political Analysis* 14(3): 353–68.

Breitmeier, H., O. Young, and M. Zürn (2006). *Analyzing International Environmental Regimes*. Cambridge (MA): MIT Press.

Bryman, A. (2006). 'Integrating Quantitative and Qualitative Research: How Is It Done?' *Qualitative Research* 6(1): 97–113.

Büthe, T. (2002). 'Taking Temporality Seriously: Modeling History and the Use of Narrative and Evidence.' *American Political Science Review* 96(3): 481–93.

Buttolph Johnson, J., H. Reynolds, and J. Mycoff (2008). *Political Science Research Methods*. Washington (DC): CQ Press.

Capoccia, G. and R. Kelemen (2007). 'The Study of Critical Junctures: Theory, Narrative, and Counterfactuals in Historical Institutionalism.' *World Politics* 59(3): 341–69.

Caramani, D. (2009). *Introduction to the Comparative Method with Boolean Algebra*. Thousand Oaks: Sage.

Checkel, J. T. (2006). 'Tracing Causal Mechanisms.' *International Studies Review* 8(2): 362–70.

Checkel, J. T. (2008). 'Process Tracing.' In *Qualitative Methods in International Relations: A Pluralist Guide*, ed. A. Klotz and D. Prakash. Basingstoke: Palgrave Macmillan, 114–27.

Collier, D. and J. Mahon (1993). 'Conceptual "Stretching" Revisited: Adapting Categories in Comparative Analysis.' *American Political Science Review* 87(4): 845–55.

Collier, D., H. E. Brady, and J. Seawright (2004). 'Sources of Leverage in Causal Inference: Toward an Alternative View of Methodology.' In *Rethinking Social Inquiry: Diverse Tools, Shared Standards*, ed. H. E. Brady and D. Collier. Lanham: Rowman & Littlefield, 229–66.

Collier, D., J. Mahoney, and J. Seawright (2004). 'Claiming Too Much: Warnings about Selection Bias.' In *Rethinking Social Inquiry: Diverse Tools, Shared Standards*, ed. H. E. Brady and D. Collier. Lanham: Rowman & Littlefield, 85–102.

Cook, T. and D. Campbell (1979). *Quasi-Experimentation: Design and Analysis Issues for Field Settings*. Boston: Houghton Mifflin.

Cruickshank, J., ed. (2003). *Critical Realism: The Difference That It Makes*. London: Routledge.

Dahl, R. A. (1967 [1961]). *Who Governs? Democracy and Power in an American City*. New Haven: Yale University Press.

David, M., ed. (2006). *Case Study Research*. London: Sage.

Dion, D. (2003). 'Evidence and Inference in the Comparative Case Study.' In *Necessary Conditions: Theory, Methodology, and Applications*, ed. G. Goertz and H. Starr. Lanham: Rowman & Littlefield, 65–94.

Duverger, M. (1969 [1954]). *Political Parties: Their Organization and Activity in the Modern State*. London: Methuen.

Eckstein, H. (1975). 'Case Study and Theory in Political Science.' In *Handbook of Political Science*, ed. F. Greenstein and N. Polsby. Reading: Addison-Wesley, 79–138.

Elster, J. (1998). 'A Plea for Mechanisms.' In *Social Mechanisms: An Analytical Approach to Social Theory*, ed. P. Hedstroem and R. Swedberg. Cambridge: Cambridge University Press, 45–73.

Elster, J. (2007). *Explaining Social Behavior: More Nuts and Bolts for the Social Sciences*. Cambridge: Cambridge University Press.

Emmenegger, P. (2010). 'The Long Road to Flexicurity: The Development of Job Security Regulations in Denmark and Sweden.' *Scandinavian Political Studies* 33(3): 271–94.

Emmenegger, P. (2011a). 'How Good Are Your Counterfactuals? Assessing Quantitative Macro-Comparative Welfare State Research with Qualitative Criteria.' *Journal of European Social Policy* 21(4): 365–80.

Emmenegger, P. (2011b). 'Job Security Regulations in Western Democracies: A Fuzzy Set Analysis.' *European Journal of Political Research* 50(3): 336–64.

Esser, H. (1993). *Soziologie: Allgemeine Grundlagen.* Frankfurt am Main: Campus.

Esser, H. (1999–2001). *Soziologie: Spezielle Grundlagen.* [Volumes 1 to 6], Frankfurt am Main: Campus.

Esser, H. (2002). 'Was könnte man (heute) unter einer "Theorie mittlerer Reichweite" verstehen?' In *Akteure – Mechanismen – Modelle: Zur Theoriefähigkeit makro-sozialer Analysen*, ed. R. Mayntz. Frankfurt am Main: Campus, 128–50.

Evans, P., D. Rueschemeyer, and T. Skocpol, eds. (1985). *Bringing the State Back in.* Cambridge: Cambridge University Press.

Falleti, T. and J. Lynch (2009). 'Context and Causal Mechanisms in Political Analysis.' *Comparative Political Studies* 42(9): 1143–66.

Faure, A. (1994). 'Some Methodological Problems in Comparative Politics.' *Journal of Theoretical Politics* 6(3): 307–22.

Fearon, J. D. (1991). 'Counterfactuals and Hypothesis Testing in Political Science.' *World Politics* 43(2): 169–95.

Fearon, J. D. and D. D. Laitin (2008). 'Integrating Qualitative and Quantitative Methods.' In *The Oxford Handbook of Political Methodology*, ed. J. Box-Steffensmeier, H. E. Brady, and D. Collier. Oxford: Oxford University Press, 756–76.

Frendreis, J. (1983). 'Explanation of Variation and Detection of Covariation: The Purpose and Logic of Comparative Analysis.' *Comparative Political Studies* 16(2): 255–72.

Friedman, M. (1966). 'The Methodology of Positive Economics.' In *Essays in Positive Economics*, ed. M. Friedman. Chicago: Chicago University Press, 3–43.

Ganghof, S. (2005). 'Kausale Perspektiven in der vergleichenden Politikwissenschaft: X-zentrierte und Y-zentrierte Forschungsdesigns.' In *Vergleichen in der Politikwissenschaft*, ed. S. Kropp and M. Minkenberg. Wiesbaden: Verlag für Sozialwissenschaften, 76–93.

Geddes, B. (1990). 'How the Cases You Choose Affect the Answer You Get: Selection Bias in Comparative Politics.' *Political Analysis* 2(1): 131–50.

Geddes, B. (1994). *Politician's Dilemma: Building State Capacity in Latin America.* Berkeley: University of California Press.

George, A. and A. Bennett (2005). *Case Studies and Theory Development in the Social Sciences.* Cambridge (MA): MIT Press.

George, A. and R. Smoke (1974). *Deterrence in American Foreign Policy: Theory and Practice.* New York: Columbia University Press.

Gerring, J. (2001). *Social Science Methodology: A Criterial Framework.* Cambridge: Cambridge University Press.

Gerring, J. (2004). 'What Is a Case Study and What Is It Good for?' *American Political Science Review* 98(2): 341–54.

Gerring, J. (2007a). *Case Study Research: Principles and Practices.* Cambridge: Cambridge University Press.

Gerring, J. (2007b). 'Is There a (Viable) Crucial-Case Method?' *Comparative Political Studies* 40(3): 231–53.

Gerring, J. (2008). 'Review Article. The Mechanismic Worldview: Thinking Inside the Box.' *British Journal of Political Science* 38(1): 161–79.

Goertz, G. (2003a). 'Cause, Correlation and Necessary Conditions.' In *Necessary Conditions: Theory, Methodology, and Applications*, ed. G. Goertz and H. Starr. Lanham: Rowman & Littlefield, 47–64.

Goertz, G. (2003b). 'The Substantive Importance of Necessary Condition Hypotheses.' In *Necessary Conditions: Theory, Methodology, and Applications*, ed. G. Goertz and H. Starr. Lanham: Rowman & Littlefield, 65–94.

Goertz, G. (2006). *Social Science Concepts: A User's Guide*. Princeton: Princeton University Press.

Goertz, G. and J. Levy (2007). 'Causal Explanation, Necessary Conditions, and Case Studies.' In *Explaining War and Peace: Case Studies and Necessary Condition Counterfactuals*, ed. G. Goertz and J. Levy. London: Routledge, 9–46.

Goertz, G. and J. Mahoney (forthcoming). *A Tale of Two Cultures: Contrasting Qualitative and Quantitative Paradigms*. Princeton: Princeton University Press.

Goffman, E. (1967). *Interaction Ritual: Essays on Face-to-Face Behavior*. Garden City (NY): Anchor Books.

Goldthorpe, J. (1997). 'Current Issues in Comparative Macrosociology: A Debate on Methodological Issues.' *Comparative Social Research* 16(1): 1–26.

Goodin, R. E. and H.-D. Klingemann (1996). 'Political Science: The Discipline.' In *A New Handbook of Political Science*, ed. R. E. Goodin and H.-D. Klingemann. Oxford: Oxford University Press, 3–49.

Greene, J., V. Caracelli, and W. Graham (1989). 'Toward a Conceptual Framework for Mixed-Method Evaluation Designs.' *Educational Evaluation and Policy Analysis* 11(3): 255–74.

Griffin, L. J. (1993). 'Narrative, Event-Structure Analysis, and Causal Interpretation in Historical Sociology.' *The American Journal of Sociology* 98(5): 1094–133.

Grofman, B., ed. (2001). *Political Science as Puzzle Solving*. Ann Arbor (MI): The University of Michigan Press.

Grzymala-Busse, A. (2011). 'Time Will Tell? Temporality and the Analysis of Causal Mechanisms and Processes.' *Comparative Political Studies* 44(9): 1267–97.

Gschwend, T. and F. Schimmelfennig (2007). 'Introduction. Designing Research in Political Science: A Dialogue Between Theory and Data.' In *Research Design in Political Science: How to Practice What They Preach*, ed. T. Gschwend and F. Schimmelfennig. Basingstoke: Palgrave Macmillan, 1–18.

Haas, P. (1992). 'Introduction: Epistemic Communities and International Policy Coordination.' *International Organization* 46(1): 1–35.

Habermas, J. (1981a). *Theorie des kommunikativen Handelns. Band 1: Handlungsrationalität und gesellschaftliche Rationalisierung*. Frankfurt am Main: Suhrkamp.

Habermas, J. (1981b). *Theorie des kommunikativen Handelns. Band 2: Zur Kritik der funktionalistischen Vernunft*. Frankfurt am Main: Suhrkamp.

Haggard, S. and B. Simmons (1987). 'Theories of International Regimes.' *International Organization* 41(3): 491–517.

Hall, P. (2003). 'Aligning Ontology and Methodology in Comparative Politics.' In *Comparative Historical Analysis in the Social Sciences*, ed. J. Mahoney and D. Rueschemeyer. Cambridge: Cambridge University Press, 373–404.

Hall, P. (2006). 'Systematic Process Analysis: When and How to Use It.' *European Management Review* 3(1): 24–31.

Hall, P. and R. Taylor (1996). 'Political Science and the Three Institutionalisms.' *Political Studies* 44(5): 936–57.

Hammersley, M. and P. Atkinson (2007). *Ethnography: Principles in Practice*, 3rd edition. New York: Routledge.

Hasenclever, A., P. Mayer, and V. Rittberger (1996). 'Interests, Power, Knowledge: The Study of International Regimes.' *Mershon International Studies Review* 40(2): 177–228.

Haverland, M. (1999). *National Autonomy, European Integration and the Politics of Packaging Waste*. Amsterdam: Thela Thesis.

Haverland, M. (2000). 'National Adaptation to the European Union: The Importance of Institutional Veto Points.' *Journal of Public Policy* 20(1): 83–103.

Haverland, M. (2005). 'Does the EU Cause Domestic Developments? The Problem of Case Selection in Europeanization Research.' *European Integration Online Papers* 9(2):

Haverland, M. (2006). 'Does the EU Cause Domestic Developments? Improving Case Selection in Europeanisation Research.' *West European Politics* 29(1): 134–46.

Haverland, M. (2007). 'Methodology.' In *Europeanization: New Research Agendas*, ed. P. Graziano and M. Vink. Basingstoke: Palgrave Macmillan, 59–70.

Hedstroem, P. and R. Swedberg (1998). 'Social Mechanisms: An Introductory Essay.' In *Social Mechanisms: An Analytical Approach to Social Theory*, ed. P. Hedstroem and R. Swedberg. Cambridge: Cambridge University Press, 1–31.

Hedstroem, P. and P. Ylikoski (2010). 'Causal Mechanisms in the Social Sciences.' *Annual Review of Sociology* 36: 49–67.

Holland, P. (1986). 'Statistics and Causal Inference.' *Journal of the American Statistical Association* 81(396): 945–60.

Howell, M. and W. Prevenier (2001). *From Reliable Sources: An Introduction to Historical Methods*. Ithaca (NY): Cornell University Press.

Immergut, E. M. (1990). 'Institutions, Veto Points, and Policy Results: A Comparative Analysis of Health Care.' *Journal of Public Policy* 10(4): 391–416.

Johnson, L. (2005). 'Constitutional Change in Local Governance: An Exploration of Institutional Entrepreneurs, Procedural Safeguards, and Selective Incentives.' Dissertation submitted to the Askew School of Public Administration and Policy, *The Florida State University*, online: http://etd.lib.fsu.edu/theses/available/etd-04152005-170723 [accessed 22 July 2011].

Joseph, J. and C. Wight, eds. (2010). *Scientific Realism and International Relations*. New York: Palgrave Macmillan.

Junk, J. (2011). 'Method Parallelization and Method Triangulation: Method Combinations in the Analysis of Humanitarian Interventions.' *German Policy Studies* 7(3): 83–116.

Junk, J. and J. Blatter (2010). 'Transnational Attention, Domestic Agenda-Setting, and International Agreement: Modelling Necessary and Sufficient Conditions for Media-Driven Humanitarian Interventions.' *WZB Discussion Paper No. SP*

IV 2010-301, online: http://bibliothek.wzb.eu/pdf/2010/iv10-301.pdf [accessed 01 November 2011].

King, G., R. O. Keohane, and S. Verba (1994). *Designing Social Inquiry: Scientific Inference in Qualitative Research*. Princeton: Princeton University Press.

King, G., R. O. Keohane, and S. Verba (2004). 'The Importance of Research Design.' In *Rethinking Social Inquiry: Diverse Tools, Shared Standards*, ed. H. E. Brady and D. Collier. Lanham: Rowman & Littlefield, 181–92.

Kingdon, J. (1984). *Agendas, Alternatives, and Public Policies*. Boston: Little, Brown and Company.

Kitschelt, H. (1986). 'Political Opportunity Structures and Political Protest: Anti-Nuclear Movements in Four Democracies.' *British Journal of Political Science* 16(1): 57–85.

Knill, C. and A. Lenschow (1998). 'Coping with Europe: The Impact of British and German Administration on the Implementation of EU Environmental Policy.' *Journal of European Public Policy* 5(4): 595–614.

Kuehn, D. and I. Rohlfing (2010). 'Causal Explanation and Multi-Method Research in the Social Sciences.' *IPSA Committee on Concepts and Methods Working Paper Series No. 26*, online: http://www.concepts-methods.org/Files/WorkingPaper/PM 26 Kuehn Rohlfing.pdf [accessed 01 November 2011].

Kurki, M. (2008). *Causation in International Relations: Reclaiming Causal Analysis*. Cambridge: Cambridge University Press.

Lakatos, I. (1970). 'Falsification and the Methodology of Scientific Research Programs.' In *Criticism and the Growth of Knowledge*, ed. I. Lakatos and A. Musgrave. Cambridge: Cambridge University Press,

Legro, J. W. (1996). 'Culture and Preferences in the International Cooperation Two-Step.' *American Political Science Review* 90(1): 118–37.

Leuffen, D. (2007). 'Case Selection and Selection Bias in Small-N Research.' In *Research Design in Political Science: How to Practice What They Preach*, ed. T. Gschwend and F. Schimmelfennig. Basingstoke: Palgrave Macmillan, 145–60.

Leuffen, D., S. Shikano, and S. Walter (2010). *Measurement and Data Aggregation in Small-N Social Scientific Research*. Paper presented at the Symposium 'Reassessing the Methodology of Process Tracing', University of Oldenburg, 26 November 2010.

Levy, J. (2002). 'Qualitative Methods in International Relations.' In *Evaluating Methodology in International Studies*, ed. F. Harvey and M. Brecher. Ann Arbor (MI): The University of Michigan Press, 432–54.

Levy, J. (2007). 'The Role of Necessary Conditions in the Outbreak of World War I.' In *Explaining War and Peace: Case Studies and Necessary Condition Counterfactuals*, ed. G. Goertz and J. Levy. London: Routledge, 47–84.

Lieberman, E. S. (2001). 'Causal Inference in Historical Institutional Analysis: A Specification of Periodization Strategies.' *Comparative Political Studies* 34(10): 1011–35.

Lieberman, E. S. (2005). 'Nested Analysis as a Mixed-Method Strategy for Comparative Research.' *American Political Science Review* 99(3): 435–52.

Lieberson, S. (1991). 'Small N's and Big Conclusions: An Examination of the Reasoning Based on a Small Number of Cases.' *Social Forces* 70(2): 307–20.

Lieberson, S. (1994). 'More on the Uneasy Case for Using Mill-Type Methods in Small-N Comparative Studies.' *Social Forces* 72(4): 1225–37.

Lieshout, R., M. Segers, and A. van der Vleuten (2004). 'De Gaulle, Moravcsik, and the Choice for Europe.' *Journal of Cold War Studies* 6(4): 89–139.

Lijphart, A. (1971). 'Comparative Politics and the Comparative Method.' *American Political Science Review* 65(3): 682–93.

Lijphart, A. (1975 [1968]). *The Politics of Accommodation: Pluralism and Democracy in the Netherlands.* Berkeley: University of California Press.

Lijphart, A. (1975). 'The Comparable-Cases Strategy in Comparative Research.' *Comparative Political Studies* 8(2): 158–77.

Lijphart, A. (1999). *Patterns of Democracy: Government Forms and Performance in Thirty-Six Countries.* New Haven: Yale University Press.

Lijphart, A. (2008). *Power Sharing and Majority Rule in Theory and Practice.* London: Routledge.

Linos, K. (2007). 'How Can International Organizations Shape National Welfare States? Evidence from Compliance with European Union Directives.' *Comparative Political Studies* 40(5): 547–70.

Locke, R. and K. Thelen (1995). 'Apples and Oranges Revisited: Contextualized Comparisons and the Study of Comparative Labor Politics.' *Politics & Society* 23(3): 337–67.

Locke, R. and K. Thelen (1998). 'Problem of Equivalence in Comparative Politics: Apples and Oranges, Again.' *Newsletter of the APSA Organized Section in Comparative Politics* 9(1): 9–12.

Lott, J. R. (2000). 'Gore Might Lose a Second Round: Media Suppressed the Bush Vote.' *Philadelphia Inquirer*, 14 November: 23A

Lyons, W. and D. Lowery (1989). 'Governmental Fragmentation versus Consolidation: Five Public-Choice Myths about How to Create Informed, Involved, and Happy Citizens.' *Public Administration Review* 49(6): 533–43.

McFarland, A. (2007). 'Neopluralism.' *Annual Review of Political Science* 10: 45–66.

Mahoney, J. (1999). 'Nominal, Ordinal, and Narrative Appraisal in Macrocausal Analysis.' *The American Journal of Sociology* 104(4): 1154–96.

Mahoney, J. (2000a). 'Path Dependence in Historical Sociology.' *Theory and Society* 29(4): 507–48.

Mahoney, J. (2000b). 'Strategies of Causal Inference in Small-N Analysis.' *Sociological Methods & Research* 28(4): 387–424.

Mahoney, J. (2003). 'Strategies of Causal Assessment in Comparative Historical Analysis.' In *Comparative Historical Analysis in the Social Sciences*, ed. J. Mahoney and D. Rueschemeyer. Cambridge: Cambridge University Press, 337–72.

Mahoney, J. (2006). 'Analyzing Path Dependence: Lessons from the Social Sciences.' In *Understanding Change: Models, Methodologies, and Metaphors*, ed. A. Wimmer and R. Kössler. Basingstoke: Palgrave Macmillan, 129–39.

Mahoney, J. and G. Goertz (2004). 'The Possibility Principle: Choosing Negative Cases in Comparative Research.' *American Political Science Review* 98(4): 653–69.

Mahoney, J. and G. Goertz (2006). 'A Tale of Two Cultures: Contrasting Quantitative and Qualitative Research.' *Political Analysis* 14(3): 227–49.

Mahoney, J. and D. Rueschemeyer, eds. (2003). *Comparative Historical Analysis in the Social Sciences.* Cambridge: Cambridge University Press.

Mahoney, J., E. Kimball, and K. Koivu (2009). 'The Logic of Historical Explanation in the Social Sciences.' *Comparative Political Studies* 42(1): 114–46.

March, J. and J. Olson (1989). *Rediscovering Institutions: The Organizational Basis of Politics.* New York: Free Press.

Marks, A. (2000). 'Allison on Essence.' *Kennedy School of Government Press Bulletin*, online: http://www.hks.harvard.edu/ksgpress/bulletin/spring2000/allison.html [accessed 11 August 2011].

Mayntz, R., ed. (2002). *Akteure – Mechanismen – Modelle: Zur Theoriefähigkeit makro-sozialer Analysen.* Frankfurt am Main: Campus.

Meier, K. (1980). 'Executive Reorganization of Government. Impact on Employment and Expenditure.' *American Journal of Political Science* 24 (3): 396–412.

Mill, J. (1875). *A System of Logic, Ratiocinative and Inductive: Being a Connected View of the Principles of Evidence and the Methods of Scientific Investigation.* London: Longmans, Green, Reader, and Dyer.

Mitchell, S. (2002). 'Contingent Generalizations: Lessons from Biology.' In *Akteure – Mechanismen – Modelle: Zur Theoriefähigkeit makro-sozialer Analysen,* ed. R. Mayntz. Frankfurt am Main: Campus, 179–95.

Moravcsik, A. (1998). *The Choice for Europe: Social Purpose and State Power from Messina to Maastricht.* London: Routledge.

Moses, J. and T. Knutsen (2007). *Ways of Knowledge: Competing Methodologies in Social and Political Research.* Basingstoke: Palgrave Macmillan.

Muno, W. (2003). 'Fallstudien und die vergleichende Methode.' In *Vergleichende Politikwissenschaftliche Methoden: Neue Entwicklungen und Diskussionen,* ed. S. Pickel, G. Pickel, H.-J. Lauth, and D. Jahn. Wiesbaden: Verlag für Sozialwissenschaften, 19–36.

Ned Lebow, R. (2000). 'What's So Different About a Counterfactual?' *World Politics* 52(4): 550–85.

Owen, J. (1997). *Liberal Peace, Liberal War: American Politics and International Security.* Ithaca (NY): Cornell University Press.

Pappi, F. (2003). 'Theorien, Methoden und Forschungsansätze.' In *Politikwissenschaft: Ein Grundkurs,* ed. H. Münkler. Hamburg: Rowohlt, 77–100.

Patzelt, W. (2005). 'Wissenschaftstheoretische Grundlagen sozialwissenschaftlichen Vergleichens.' In *Vergleichen in der Politikwissenschaft,* ed. S. Kropp and M. Minkenberg. Wiesbaden: Verlag für Sozialwissenschaften, 16–54.

Peled, A. (2002). 'Why Style Matters: A Comparison of Two Administrative Reform Initiatives in the Israeli Public Sector, 1989–1998.' *Journal of Public Administration Research and Theory* 12(2): 217–40.

Pierson, P. (2000a). 'Increasing Returns, Path Dependence, and the Study of Politics.' *American Political Science Review* 94(2): 251–67.

Pierson, P. (2000b). 'Not Just What, but When: Timing and Sequence in Political Processes.' *Studies in American Political Development* 14(1): 72–92.

Pierson, P. (2004). *Politics in Time: History, Institutions, and Social Analysis.* Princeton: Princeton University Press.

Przeworski, A. and H. Teune (1970). *The Logic of Comparative Social Inquiry.* New York: Wiley & Sons.

Ragin, C. (1987). *The Comparative Method: Moving beyond Qualitative and Quantitative Strategies.* Berkeley: University of California Press.

Ragin, C. (1992). ' "Casing" and the Process of Social Inquiry.' In *What Is a Case? Exploring the Foundations of Social Inquiry,* ed. C. Ragin and H. Becker. Cambridge: Cambridge University Press, 217–26.

Ragin, C. (2000). *Fuzzy-Set Social Science.* Chicago: University of Chicago Press.

Ragin, C. (2004). 'Turning the Tables: How Case-Oriented Research Challenges Variable-Oriented Research.' In *Rethinking Social Inquiry: Diverse Tools, Shared Standards*, ed. H. E. Brady and D. Collier. Lanham: Rowman & Littlefield, 123–38.

Ragin, C. (2008). *Redesigning Social Inquiry: Fuzzy Sets and beyond.* Chicago: University of Chicago Press.

Rhodes, S. and A. Harutyunyan (2010). 'Extending Citizenship to Emigrants: Democratic Contestation and a New Global Norm.' *International Political Science Review* 31(4): 470–93.

Rihoux, B. (2008). 'Case-Oriented Configurational Research: Qualitative Comparative Analysis (QCA), Fuzzy Sets, and Related Techniques.' In *The Oxford Handbook of Political Methodology*, ed. J. Box-Steffensmeier, H. E. Brady, and D. Collier. Oxford: Oxford University Press, 722–36.

Rihoux, B. and G. de Meur (2009). 'Crisp-Set Qualitative Comparative Analysis (csQCA).' In *Configurational Comparative Methods: Qualitative Comparative Analysis (QCA) and Related Techniques*, ed. B. Rihoux and C. Ragin. Thousand Oaks: Sage, 33–68.

Rihoux, B. and C. Ragin, eds. (2009). *Configurational Comparative Methods: Qualitative Comparative Analysis (QCA) and Related Techniques.* Thousand Oaks: Sage.

Rihoux, B., D. Bol, and I. Rezsöhazy (2011). 'Qualitative Comparative Analysis in Public Policy Analysis: An Extensive Review.' *German Policy Studies*, 9–82.

Rohlfing, I. (2008). 'What You See and What You Get: Pitfalls and Principles of Nested Analysis in Comparative Research.' *Comparative Political Studies* 41(11): 1492–514.

Rohlfing, I. and C. Schneider (2011). 'Case Selection for Process Tracing after Regression Analysis and Qualitative Comparative Analysis: A Comparative Discussion.' Paper prepared for the 'Workshop on Comparative Methodology', University of Southern Denmark, Odense, May 25–26, 2011.

Rueschemeyer, D. (2009). *Usable Theory: Analytical Tools for Social and Political Research.* Princeton: Princeton University Press.

Rueschemeyer, D. and J. Stephens (1997). 'Comparing Historical Sequences: A Powerful Tool for Causal Analysis.' In *Methodological Issues in Comparative Social Science*, ed. L. Mjoset, F. Engelstad, G. Borchmann, R. Kalleberg, and A. Leira. London: JAI Press, 55–72.

Sabatier, P. (1993). 'Policy change over a decade and more.' In *Policy Change and Learning: An Advocacy Coalition Approach*, ed. P. Sabatier and H. Jenkins-Smith. Boulder (CO): Westview Press, 13–40.

Sabatier, P. and H. Jenkins-Smith, eds. (1993). *Policy Change and Learning: An Advocacy Coalition Approach.* Boulder (CO): Westview Press.

Sagan, S. (1993). *The Limits of Safety: Organizations, Accidents, and Nuclear Weapons.* Princeton: Princeton University Press.

Sager, F. (2002). *Vom Verwalten des urbanen Raumes: Institutionelle Bedingungen von Politikkoordination am Beispiel der Raum- und Verkehrsplanung in städtischen Gebieten.* Bern: Haupt.

Sager, F. (2005). 'Metropolitan Institutions and Policy Coordination: The Integration of Land Use and Transport Policies in Swiss Urban Areas.' *Governance* 18(2): 227–56.

Sager, F. (2006). 'Policy Coordination in the European Metropolis: A Meta-Analysis.' *West European Politics* 29(3): 433–60.

Sartori, G., ed. (1984). *Social Science Concepts: A Systematic Analysis.* London: Sage.

Scharpf, F. (1997). *Games Real Actors Play: Actor-Centered Institutionalism in Policy Research.* Boulder (CO): Westview Press.

Schimmelfennig, F. (2001). 'The Community Trap: Liberal Norms, Rhetorical Action, and the Eastern Enlargement of the European Union.' *International Organization* 55(1): 47–80.

Schimmelfennig, F. (2003). *The EU, NATO and the Integration of Europe: Rules and Rhetoric.* Cambridge: Cambridge University Press.

Schneider, C. (2009). *The Consolidation of Democracy: Comparing Europe and Latin America.* London: Routledge.

Schneider, C. and C. Wagemann (2007). *Qualitative Comparative Analysis (QCA) und Fuzzy Sets: Ein Lehrbuch für Anwender und jene, die es werden wollen.* Opladen: Barbara Budrich Publishers.

Seawright, J. and D. Collier (2004). 'Glossary of Selected Terms.' In *Rethinking Social Inquiry: Diverse Tools, Shared Standards*, ed. H. E. Brady and D. Collier. Lanham: Rowman & Littlefield, 273–313.

Seawright, J. and J. Gerring (2008). 'Case-Selection Techniques in Case Study Research: A Menu of Qualitative and Quantitative Options.' *Political Research Quarterly* 61(2): 294–308.

Sewell, W. (2005). *The Logics of History: Social Theory and Social Transformation.* Chicago: Chicago University Press.

Skocpol, T. (1979). *States and Social Revolutions: A Comparative Analysis of France, Russia, and China.* Cambridge: Cambridge University Press.

Stake, R. (1995). *The Art of Case Study Research.* London: Sage.

Tannenwald, N. (1999). 'The Nuclear Taboo: The United States and the Normative Basis of Nuclear Non-Use.' *International Organization* 53(3): 433–68.

Tannenwald, N. (2007). *The Nuclear Taboo: The United States and the Non-Use of Nuclear Weapons Since 1945.* Cambridge: Cambridge University Press.

Tetlock, B. and A. Belkin, eds. (1996a). *Counterfactual Thought Experiments in World Politics: Logical, Methodological, and Psychological Perspectives.* Princeton: Princeton University Press.

Tetlock, B. and A. Belkin (1996b). 'Counterfactual Thought Experiments in World Politics: Logical, Methodological, and Psychological Perspectives.' In *Counterfactual Thought Experiments in World Politics: Logical, Methodological, and Psychological Perspectives*, ed. B. Tetlock and A. Belkin. Princeton: Princeton University Press, 1–38.

Tilly, C. (2008). *Explaining Social Processes.* Boulder (CO): Paradigm Publishers.

Turner, J. (2003 [1974]). *The Structure of Sociological Theory.* Belmont (CA): Thomson Wadsworth.

van Evera, S. (1997). *Guide to Methods for Students of Political Science.* Ithaca (NY): Cornell University Press.

Vennesson, P. (2008). 'Case Studies and Process Tracing: Theories and Practices.' In *Approaches and Methodologies in the Social Sciences: A Pluralist Perspective*, ed. D. Della Porta and M. Keating. Cambridge: Cambridge University Press, 223–39.

Wendt, A. (1999). *Social Theory of International Politics.* Cambridge: Cambridge University Press.

Wight, C. (2006). *Agents, Structures and International Relations: Politics as Ontology.* Cambridge: Cambridge University Press.

Wilson, E. J. and D. T. Wilson (1988). ' "Degrees of Freedom" in Case Research of Behavioral Theories of Group Buying.' *Advances in Consumer Research* 15: 587–94.

Wilson, E. J. and A. G. Woodside (1999). 'Degrees-of-Freedom Analysis of Case Data in Business Marketing Research.' *Industrial Marketing Management* 28(3): 215–29.

Wolf, F. (2010). 'Enlightened Eclecticism or Hazardous Hotchpotch? Mixed Methods and Triangulation Strategies in Comparative Public Policy Research.' *Journal of Mixed Methods Research* 4(2): 144–67.

Yin, R. (2009). *Case Study Research*, 4th edition. Thousand Oaks: Sage.

Zangl, B. (2008). 'Judicialization Matters! A Comparison of Dispute Settlement Under GATT and the WTO.' *International Studies Quarterly* 52(4): 825–54.

Index

Action-formation mechanisms,
  see mechanisms
Ad-hoc explanation, 171
Advocacy Coalition Framework, 6,
  172, 221
Agency-structure problem, 7
Allison, Graham T., 2–4, 147, 148,
  149, 150, 151, 158, 160, 171, 173,
  178, 182–3, 188
American Politics, 6
analytic narratives, 134
anti-foundationalist stance, 10, 11
applied research, 36, 44, 53, 69
archival work, 106
autonomous causality, 24, 26, 41

background concept, 63
Bayesian approach, 176, 177, 194
behavioral theories, 97, 117, 132, 157,
  159, 193
Blatter, Joachim, 89, 103, 148, 151,
  172, 174, 194, 201–2, 219–23
Boolean Algebra, 41
Brady, Henry, 83, 85, 89, 123–7

case selection, 14, 16, 24, 25, 33, 34,
  38, 41, 42–4, 49, 50, 56, 58, 63,
  72, 76, 87, 99–105, 147, 150,
  176–8, 211, 214, 216, 224, 227,
  229, 235
case-centered, 18, 135, 141
cases
  accessible, 25, 26, 82, 102, 103
  deviant, 207, 226–8
  negative, 101, 104, 105, 127, 216,
    217
  positive, 26, 100, 101–2, 108, 113,
    127, 216–7
  possible, 25, 26, 82, 101, 104, 127,
    225
  typical, 226, 231

case studies
  definitions, 18–20
  explorative, 225
  casing, 19
causal chains, 27, 29, 85, 94, 97, 105,
  109, 110, 113, 119–22, 124, 127,
  128, 129, 131, 137, 179, 217, 218,
  235
causal complexity, 80, 91, 119, 136
causal configurations, 26, 27, 30, 31,
  92–5, 97, 98, 104, 106, 107,
  134–6, 138, 142, 197, 209, 210,
  211, 217, 231, 232, 234
causal conjunctions, 4, 27, 83, 85, 89,
  94, 97, 124, 127, 128, 129, 131,
  217, 218, 235
causal diversity, 136
causal effect, 27, 29, 37–8, 40, 43, 54,
  56, 57, 61, 62, 94, 212, 213,
  224–30
causal heterogeneity, 80, 82, 89, 231,
  236,
  see also causal complexity
causality
  additive, 90, 93, 94, 97, 98, 128
  autonomous, 24, 26, 40, 41
  configurational, 12, 18, 40, 41, 63,
    80, 87, 90, 92, 94–8, 114, 124,
    140, 143, 207, 231
  interactive, 90, 93, 94, 97, 98
  recursive, 131
causal mechanisms, 17, 19, 29, 52, 53,
  72, 86, 88, 95–9, 103, 106, 110,
  114, 115, 118, 122, 125, 130–42,
  174, 201, 204, 223, 225, 227, 236
  see also social mechanisms
causal narratives, 109, 119, 128, 130,
  135
causal pathways, 52, 58, 60, 106, 110,
  111, 130, 131, 139, 224–7
causal power, 94, 145

257

9 781137 472571